# THE BOOK OF SECOND SAMUEL

# EXPOSITORY LECTURES

## ON

# THE BOOK OF SECOND SAMUEL

### WILLIAM GARDEN BLAIKIE

SOLID GROUND CHRISTIAN BOOKS
BIRMINGHAM, ALABAMA USA

Solid Ground Christian Books
2090 Columbiana Rd, Suite 2000
Birmingham, AL 35216
205-443-0311
sgcb@charter.net
http://solid-ground-books.com

**Expository Lectures on the Book of Second Samuel**

William Garden Blaikie (1820-1899)

First published in 1887-1888

*Solid Ground Classic Reprints*

First printing of new edition November 2005

Cover work by Borgo Design, Tuscaloosa, AL
Contact them at nelbrown@comcast.net

*Cover image is David Mourns the Death of Absalom,*
*in 2 Samuel 18:31-33, done by Gustave Dore (1832-1883).*

ISBN: 1-59925-027-6

# CONTENTS.

---

# CHAPTER I.

*DAVID'S LAMENT FOR SAUL AND JONATHAN.*

2 SAMUEL i.

DAVID had returned to Ziklag from the slaughter of the Amalekites only two days before he heard of the death of Saul. He had returned weary enough, we may believe, in body, though refreshed in spirit by the recovery of all that had been taken away, and by the possession of a vast store of booty besides. But in the midst of his success, it was discouraging to see nothing but ruin and confusion where the homes of himself and his people had recently been ; and it must have needed no small effort even to plan, and much more to execute, the reconstruction of the city. But besides this, a still heavier feeling must have oppressed him. What had been the issue of that great battle at Mount Gilboa ? Which army had conquered ? If the Israelites were defeated, what would be the fate of Saul and Jonathan ? Would they be prisoners now in the hands of the Philistines ? And if so, what would be his duty in regard to them ? And what course would it be best for him to take for the welfare of his ruined and distracted country ?

He was not kept long in suspense. An Amalekite from the camp of Israel, accustomed, like the Bedouin generally, to long and rapid runs, arrived at Ziklag, bearing on his body all the tokens of a disaster, and did obeisance to David, as now the legitimate occupant of the throne. David must have surmised at a glance how matters stood. His questions to the Amalekite elicited an account of the death of Saul materially different from that given in a former part of the history, " As I happened by chance upon Mount Gilboa, behold Saul leaned upon his spear; and lo, the chariots and the horsemen followed hard after him. And when he looked behind him, he saw me and called unto me. And I answered, Here am I. And he said unto me, Who art thou ? And I answered him, I am an Amalekite. And he said unto me, Stand, I pray thee, beside me, and slay me, for anguish hath taken hold of me : because my life is yet whole in me. So I stood beside him and slew him, because I was sure that he could not live after that he was fallen ; and I took the crown that was upon his head, and the bracelet that was upon his arm, and have brought them hither to my lord." There is no reason to suppose that this narrative of Saul's death, in so far as it differs from the previous one, is correct. That this Amalekite was somehow near the place where Saul fell, and that he witnessed all that took place at his death, there is no cause to doubt. That when he saw that both Saul and his armour-bearer were dead he removed the crown and the bracelet from the person of the fallen king, and stowed them away among his own accoutrements, may likewise be accepted without any difficulty. Then, managing to escape, and considering what he would do with the ensigns of royalty, he decided to carry them to David. To David he accordingly brought them, and no doubt it was to ingratiate himself the more with him, and to establish the stronger claim

to a splendid recompense, that he invented the story of
Saul asking him to kill him, and of his complying with
the king's order, and thus putting an end to a life
which already was obviously doomed.

In his belief that his pretended despatching of the
king would gratify David, the Amalekite undoubtedly
reckoned without his host; but such things were so
common, so universal in the East, that we can hardly
divest ourselves of a certain amount of compassion for
him.   Probably there was no other kingdom, round
and round, where this Amalekite would not have found
that he had done a wise thing in so far as his own
interests were concerned.   For helping to despatch a
rival, and to open the way to a throne, he would
probably have received cordial thanks and ample gifts
from one and all of the neighbouring potentates.   To
David, the matter appeared in a quite different light.
He had none of that eagerness to occupy the throne on
which the Amalekite reckoned as a universal instinct
of human nature.   And he had a view of the sanctity
of Saul's life which the Amalekite could not understand.
His being the Lord's anointed ought to have withheld
this man from hurting a hair of his head.   Sadly
though Saul had fallen back, the divinity that doth
hedge a king still encompassed him.   " Touch not
mine anointed " was still God's word concerning him.
This miserable Amalekite, a member of a doomed race,
appeared to David by his own confession not only a
murderer, but a murderer of the deepest dye.   He had
destroyed the life of one who in an eminent sense was
" the Lord's anointed."   He had done what once and
again David had himself shrunk from doing.   It is no
wonder that David was at once horrified and provoked,
—horrified at the unblushing criminality of the man ;

provoked at his effrontery, at his doing without the slightest compunction what, at an immense sacrifice, he had twice restrained himself from doing. No doubt he was irritated, too, at the bare supposition on which the Amalekite reckoned so securely, that such a black deed could be gratifying to David himself. So without a moment's hesitation, and without allowing the astonished youth a moment's preparation, he caused an attendant to fall upon him and kill him. His sentence was short and clear, " Thy blood be upon thy head ; for thy mouth hath testified against thee saying, I have slain the Lord's anointed."

In this incident we find David in a position in which good men are often placed, who profess to have regard to higher principles than the men of the world in regulating their lives, and especially in the estimate which they form of their worldly interests and considerations. That such men are sincere in the estimate they thus profess to follow is what the world is very slow to believe. Faith in any moral virtue that rises higher than the ordinary worldly level is extremely rare among men. The world fancies that every man has his price—sometimes that every woman has her price. Virtue of the heroic quality that will face death itself rather than do wrong is what it is most unwilling to believe in. Was it not this that gave rise to the memorable trial of Job ? Did not the great enemy, representing here the spirit of the world, scorn the notion that at bottom Job was in any way better than his neighbours, although the wonderful prosperity with which he had been gifted made him appear more ready to pay honour to God ? It is all a matter of selfishness, was Satan's plea ; take away his prosperity, and lay a painful malady on his body, his religion will vanish, he will curse Thee to Thy face.  He would not give Job credit for anything like disinterested virtue—anything like genuine reverence for God.  And was it not on the same principle the tempter acted when he brought his threefold temptation to our Lord in the wilderness ? He did not believe in the superhuman virtue of Jesus ; he did not believe in His unswerving loyalty to truth and duty.  He did not believe that He was proof at once against the lust of the flesh, and the lust of the eye, and the pride of life.  At least he did not believe till he tried, and had to retreat defeated.  When the end of His life drew near Jesus could say, " The prince of this world cometh, but hath nothing in Me."  There was no weakness in Jesus to which he could fasten his cord—no trace of that worldliness by which he had so often been able to entangle and secure his victims.

So likewise Simon the sorcerer fancied that he only needed to offer money to the Apostles to secure from them the gift of the Holy Ghost.  " Thy money perish with thee ! " was the indignant rebuke of Peter.  It is the same refusal to believe in the reality of high principle that has made so many a persecutor fancy that he could bend the obstinacy of the heretic by the terrors of suffering and torture.  And on the other hand, no nobler sight has ever been presented than when this incredulous scorn of the world has been rebuked by the firmness and triumphant faith of the noble martyr.  What could Nebuchadnezzar have thought when the three Hebrew children were willing to enter the fiery furnace ?  What did Darius think of Daniel when he shrank not from the lions' den ?  How many a rebuke and surprise was furnished to the rulers of this world in the early persecutions of the Christians, and to the champions of the Church of Rome in the splendid defiance hurled against them by the Protestant martyrs! The men who formed the Free Church of Scotland were utterly discredited when they affirmed that rather than surrender the liberties of their Church they would part with every temporal privilege which they had enjoyed from connection with the State. Such is the spirit of the world; if it will not rise to the apparent level of the saints, it delights to pull down the saints to its own. These pretences to superior virtue are hypocrisy and pharisaism; test their professions by their worldly interests, and you will find them soon enough on a level with yourselves.

The Amalekite that thought to gratify David by pretending that he had slain his rival had no idea that he was wronging him; in his blind innocency he seems to have assumed as a matter of course that David would be pleased. It is not likely the Amalekite had ever heard of David's noble magnanimity in twice sparing Saul's life when he had an excellent pretext for taking it, if his conscience had allowed him. He just assumed that David would feel as he would have felt himself. He simply judged of him by his own standard. His object was to show how great a service he had rendered him, and thus establish a claim to a great reward. Never did heartless selfishness more completely overreach itself. Instead of a reward, this impious murderer had earned a fearful punishment. An Israelite might have had a chance of mercy, but an Amalekite had none—the man was condemned to instant death. One can hardly fancy his bewilderment,—what a strange man was this David! What a marvellous reverence he had for God! To place him on a throne was no favor, if it involved doing anything against "the Lord's anointed!" And yet who shall say that in his estimate of this proceeding David did more than recognize the obligation of the first commandment? To him God's will was all in all.

Dismissing this painful episode, we now turn to contemplate David's conduct after the intelligence reached him that Saul was dead. David was now just thirty (2 Sam. v. 4); and never did man at that age, or at any age, act a finer part. The death, and especially the sudden death, of a relative or a friend has usually a remarkable effect on the tender heart, and especially in the case of the young. It blots out all remembrance of little injuries done by the departed; it fills one with regret for any unkind words one may have spoken, or any unkind deeds one may ever have done to him. It makes one very forgiving. But it must have been a far more generous heart than the common that could so soon rid itself of every shred of bitter feeling toward Saul— that could blot out, in one great act of forgiveness, the remembrance of many long years of injustice, oppression, and toil, and leave no feelings but those of kindness, admiration, and regret, called forth by the contemplation of what was favourable in Saul's character. How beautiful does the spirit of forgiveness appear in such a light! Yet how hard do many feel it to be to exercise this spirit in any case, far less in all cases! How terrible a snare the unforgiving spirit is liable to be to us, and how terrible an obstacle to peaceful communion with God! "For if ye forgive not men their trespasses, neither will your Father in heaven forgive your trespasses."

The feelings of David toward Saul and Jonathan were permanently embodied in a song which he composed for the occasion. It seems to have been called "The Song of the Bow," so that the rendering of the Revised

Version—"he taught them the Song of the Bow," gives
a much better sense than the old—"he taught them the
use of the bow." The song was first written in the
book of Jasher; and it was ordered by David to be
taught to the people as a permanent memorial of their
king and his eldest son. The writing of such a song,
the spirit of admiration and eulogy which pervades it,
and the unusual enactment that it should be taught to
the people, show how far superior David was to the
ordinary feelings of jealousy, how full his heart was of
true generosity. There was, indeed, a political end
which it might advance; it might conciliate the supporters of Saul, and smooth David's way to the throne.
But there is in it such depth and fulness of feeling
that one can think of it only as a genuine cardiphonia
—a true voice of the heart. The song dwells on all
that could be commended in Saul, and makes no allusion
to his faults. His courage and energy in war, his happy
co-operation with Jonathan, his advancement of the
kingdom in elegance and comfort, are all duly celebrated.
David appears to have had a real affection for Saul, if
only it had been allowed to bloom and flourish. His
martial energy had probably awakened his admiration
before he knew him personally; and when he became
his minstrel, his distressed countenance would excite
his pity, while his occasional gleams of generous feeling
would thrill his heart with sympathy. The terrible
effort of Saul to crush David was now at an end, and
like a lily released from a heavy stone, the old attachment bloomed out speedily and sweetly. There would
be more true love in families and in the world, more
of expansive, responsive affection, if it were not so
often stunted by reserve on the one hand, and crushed
by persecution on the other.

The song embalms very tenderly the love of Jonathan
for David. Years had probably elapsed since the two
friends met, but time had not impaired the affection and
admiration of David. And now that Jonathan's light
was extinguished, a sense of desolation fell on David's
heart, and the very throne that invited his occupation seemed dark and dull under the shadow cast on
it by the death of Jonathan. As a prize of earthly
ambition it would be poor indeed; and if ever it had
seemed to David a proud distinction to look forward
to, such a feeling would appear very detestable when
the same act that opened it up to him had deprived
him for ever of his dearest friend, his sweetest source
of earthly joy. The only way in which it was possible
for David to enjoy his new position was by losing sight
of himself; by identifying himself more closely than
ever with the people; by regarding the throne as only
a position for more self-denying labours for the good
of others. And in the song there is evidence of the
great strength and activity of this feeling. The sentiment of patriotism burns with a noble ardour; the
national disgrace is most keenly felt; the thought of
personal gain from the death of Saul and Jonathan is
entirely swallowed up by grief for the public loss.
" Tell it not in Gath, publish it not in the streets of
Askelon; lest the daughters of the Philistines rejoice,
lest the daughters of the uncircumcised triumph!" In
David's view, it is no ordinary calamity that has fallen
on Israel. It is no common men that have fallen, but
" the beauty of Israel," her ornament and her glory,
men that were never known to flinch or to flee from
battle, men that were " swifter than eagles, and stronger
than lions." It is not in any obscure corner that they
have fallen, but "on her high places," on Mount Gilboa,

at the head of a most conspicuous and momentous enterprise. Such a national loss was unprecedented in the history of Israel, and it seems to have affected David and the nation generally as the slaughter at Flodden affected the Scots, when it seemed as if all that was great and beautiful in the nation perished—"the flowers o' the forest were a' weed awa'."

A word on the general structure of this song. It is not a song that can be classed with the Psalms. Nor can it be said that in any marked degree it resembles the tone or spirit of the Psalms. Yet this need not surprise us, nor need it throw any doubt either as to the authorship of the song or the authorship of the Psalms. The Psalms, we must remember, were avowedly composed and designed for use in the worship of God. If the Greek term *psalmoi* denotes their character, they were songs designed for use in public worship, to be accompanied with the lyre, or harp, or other musical instruments suitable for them. The special sphere of such songs was—the relation of the human soul to God. These songs might be of various kinds—historical, lyrical, dramatical; but in all cases the paramount subject was, the dealings of God with man, or the dealings of man with God. It was in this class of composition that David excelled, and became the organ of the Holy Ghost for the highest instruction and edification of the Church in all ages. But it does not by any means follow that the poetical compositions of David were restricted to this one class of subject. His muse may sometimes have taken a different course. His poems were not always directly religious. In the case of this song, whose original place in the book of Jasher indicated its special character, there is no mention of the relation of Saul and Jonathan to God.

The theme is, their services to the nation, and the national loss involved in their death. The soul of the poet is profoundly thrilled by their death, occurring in such circumstances of national disaster. No form of words could have conveyed more vividly the idea of unprecedented loss, or thrilled the nation with such a sense of calamity. There is not a line of the song but is full of life, and hardly one that is not full of beauty. What could more touchingly indicate the fatal nature of the calamity than that plaintive entreaty—" Tell it not in Gath, publish it not in the streets of Askelon "? How could the hills be more impressively summoned to show their sympathy than in that invocation of everlasting sterility—" Ye mountains of Gilboa, let there be no dew, neither let there be rain upon you, or fields of offerings "? What gentler veil could be drawn over the horrors of their bloody death and mutilated bodies than in the tender words, " Saul and Jonathan were loving and pleasant in their lives, and in their deaths they were not divided "? And what more fitting theme for tears could have been furnished to the daughters of Israel, considering what was probably the prevalent taste, than that Saul had " clothed them with scarlet and other delights, and put on ornaments of gold upon their apparel "? Up to this point Saul and Jonathan are joined together; but the poet cannot close without a special lamentation for himself over him whom he loved as his own soul. And in one line he touches the very kernel of his own loss, as he touches the very core of Jonathan's heart—"thy love to me was wonderful, passing the love of women." Such is the Song of the Bow. It hardly seems suitable to attempt to draw spiritual lessons out of a song, which, on purpose, was placed in a different category. Surely it is enough to point out the exceeding beauty and generosity of spirit which sought in this way to embalm the memory and perpetuate the virtues of Saul and Jonathan; which blended together in such melodious words a deadly enemy and a beloved friend; which transfigured one of the lives so that it shone with the lustre and the beauty of the other; which sought to bury every painful association, and gave full and unlimited scope to the charity that thinketh no evil. *De mortuis nil nisi bonum,* was a heathen maxim,—"Say nothing but what is good of the dead." Surely no finer exemplification of the maxim was ever given than in this "Song of the Bow."

To "thoughts that breathe and words that burn," like those of this song, David could not have given expression without having his whole soul stirred with the desire to repair the national disaster, and by God's help bring back prosperity and honour to Israel. Thus, both by the afflictions that saddened his heart and the stroke of prosperity that raised him to the throne, he was impelled to that course of action which is the best safeguard under God against the hurtful influences both of adversity and prosperity. Affliction might have driven him into his shell, to think only of his own comfort; prosperity might have swollen him with a sense of his importance, and tempted him to expect universal admiration;—both would have made him unfit to rule; by the grace of God he was preserved from both. He was induced to gird himself for a course of high exertion for the good of his country; the spirit of trust in God, after its long discipline, had a new field opened for its exercise; and the self-government acquired in the wilderness was to prove its usefulness in a higher sphere. Thus the providence of his heavenly

Father was gradually unfolding His purposes concerning him ; the clouds were clearing off his horizon ; and the " all things " that once seemed to be "against him " were now plainly " working together for his good."

# CHAPTER II

2 SAMUEL ii. 1-7.

THE death of Saul did not end David's troubles. nor was it for a good many years that he became free to employ his whole energies for the good of the kingdom. It appears that his chastisement for his unbelieving spirit, and for the alliance with Achish to which it led, was not yet completed. The more remote consequences of that step were only beginning to emerge, and years elapsed before its evil influence ceased altogether to be felt. For in allying himself with Achish, and accompanying his army to the plain of Esdraelon, David had gone as near to the position of a traitor to his country as he could have gone without actually fighting against it. That he should have acted as he did is one of the greatest mysteries of his life; and the reason why it has not attracted more notice is simply because the worst consequences of it were averted by his dismissal from the Philistine army through the jealousy and suspicion of their lords. But for that step David must have been guilty of gross treachery either in one direction or another; either to his own countrymen, by fighting against them in the Philistine army; or to King Achish, by suddenly turning against him in the heat of the battle, and creating a diversion

which might have given a new chance to his countrymen. In either case the proceeding would have been
most reprehensible.

But to his own countrymen he would have made
himself especially obnoxious if he had lent himself to
Achish in the battle. Whether he contemplated treachery to Achish is a secret that seems never to have
gone beyond his own bosom. All the appearances
favoured the supposition that he would fight against his
country, and we cannot wonder if, for a long time, this
made him an object of distrust and suspicion. If we
would understand how the men of Israel must have
looked on him, we have only to fancy how we should
have viewed a British soldier if, with a troop of his
countrymen, he had followed Napoleon to the field of
Waterloo, and had been sent away from the French
army only through the suspicion of Napoleon's generals.
In David's case, all his former achievements against the
Philistines, all that injustice from Saul which had driven
him in despair to Achish, his services against the
Amalekites, his generous use of the spoil, as well as
his high personal character, did not suffice to counteract
the bad impression of his having followed Achish to
battle. For after a great disaster the public mind is
exasperated; it is eager to find a scapegoat on whom
to throw the blame, and it is unmeasured in its denun-
ciations of any one who can be plausibly assailed.
Beyond all doubt, angry and perplexed as the nation
was, David would come in for a large share of the
blame; his alliance with Achish would be denounced
with unmeasured bitterness ; and, probably enough, he
would have to bear the brunt of many a bitter calumny
in addition, as if he had instigated Achish, and given
him information which had helped him to conquer.

His own tribe, the tribe of Judah, was far the friendliest, and the most likely to make allowance for the position in which he had been placed. They were his own flesh and blood; they knew the fierce and cruel malignity with which Saul had hunted him down, and they knew that, as far as appearances went, his chances of getting the better of Saul's efforts were extremely small, and the temptation to throw himself into the hands of Achish correspondingly great. Evidently, therefore, the most expedient course he could now take was to establish himself in some of the cities of Judah. But in that frame of recovered loyalty to God in which he now was, he declined to take this step, indispensable though it seemed, until he had got Divine direction regarding it. " It came to pass, after this, that David inquired of the Lord saying, Shall I go up to any of the cities of Judah ? And the Lord said unto him, Go up. And David said, Whither shall I go up ? And He said, Unto Hebron." The form in which he made the inquiry shows that to his mind it was very clear that he ought to go up to one or another of the cities of Judah; his advisers and companions had probably the same conviction; but notwithstanding, it was right and fitting that no such step should be taken without his asking direction from God. And let us observe that, on this occasion, prayer was not the last resort of one whom all other refuge had failed, but the first resort of one who regarded the Divine approval as the most essential element for determining the propriety of the undertaking.

It is interesting and instructive to ponder this fact. The first thing done by David, after virtually acquiring a royal position, was to ask counsel of God. His royal administration was begun by prayer. And there was a singular appropriateness in this act. For the great characteristic of David, brought out especially in his Psalms, is the reality and the nearness of his fellowship with God. We may find other men who equalled him in every other feature of character—who were as full of human sympathy, as reverential, as self-denying, as earnest in their efforts to please God and to benefit men; but we shall find no one who lived so closely under God's shadow, whose heart and life were so influenced by regard to God, to whom God was so much of a personal Friend, so blended, we may say, with his very existence. David therefore is eminently himself when asking counsel of the Lord. And would not all do well to follow him in this? True, he had supernatural methods of doing this, and you have only natural; he had the Urim and Thummim, you have only the voice of prayer; but this makes no real difference, for it was only in great national matters that he made use of the supernatural method; in all that concerned his personal relations to God it was the other that he employed. And so may you. But the great matter is to resemble David in his profound sense of the infinite value and reality of Divine direction. Without this your prayers will always be more or less matters of formality. And being formal, you will not feel that you get any good of them. Is it really a profound conviction of yours that in every step of your life God's direction is of supreme value? That you dare not even change your residence with safety without being directed by Him? That you dare not enter on new relations in life,—new business, new connections, new recreations—without seeking the Divine countenance? That endless difficulties, troubles, complications, are liable to arise, when you simply follow your own notions or inclinations without consulting the Lord ? And under the influence of that conviction do you try to follow the rule, " In all thy ways acknowledge Him "? And do you endeavour to get from prayer a trustful rest in God, an assurance that He will not forsake you, a calm confidence that He will keep His word ? Then, indeed, you are treading in David's footsteps, and you may expect to share his privilege—Divine direction in your times of need.

The city of Hebron, situated about eighteen miles to the south of Jerusalem, was the place to which David was directed to go. It was a place abounding in venerable and elevating associations. It was among the first, if not the very first, of the haunts of civilized men in the land—so ancient that it is said to have been built seven years before Zoan in Egypt (Numb. xiii. 22). The father of the faithful had often pitched his tent under its spreading oaks, and among its olive groves and vine-clad hills the gentle Isaac had meditated at eventide. There Abraham had watched the last breath of his beloved Sarah, the partner of his faith and the faithful companion of his wanderings ; and there from the sons of Heth he had purchased the sepulchre of Machpelah, where first Sarah's body, then his own, then that of Isaac were laid to rest. There Joseph and his brethren had brought up the body of Jacob, in fulfilment of his dying command, laying it beside the bones of Leah. It had been a halting-place of the twelve spies when they went up to search the land ; and the cluster of grapes which they carried back was cut from the neighbouring valley, where the finest grapes of the country are found to this day. The s ght of its venerable cave had doubtless served to raise the faith and courage of Joshua and Caleb, when the other spies became so feeble and so faithless. In the division of the land it had been assigned to Caleb, one of the best and noblest spirits the nation ever produced; afterwards it was made one of the Levitical cities of refuge. More recently, it had been one of the places selected by David to receive a portion of the Amalekite spoil. No place could have recalled more vividly the lessons of departed worth and the victories of early faith, or abounded more in tokens of the blessedness of fully following the Lord. It was a token of God's kindness to David that He directed him to make this city his headquarters. It was equivalent to a new promise that the God of Abraham and of Isaac and Jacob would be the God of David, and that his public career would prepare the way for the mercies in the prospect of which they rejoiced, and sustain the hope to which they looked forward, though they did not in their time see the promise realised.

It was a further token of God's goodness that no sooner had David gone up to Hebron than "the men of Judah came and anointed him king over the house of Judah." Judah was the imperial or premier tribe, and though this was not all that God had promised to David, it was a large instalment. The occasion might well awaken mingled emotions in his breast—gratitude for mercies given and solicitude for the responsibility of a royal position. With his strong sense of duty, his love of righteousness and hatred of wickedness, we should expect to find him strengthening himself in the purpose to rule only in the fear of God. It is just such views and purposes as these we find expressed in the hundred and first Psalm, which internal

evidence would lead us to assign to this period of his
life :—

> " I will sing of mercy and of judgment :
> Unto Thee, O Lord, will I sing.
> I will behave myself wisely in a perfect way.
> O when wilt Thou come unto me?
> I will walk within my house with a perfect heart.
> I will set no base thing before mine eyes :
> I hate the work of them that turn aside ;
> It shall not cleave to me.
> A froward heart shall depart from me :
> I will know no evil thing.
> Whoso privily slandereth his neighbour, him will I destroy ;
> Him that hath an high look and a proud heart will not I suffer.
> Mine eyes shall be upon the faithful of the land that they may
>     dwell with me :
> He that walketh in a perfect way, he shall minister unto me.
> He that worketh deceit shall not dwell within my house ;
> He that speaketh falsehood shall not be established before mine
>     eyes.
> Morning by morning will I destroy all the wicked of the land ;
> To cut off all the workers of iniquity from the city of the Lord." *

By a singular coincidence, the first place to which
the attention of David was called, after his taking possession of the royal position, was the same as that to
which Saul had been directed in the same circumstances
—namely, Jabesh-gilead. It was far away from
Hebron, on the other side of Jordan, and quite out

---

* From the use of the expression "city of the Lord," it has been
inferred by some critics that this Psalm must have been written after
the capture and consecration of Jerusalem. But there is no reason why
Hebron might not have been called at that time "the city of the Lord."
The Lord had specially designated it as the abode of David ; and that
alone entitled it to be so called. Those who have regarded this Psalm
as a picture of a model household or family have never weighed the
force of the last line, which marks the position of a king, not a father.
The Psalm is a true statement of the principles usually followed by
David in public rule, but not in domestic administration.

of the scope of David's former activities ; but he recognised a duty to its people, and he hastened to perform it. In the first place, he sent them a gracious and grateful message of thanks for the kindness shown to Saul, the mark of respect they had paid him in burying his body. Every action of David's in reference to his great rival evinces the superiority of his spirit to that which was wont to prevail in similar circumstances. Within the Scriptures themselves we have instances of the dishonour that was often put on the body of a conquered rival. The body of Jehoram, cast ignominiously by Jehu, in mockery of his royal state, into the vineyard of Naboth, which his father Ahaz had unrighteously seized, and the body of Jezebel, flung out of the window, trodden under foot, and devoured by dogs are instances readily remembered. The shocking fate of the dead body of Hector, dragged thrice round the walls of Troy after Achilles' chariot, was regarded as only such a calamity as might be looked for amid the changing fortunes of war. Mark Antony is said to have broken out into laughter at the sight of the hands and head of Cicero, which he had caused to be severed from his body. The respect of David for the person of Saul was evidently a sincere and genuine feeling ; and it was a sincere pleasure to him to find that this feeling had been shared by the Jabeshites, and manifested in their rescuing Saul's body and consigning it to honourable burial.

In the next place, he invokes on these people a glowing benediction from the Lord : " The Lord show kindness and truth to you ; " and he expresses his purpose also to requite their kindness himself. " Kindness and truth." There is something instructive in the combination of these two words. It is the Hebrew way of expressing "true kindness," but even in that form, the words suggest that kindness is not always true kindness, and mere kindness cannot be a real blessing unless it rest on a solid basis. There is in many men an amiable spirit which takes pleasure in gratifying the feelings of others. Some manifest it to children by loading them with toys and sweetmeats, or taking them to amusements which they know they like. But it does not follow that such kindness is always true kindness. To please one is not always the kindest thing you can do for one, for sometimes it is a far kinder thing to withhold what will please. True kindness must be tested by its ultimate effects. The kindness that loves best to improve our hearts, to elevate our tastes, to straighten our habits, to give a higher tone to our lives, to place us on a pedestal from which we may look down on conquered spiritual foes, and on the possession of what is best and highest in human attainment,—the kindness that bears on the future, and especially the eternal future, is surely far more true than that which, by gratifying our present feelings, perhaps confirms us in many a hurtful lust. David's prayer for the men of Jabesh was an enlightened benediction : " God show you kindness and truth." And so far as he may have opportunity, he promises that he will show them the same kindness too.

We need not surely dwell on the lesson which this suggests. Are you kindly disposed to any one ? You wish sincerely to promote his happiness, and you try to do so. But see well to it that your kindness is true. See that the day shall never come when that which you meant so kindly will turn out to have been a snare, and perhaps a curse. Think of your friend as an immortal being, with either heaven or hell before him, and consider what genuine kindness requires of you in such a case. And in every instance beware of the kindness which shakes the stability of his principles, which increases the force of his temptations, and makes the narrow way more distasteful and difficult to him than ever.

There can be no doubt that David was moved by considerations of policy as well as by more disinterested motives in sending this message and offering this prayer for the men of Jabesh-gilead. Indeed, in the close of his message he invites them to declare for him, and follow the example of the men of Judah, who have made him king. The kindly proceeding of David was calculated to have a wider influence than over the men of Jabesh, and to have a conciliating effect on all the friends of the former king. It would have been natural enough for them to fear, considering the ordinary ways of conquerors and the ordinary fate of the friends of the conquered, that David would adopt very rigid steps against the friends of his persecutors. By this message sent across the whole country and across the Jordan, he showed that he was animated by the very opposite spirit : that, instead of wishing to punish those who had served with Saul, he was quite disposed to show them favour. Divine grace, acting on his kindly nature, made him forgiving to Saul and all his comrades, and presented to the world the spectacle of an eminent religious profession in harmony with a noble generosity.

But the spirit in which David acted towards the friends of Saul did not receive the fitting return. The men of Jabesh-gilead appear to have made no response to his appeal. His peaceable purpose was defeated through Abner, Saul's cousin and captain-general of his army, who set up Ishbosheth, one of Saul's sons, as

king in opposition to David. Ishbosheth himself was
but a tool in Abner's hands, evidently a man of no
spirit or activity; and in setting him up as a claimant
for the kingdom, Abner very probably had an eye to
the interests of himself and his family. It is plain that
he acted in this matter in that spirit of ungodliness and
wilfulness of which his royal cousin had given so many
proofs; he knew that God had given the kingdom to
David, and afterwards taunted Ishbosheth with the fact
(iii. 9); perhaps he looked for the reversion of the
throne if Ishbosheth should die, for it needed more than
an ordinary motive to go right in opposition to the
known decree of God. The world's annals contain
too many instances of wars springing from no higher
motive than the ambition of some Diotrephes to have
the pre-eminence. You cry shame on such a spirit;
but while you do so take heed lest you share it yourselves. To many a soldier war is welcome because it
is the pathway to promotion, to many a civilian because
it gives for the moment an impulse to the business
with which he is connected. How subtle and dangerous is the feeling that secretly welcomes what may
spread numberless woes through a community if only
it is likely to bring some advantage to ourselves!
O God, drive selfishness from the throne of our hearts,
and write on them in deepest letters Thine own holy
law, " Thou shalt love thy neighbour as thyself."

The place chosen for the residence of Ishbosheth
was Mahanaim, in the half-tribe of Manasseh, on the
east side of the Jordan. It is a proof how much the
Philistines must have dominated the central part of the
country that no city in the tribe of Benjamin and no
place even on the western side of the Jordan could be
obtained as a royal seat for the son of Saul. Surely

this was an evil omen. Ishbosheth's reign, if reign it might be called, lasted but two short years. No single event took place to give it lustre. No city was taken from the Philistines, no garrison put to flight, as at Michmash. No deed was ever done by him or done by his adherents of which they might be proud, and to which they might point in justification of their resistance to David. Ishbosheth was not the wicked man in great power, spreading himself like the green bay-tree, but a short-lived, shrivelled plant, that never rose above the humiliating circumstances of its origin. Men who have defied the purpose of the Almighty have often grown and prospered, like the little horn of the Apocalypse ; but in this case of Ishbosheth little more than one breath of the Almighty sufficed to wither him up. Yes, indeed, whatever may be the immediate fortunes of those who unfurl their own banner against the clear purpose of the Almighty, there is but one fate for them all in the end—utter humiliation and defeat. Well may the Psalm counsel all, " Kiss ye the Son, lest He be angry, and ye perish from the way, if once His wrath is kindled but a little. Blessed are all they that put their trust in Him."

# CHAPTER III.

## BEGINNING OF CIVIL WAR.

### 2 Samuel ii. 12—32

THE well-meant and earnest efforts of David to ward off strife and bring the people together in reccgnising him as king were frustrated, as we have seen, through the efforts of Abner. Unmoved by the solemn testimony of God, uttered again and again through Samuel, that He had rejected Saul and found as king a man after His own heart; unmoved by the sad proceedings at Endor, where, under such awful circumstances, the same announcement of the purpose of the Almighty had been repeated; unmoved by the doom of Saul and his three sons on Mount Gilboa, where such a striking proof of the reality of God's judgment on his house had been given; unmoved by the miserable state of the kingdom, overrun and humiliated by the Philistines and in the worst possible condition to bear the strain of a civil war,—this Abner insisted on setting up Ishbosheth and endeavouring to make good his claims by the sword. It was never seen more clearly how "one sinner destroyeth much good."

As to the immediate occasion of the war, David was quite innocent, and Abner alone was responsible; but to a feeling and patriotic heart like David's, the war itself must have been the occasion of bitter distress

Did it ever occur to him to think that in a sense he was now brought, against his will, into the position which he had professed to King Achish to be willing to occupy, or that, placed as he now was in an attitude of opposition to a large section of his countrymen, he was undergoing a chastisement for what he was rash enough to say and to do then ?

In the commencement of the war, the first step was taken by Abner. He went out from Mahanaim, descended the Jordan valley, and came to Gibeon, in the tribe of Benjamin, a place but a few miles distant from Gibeah, where Saul had reigned. His immediate object probably was to gain such an advantage over David in that quarter as would enable him to establish Ishbosheth at Gibeah, and thus bring to him all the prestige due to the son and successor of Saul. We must not forget that the Philistines had still great influence in the land, and very likely they were in possession of Gibeah, after having rifled Saul's palace and appropriated all his private property. With this powerful enemy to be dealt with ultimately, it was the interest of Abner to avoid a collision of the whole forces on either side, and spare the slaughter which such a contest would have involved. There is some obscurity in the narrative now before us, both at this point and at other places. But it would appear that, when the two armies were ranged on opposite sides of the "pool" or reservoir at Gibeon, Abner made the proposal to Joab that the contest should be decided by a limited number of young men on either side, whose encounter would form a sort of play or spectacle, that their brethren might look on, and, in a sense, enjoy. In the circumstances, it was a wise and humane proposal, although we get something of a shock from the frivolous

spirit that could speak of such a deadly encounter as
" play."

David was not present with his troops on this
occasion, the management of them being entrusted to
Joab, his sister's son.   Here was another of the difficulties of David—a difficulty which embarrassed him
for forty years.   He was led to commit the management of his army to his warlike nephew, although he
appears to have been a man very unlike himself.   Joab
is much more of the type of Saul than of David.   He
is rough, impetuous, worldly, manifesting no faith, no
prayerfulness, no habit or spirit of communion with
God.   Yet from the beginning he threw in his lot
with David ; he remained faithful to him in the insurrection of Absalom ; and sometimes he gave him advice
which was more worthy to be followed than his own
devices.   But though Joab was a difficulty to David,
he did not master him.   The course of David's life and
the character of his reign were determined mainly by
those spiritual feelings with which Joab appears to
have had no sympathy.   It was unfortunate that the
first stage of the war should have been in the hands of
Joab ; he conducted it in a way that must have been
painful to David ; he stained it with a crime that gave
him bitter pain.

The practice of deciding public contests by a small
and equal number of champions on either side, if not a
common one in ancient times, was, at any rate, not very
rare.   Roman history furnishes some memorable instances of it : that of Romulus and Aruns, and that of
the Horatii and the Curiatii ; while the challenge of
Goliath and the proposal to settle the strife between
the Philistines and the Hebrews according to the result
of the duel with him had taken place not many years

before.    The young men were accordingly chosen, twelve on either side; but they rushed against each other with such impetuosity that the whole of them fell together, and the contest remained undecided as before. Excited probably by what they had witnessed, the main forces on either side now rushed against each other; and when the shock of battle came, the victory fell to the side of David, and Abner and his troops were signally defeated.    On David's side, there was not a very serious loss, the number of the slain amounting to twenty; but on the side of Abner the loss was three hundred and sixty.    To account for so great an inequality we must remember that in Eastern warfare it was in the pursuit that by far the greatest amount of slaughter took place.    That obstinate maintenance of their ground which is characteristic of modern armies seems to have been unknown in those times.    The superiority of one of the hosts over the other appears usually to have made itself felt at the beginning of the engagement; the opposite force, seized with panic, fled in confusion, followed close by the conquerors, whose weapons, directed against the backs of the fugitive, were neither caught on shields, nor met by counter-volleys.    Thus it was that Joab's loss was little more than the twelve who had fallen at first, while that of Abner was many times more.

Among those who had to save themselves by flight after the battle was Abner, the captain of the host. Hard in pursuit of him, and of him only, hastened Asahel, the brother of Joab.    It is not easy to understand all the circumstances of this pursuit.    We cannot but believe that Asahel was bent on killing Abner, but probably his hope was that he would get near enough to him to discharge an arrow at him, and that in doing so he would incur no personal danger.   But Abner appears to have remarked him, and to have stopped his flight and faced round to meet him.   Abner seems to have carried sword and spear; Asahel had probably nothing heavier than a bow.   It was fair enough in Abner to propose that if they were to be opponents, Asahel should borrow armour, that they might fight on equal terms.   But this was not Asahel's thought.   He seems to have been determined to follow Abner, and take his opportunity for attacking him in his own way. This Abner would not permit; and, as Asahel would not desist from his pursuit, Abner, rushing at him, struck him with such violence with the hinder end of his spear that the weapon came out behind him.   " And Asahel fell down there, and died in the same place ; and it came to pass that as many as came to the place where Asahel fell down and died stood still."   Asahel was a man of consequence, being brother of the commander of the army and nephew of the king.   The death of such a man counted for much, and went far to restore the balance of loss between the two contending armies.   It seems to have struck a horror into the hearts of his fellow-soldiers ; it was an awful incident of the war. It was strange enough to see one who an hour ago was so young, so fresh and full of life, stretched on the ground a helpless lump of clay ; but it was more appalling to remember his relation to the two greatest men of the nation—David and Joab.   Certainly war is most indiscriminate in the selection of its victims ; commanders and their brothers, kings and their nephews, being as open to its catastrophes as any one else.   Surely it must have sent a thrill through Abner to see among the first victims of the strife which he had kindled one whose family stood so high, and whose

death would exasperate against him so important a
person as his brother Joab.

The pursuit of the defeated army was by-and-bye
ii terrupted by nightfall. In the course of the evening
tl.e fugitives somewhat rallied, and concentrated on the
top of a hill, in the wilderness of Gibeon. And here
the two chiefs held parley together. The proceedings
were begun by Abner, and begun by a question that
was almost insolent. " Abner called to Joab and said,
Shall the sword devour for ever? knowest thou not
that it will be bitterness in the latter end? how long
shall it be ere thou bid the people return from following
their brethren?" It was an audacious attempt to
throw on Joab and Joab's master the responsibility of
the war. We get a new glimpse of Abner's character
here. If there was a fact that might be held to be
beyond the possibility of question, it was that Abner
had begun the contest. Had not he, in opposition to
the Divine King of the nation, set up Ishbosheth against
the man called by Jehovah? Had not he gathered the
army at Mahanaim, and moved towards Gibeon, on
express purpose to exclude David, and secure for his
nominee what might be counted in reality, and not in
name only, the kingdom of Israel? Yet he insolently
demanded of Joab, "Shall the sword devour for ever?"
He audaciously applies to Joab a maxim that he had
not thought of applying to himself in the morning—
"Knowest thou not that it will be bitterness in the
latter end?" This is a war that can be terminated
only by the destruction of one half of the nation; it
will be a bitter enough consummation, which half
soever it may be. Have you no regard for your
" brethren," against whom you are fighting, that you
are holding on in this remorseless way?

It may be a marvellously clever thing, in this audacious manner, to throw upon an opponent all the blame which is obviously one's own. But no good man will do so. The audacity that ascribes its own sins to an opponent is surely the token of a very evil nature. We have no reason to form a very high opinion of Joab, but of his opponent in this strife our judgment must be far worse. An insincere man, Abner could have no high end before him. If David was not happy in his general, still less was Ishbosheth in his.

Joab's answer betrayed a measure of indignation. " As God liveth, unless thou hadst spoken, surely then in the morning the people had gone up every one from following his brother." There is some ambiguity in these words. The Revised Version renders, " If thou hadst not spoken, surely then in the morning the people had gone away, nor followed every one his brother." The meaning of Joab seems to be that, apart from any such ill-tempered appeal as Abner's, it was his full intention in the morning to recall his men from the pursuit, and let Abner and his people go home without further harm. Joab shows the indignation of one credited with a purpose he never had, and with an inhumanity and unbrotherliness of which he was innocent. Why Joab had resolved to give up further hostilities at that time, we are not told. One might have thought that had he struck another blow at Abner he might have so harassed his force as to ruin his cause, and thus secure at once the triumph of David. But Joab probably felt very keenly what Abner accused him of not feeling : that it was a miserable thing to destroy the lives of so many brethren. The idea of building up David's throne on the dead bodies of his subjects he must have known to be extremely distasteful to David himself. Civil war is such a horrible thing, that a general may well be excused who accepts any reason for stopping it. If Joab had known what was to follow he might have taken a different course. If he had foreseen the "long war" that was to be between the house of Saul and the house of David, he might have tried on this occasion to strike a decisive blow, and pursued Abner's men until they were utterly broken. But that day's work had probably sickened him, as he knew it would sicken David ; and leaving Abner and his people to make their way across the Jordan, he returned to bury his brother, and to report his proceedings to David at Hebron.

And David must have grieved exceedingly when he heard what had taken place. The slaughter of nearly four hundred of God's nation was a terrible thought; still more terrible it was to think that in a sense he had been the occasion of it—it was done to prevent him from occupying the throne. No doubt he had reason to be thankful that when fighting had to be done, the issue was eminently favourable to him and his cause. But he must have been grieved that there should be fighting at all. He must have felt somewhat as the Duke of Wellington felt when he made the observation that next to the calamity of losing a battle was that of gaining a victory. Was this what Samuel had meant when he came that morning to Bethlehem and anointed him in presence of his family? Was this what God designed when He was pleased to put him in the place of Saul? If this was a sample of what David was to bring to his beloved people, would it not have been better had he never been born? Very strange must God's ways have appeared to him. How different were his desires, how different his dreams of what

should be done when he got the kingdom, from **this**
day's work! Often he had thought how he would drive
out the enemies of his people; how he would secure
tranquillity and prosperity to every Hebrew homestead;
how he would aim at their all living under their vine
and under their fig-tree, none making them afraid.
But now his reign had begun with bloodshed, and
already desolation had been carried to hundreds of his
people's homes.  Was this the work, O God, for which
Thou didst call me from the sheep-folds?  Should I not
have been better employed "following the ewes great
with young," and protecting my flock from the lion and
the bear, rather than sending forth men to stain the
soil of the land with the blood of the people and carry
to their habitations the voice of mourning and woe?

If David's mind was exercised in this way by the
proceedings near the pool of Gibeon, all his trust and
patience would be needed to wait for the time when
God would vindicate His way.  After all, was not his
experience somewhat like that of Moses when he first
set about the deliverance of his people?  Did he not
appear to do more harm than good?  Instead of
lightening the burdens of his people, did he not cause
an increase of their weight?  But has it not been the
experience of most men who have girded themselves
for great undertakings in the interest of their brethren?
Nay, was it not the experience of our blessed Lord Himself?  At His birth the angels sang, " Glory to God in
the highest; on earth peace; goodwill to men!"  And
almost the next event was the massacre at Bethlehem,
and Jesus Himself even in His lifetime found cause to
say, "Think not that I am come to send peace on
the earth; I am not come to send peace, but a sword."
What a sad evidence of the moral disorder of the

world ! The very messengers of the God of peace
are not allowed to deliver their messages in peace,
but even as they advance toward men with smiles and
benedictions, are fiercely assailed, and compelled to
defend themselves by violence.    Nevertheless the
angels' song is true.    Jesus did come to bless the
world with peace.    " Peace I leave with you ; My peace
I give unto you ; not as the world giveth give I unto
you."    The resistance of His enemies was essentially
a feeble resistance, and that stronger spirit of peace
which Jesus brought in due time prevailed mightily
in the earth.    So with the bloodshed in David's reign.
It did not hinder David from being a great benefactor
to his kingdom in the end.    It did not annul the
promise of God.    It did not neutralise the efficacy of
the holy oil.    This was just one of the many ways
in which his faith and his patience were tried.    It must
have shown him even more impressively than anything that had yet happened the absolute necessity of
Divine direction in all his ways.    For it is far easier
for a good man to bear suffering brought on himself by
his actions, than to see suffering and death entailed on
his brethren in connection with a course which has
been taken by him.

In that audacious speech which Abner addressed
to Joab, there occurs an expression worthy of being
taken out of the connection in which it was used and
of being viewed with wider reference.    " Knowest
thou not that it will be bitterness in the latter end ? "
Things are to be viewed by rational beings not merely
in their present or immediate result, but in their final
outcome, in their ultimate fruits.    A very commonplace
truth, I grant you, this is, but most wholesome, most
necessary to be cherished.    For how many of the

miseries and how many of the worst sins of men come
of forgetting the " bitterness in the latter end " which
evil beginnings give rise to! It is one of the most
wholesome rules of life never to do to-day what you
shall repent of to-morrow. Yet how constantly is the
rule disregarded! Youthful child of fortune, who are
revelling to-day in wealth which is counted by
hundreds of thousands, and which seems as if it could
never be exhausted, remember how dangerous those
gambling habits are into which you are falling;
remember that the gambler's biography is usually a
short, and often a tragic, one ; and when you hear the
sound of the pistol with which one like yourself has
ended his miserable existence, remember it all
began by disregarding the motto, written over the
gambler's path, " Knowest thou not that it will be
bitterness in the latter end?" You merry-hearted
and amusing companion, to whom the flowing bowl,
and the jovial company, and the merry jest and lively
song are so attractive, the more you are tempted
to go where they are found remember that rags and
dishonour, dirt and degradation, form the last stage of
the journey,—" the latter end bitterness " of the course
you are now following. You who are wasting in
idleness the hours of the morning, remember how
you will repent of it when you have to make up your
leeway by hard toil at night. I have said that things
are to be viewed by rational beings in their relations to
the future as well as the present. It is not the part
of a rational being to accumulate disaster, distress,
and shame for the future. Men that are rational will
far rather suffer for the present if they may be free
from suffering hereafter. Benefit societies, life in-
surance, annuity schemes—what are they all but the

devices of sensible men desirous to ward off even the possibility of temporal " bitterness in the latter end " ? And may not this wisdom, this good sense, be applied with far more purpose to the things that are unseen and eternal ?   Think of the " bitterness in the end " that must come of neglecting Christ, disregarding conscience, turning away from the Bible, the church, the Sabbath, grieving the Spirit, neglecting prayer !   Will not many a foretaste of this bitterness visit you even while yet you are well, and all things are prospering with you ? Will it not come on you with overpowering force while you lie on your death-bed ?   Will it not wrap your soul in indescribable anguish through all eternity ?

Think then of this " bitterness in the latter end " ! Now is the accepted time.   In the deep consciousness of your weakness, let your prayer be that God would restrain you from the folly to which your hearts are so prone, that, by His Holy Spirit, He would work in you both to will and to do of His good pleasure.

# CHAPTER IV.

## *CONCLUSION OF THE CIVIL WAR.*

### 2 SAMUEL iii. 1—21.

THE victory at the pool of Gibeon was far from ending the opposition to David. In vain, for many a day, weary eyes looked out for the dove with the olive leaf. "There was long war between the house of Saul and the house of David." The war does not seem to have been carried on by pitched battles, but rather by a long series of those fretting and worrying little skirmishes which a state of civil war breeds, even when the volcano is comparatively quiet. But the drift of things was manifest. "David waxed stronger and stronger; but the house of Saul waxed weaker and weaker." The cause of the house of Saul was weak in its invisible support because God was against it; it was weak in its champion Ishbosheth, a feeble man, with little or no power to attract people to his standard; its only element of strength was Abner, and even he could not make head against such odds. Good and evil so often seem to balance each other, existing side by side in a kind of feeble stagnation, and giving rise to such a dull feeling on the part of onlookers, that we cannot but think with something like envy of the followers of David even under the pain of a civil war,

cheered as they were by constant proofs that their cause
was advancing to victory.

And now we get a glimpse of David's domestic mode
of life, which, indeed, is far from satisfactory. His
wives were now six in number; of some of them we
know nothing; of the rest what we do know is not
always in their favour. The earliest of all was
"Ahinoam, the Jezreelitess." Her native place, or the
home of her family, was Jezreel, that part of the plain
of Esdraelon where the Philistines encamped before
Saul was defeated (1 Sam. xxix. 12), and afterwards, in
the days of Ahab, a royal residence of the kings of
Israel (1 Kings xviii. 46) and the abode of Naboth,
who refused to part with his vineyard in Jezreel to the
king (1 Kings xxi.). Of Ahinoam we find absolutely
no mention in the history; if her son Amnon, the
oldest of David's family, reflected her character, we
have no reason to regret the silence (2 Sam. xiii.).
The next of his wives was Abigail, the widow of Nabal
the Carmelite, of whose smartness and excellent
management we have a full account in a former part
of the history. Her son is called Chileab, but in the
parallel passage in Chronicles Daniel; we can only
guess the reason of the change; but whether it was
another name for the same son, or the name of
another son, the history is silent concerning him, and
the most probable conjecture is that he died early.
His third wife was Maachah, the daughter of Talmai
the Geshurite. This was not, as some have rather
foolishly supposed, a member of those Geshurites in
the south against whom David led his troop (1 Sam.
xxvii. 8), for it is expressly stated that of that tribe "he
left neither man nor woman alive." It was of Geshur
in Syria that Talmai was king (2 Sam. xv. 8); it

formed one of several little principalities lying between
Mount Hermon and Damascus : but we cannot commend the alliance ; for these kingdoms were idolatrous,
and unless Maachah was an exception, she must have
introduced idolatrous practices into David's house.   Of
the other three wives we have no information.   And
in regard to the household which he thus established
at Hebron, we can only regret that the king of Israel
did not imitate the example that had been set there
by Abraham, and followed in the same neighbourhood
by Isaac.   What a different complexion would have
been given to David's character and history if he had
shown the self-control in this matter that he showed in
his treatment of Saul !   Of how many grievous sins
and sorrows did he sow the seed when he thus multiplied wives to himself !   How many a man, from his
own day down to the days of Mormonism, did he
silently encourage in licentious conduct, and furnish
with a respectable example and a plausible excuse for
it !   How difficult did he make it for many who cannot
but acknowledge the bright aspect of his spiritual life
to believe that even in that it was all good and genuine!
We do not hesitate to ascribe to the life of David
an influence on successive generations on the whole
pure and elevating ; but it is impossible not to own
that by many, a justification of relaxed principle and
unchaste living has been drawn from his example.

We have already said that polygamy was not imputed
to David as a sin in the sense that it deprived him of
the favour of God.   But we cannot allow that this permission was of the nature of a boon.   We cannot but
feel how much better it would have been if the seventh
commandment had been read by David with the same
absolute, unbending limitation with which it is read by

**us.** It would have been better for him and better **for** his house.   Puritan strictness of morals is, after all, **a** right wholesome and most blessed thing.   Who shall say that the sum of a man's enjoyment is not far greatest in the end of life when he has kept with un- flinching steadfastness his early vow of faithfulness, and, as his reward, has never lost the freshness and the flavour of his first love, nor ceased to find in his ever- faithful partner that which fills and satisfies his heart? Compared to this, the life of him who has flitted from one attachment to another, heedless of the soured feel- ings or, it may be, the broken hearts he has left behind, and whose children, instead of breathing the sweet spirit of brotherly and sisterly love, scowl at one another with the bitter feelings of envy, jealousy, and hatred, is like an existence of wild fever compared to the pure tranquil life of a child.

In such a household as David's, occasions of estrange- ment must have been perpetually arising among the various branches, and it would require all his wisdom and gentleness to keep these quarrels within moderate bounds.   In his own breast, that sense of delicacy, that instinct of purity, which exercises such an influence on a godly family, could not have existed ; the necessity of reining in his inclinations in that respect was not acknowledged ; and it is remarkable that in the confes- sions of the fifty-first Psalm, while he specifies the sins of blood-guiltiness and seems to have been over- whelmed by a sense of his meanness, injustice, and selfishness, there is no special allusion to the sin of adultery, and no indication of that sin pressing very heavily upon his conscience.

Whether it be by design or not, it is an instructive circumstance that it is immediately after this glimpse

of David's domestic life that we meet with a sample
of the kind of evils which the system of royal harems
is ever apt to produce.   Saul too had had his harem ;
and it was a rule of succession in the East that the
harem went with the throne.   To take possession of
the one was regarded as equivalent to setting up a
claim to the other.   When therefore Ishbosheth heard
that Abner had taken one of his father's concubines,
he locked on it as a proof that Abner had an eye to the
throne for himself.   He accordingly demanded an explanation from Abner, but instead of explanation or
apology, he received a volley of rudeness and defiance.
Abner knew well that without him Ishbosheth was but
a figure-head, and he was enraged by treatment that
seemed to overlook all the service he had rendered him
and to treat him as if he were some second or third-
rate officer of a firm and settled kingdom.   Perhaps
Abner had begun to see that the cause of Ishbosheth
was hopeless, and was even glad in his secret heart of
an excuse for abandoning an undertaking which could
bring neither success nor honour.   "Am I a dog's head,
which against Judah do show kindness this day unto
the house of Saul thy father, to his brethren, and to his
friends, and have not delivered thee into the hand of
David, that thou chargest me to-day with a fault
concerning this woman ?   So do God to Abner, and
more also, except, as the Lord hath sworn to David,
even so I do to him, to translate the kingdom from the
house of Saul, and to set up the throne of David over
Israel and over Judah from Dan even to Beersheba."

The proverb says, "When rogues fall out, honest
men get their own."   How utterly unprincipled the
effort of Abner and Ishbosheth was is evident from
the confession of the former that God had sworn to

David to establish his throne over the whole land. Their enterprise therefore bore impiety on its very face ; and we can only account for their setting their hands to it on the principle that keen thirst for worldly advantage will drive ungodly men into virtual atheism, as if God were no factor in the affairs of men, as if it mattered not that He was against them, and that it is only when their schemes show signs of coming to ruin that they awake to the consciousness that there is a God after all! And how often we see that godless men banded together have no firm bond of union; the very passions which they are united to gratify begin to rage against one another ; they fall into the pit which they digged for others ; they are hanged on the gallows which they erected for their foes.

The next step in the narrative brings us to Abner's offer to David to make a league with him for the undisputed possession of the throne. Things had changed now very materially from that day when, in the wilderness of Judah, David reproached Abner for his careless custody of the king's person (1 Sam. xxvi. 14). What a picture of feebleness David had seemed then, while Saul commanded the whole resources of the kingdom! Yet in that day of weakness David had done a noble deed, a deed made nobler by his very weakness, and he had thereby shown to any that had eyes to see which party it was that had God on its side. And now this truth concerning him, against which Abner had kicked and struggled in vain, was asserting itself in a way not to be resisted. Yet even now there is no trace of humility in the language of Abner. He plays the great man still. " Behold, my hand shall be with thee, to bring about all Israel to thee." He approaches King David, not as one who has done him a great wrong, but as one who offers to do him a great favour.   There is no word of regret for his having opposed what he knew to be God's purpose and promise, no apology for the disturbance he had wrought in Israel, no excuse for all the distress which he had caused to David by keeping the kingdom and the people at war.   He does not come as a rebel to his sovereign, but as one independent man to another.  Make a league with me.   Secure me from punishment ; promise me a reward.   For this he simply offers to place at David's disposal that powerful hand of his that had been so mighty for evil.   If he expected that David would leap into his arms at the mention of such an offer, he was mistaken.   This was not the way for a rebel to come to his king.   David was too much dissatisfied with his past conduct, and saw too clearly that it was only stress of weather that was driving him into harbour now, to show any great enthusiasm about his offer.   On the contrary, he laid down a stiff pre-liminary condition ; and with the air of one who knew his place and his power, he let Abner know that if that condition were not complied with, he should not see his face.   We cannot but admire the firmness shown in this mode of meeting Abner's advances ; but we are somewhat disappointed when we find what the condition was—that Michal, Saul's daughter, whom he had espoused for a hundred foreskins of the Philistines, should be restored to him as his wife.   The demand was no doubt a righteous one, and it was reasonable that David should be vindicated from the great slur cast on him when his wife was given to another ; moreover, it was fitted to test the genuineness of Abner's advances, to show whether he really meant to acknow-ledge the royal rights of David ; but we wonder that, with six wives already about him, he should be so eager for another, and we shrink from the reason given for the restoration—not that the marriage tie was inviolable, but that he had paid for her a very extraordinary dowry. And most readers, too, will feel some sympathy with the second husband, who seems to have had a strong affection for Michal, and who followed her weeping, until the stern military voice of Abner compelled him to return. All we can say about him is, that his sin lay in receiving another man's wife and treating her as his own; the beginning of the connection was unlawful, although the manner of its ending on his part was creditable. Connections formed in sin must sooner or later end in suffering; and the tears of Phaltiel would not have flowed now if that unfortunate man had acted firmly and honourably when Michal was taken from David.

But it is not likely that in this demand for the restoration of Michal David acted on purely personal considerations. He does not seem to have been above the prevalent feeling of the East which measured the authority and dignity of the monarch by the rank and connections of his wives. Moreover, as David laid stress on the way in which he got Michal as his wife, it is likely that he desired to recall attention to his early exploits against the Philistines. He had probably found that his recent alliance with King Achish had brought him into suspicion; he wished to remind the people therefore of his ancient services against those bitter and implacable enemies of Israel, and to encourage the expectation of similar exploits in the future. The purpose which he thus seems to have had in view was successful. For when Abner soon after made a representation to the elders of Israel in favour of King David

and reminded tl em of the promise which God had made
regarding him, it was to this effect : " By the hand of
My servant David I will save My people Israel out of
the hand of the Philistines and out of the hand of all
their enemies." It seems to have been a great step
towards David's recognition by the whole nation that
they came to have confidence in him in leading them
against the Philistines. Thus he received a fresh proof
of the folly of his distrustful conclusion, "There is
nothing better for me than that I should escape into the
land of the Philistines." It became more and more
apparent that nothing could have been worse.

One is tempted to wonder if David ever sat down to
consider what would probably have happened if, instead
of going over to the Philistines, he had continued to
abide in the wilderness of Judah, braving the dangers
of the place and trusting in the protection of his God.
Some sixteen months after, the terrible invasion of the
Philistines took place, and Saul, overwhelmed with
terror and despair, was at his wits' end for help. How
natural it would have been for him in that hour of
despair to send for David if he had been still in the
country and ask his aid! How much more in his own
place would David have appeared bravely fronting the
Philistines in battle, than hovering in the rear of Achish
and pretending to feel himself treated ill because the
Philistine lords had required him to be sent away!
Might he not have been the instrument of saving his
country from defeat and disgrace? And if Saul and
Jonathan had fallen in the battle, would not the whole
nation have turned as one man to him, and would not
that long and cruel civil war have been entirely averted?
It is needless to go back on the past and think how
much better we could have acted if unavailing regret is

to be the only result of the process ; but it is a salutary
and blessed exercise if it tends to fix in our minds—
what we doubt not it fixed in David's—how infinitely
better for us it is to follow the course marked out for us
by our heavenly Father, with all its difficulties and
dangers, than to walk in the light of our own fire and
in the sparks of our own kindling.

It appears that Abner set himself with great vigour
to fulfil the promise made by him in his league with
David. First, he held communication with the representatives of the whole nation, " the elders of Israel,"
and showed to them, as we have seen—no doubt to
his own confusion and self-condemnation—how God had
designated David as the king through whom deliverance would be granted to Israel from the Philistines
and all their other enemies. Next, remembering that
Saul was a member of the tribe of Benjamin, and
believing that the feeling in favour of his family would
be eminently strong in that tribe, he took special pains
to attach them to David, and as he was himself
likewise a Benjamite, he must have been eminently
useful in this service. Thirdly, he went in person to
Hebron, David's seat,  to speak in the ears of David
all that seemed good to Israel and to the whole house
of Benjamin." Finally, after being entertained by
David at a great feast, he set out to bring about a
meeting of the whole congregation of Israel, that they
might solemnly ratify the appointment of David as
king, in the same way as, in the early days of Saul,
Samuel had convened the representatives of the
nation at Gilgal (1 Sam. xi. 15). That in all this
Abner was rendering a great service both to David and
the nation cannot be doubted. He was doing what no
other man in Israel could have done at the time for

establishing the throne of David and ending the civil war. Having once made overtures to David, he showed an honourable promptitude in fulfilling the promise under which he had come. No man can atone for past sin by doing his duty at a future time; but if anything could have blotted out from David's memory the remembrance of Abner's great injury to him and to the nation, it was the zeal with which he exerted himself now to establish David's claims over all the country, and especially where his cause was feeblest—in the tribe of Benjamin.

It must have been a happy day in David's history when Abner set out from Hebron to convene the assembly of the tribes that was to call him with one voice to the throne. It was the day long looked for come at last. The dove had at length come with the olive leaf, and peace would now reign among all the tribes of Israel. And we may readily conceive him, with this prospect so near, expressing his feelings, if not in the very words of the thirty-seventh Psalm, at any rate in language of similar import :—

" Fret not thyself because of evil-doers,
    Neither be thou envious against them that work unrighteousness
    For they shall soon be cut down like the grass,
    And wither as the green herb.
    Trust in the Lord and do good ;
    Dwell in the land, and follow after faithfulness.
    Delight thyself also in the Lord,
    And He shall give thee the desires of thine heart.
    Commit thy way unto the Lord,
    Trust also in Him, and He shall bring it to pass.
    And He shall make thy righteousness to go forth as the light,
    And thy judgment as the noonday.
    Rest in the Lord and wait patiently for Him ;
    Fret not thyself because of him that prospereth in his way,
    Because of the man who bringeth wicked devices to pass.

For evil-doers shall be cut off ;
But those that wait on the Lord, they shall inherit the land."

But a crime was now on the eve of being perpetrated destined for the time to scatter all King David's pleasing expectations and plunge him anew into the depths of distress.

# CHAPTER V.

*ASSASSINATION OF ABNER AND ISHBOSHETH.*

2 SAMUEL iii. 22—39 ; iv.

I T is quite possible that, in treating with Abner, David showed too complacent a temper, that he treated too lightly his appearance in arms against him at the pool of Gibeon, and that he neglected to demand an apology for the death of Asahel. Certainly it would have been wise had some measures been taken to soothe the ruffled temper of Joab and reconcile him to the new arrangement  This, however, was not done. David was so happy in the thought that the civil war was to cease, and that all Israel were about to recognise him as their king, that he would not go back on the past, or make reprisals even for the death of Asahel. He was willing to let bygones be bygones.  Perhaps, too, he thought that if Asahel met his death at the hand of Abner, it was his own rashness that was to blame for it.  Anyhow he was greatly impressed with the value of Abner's service on his behalf, and much interested in the project to which he was now going forth—gathering all Israel to the king, to make a league with him and bind themselves to his allegiance.

In these measures Joab had not been consulted. When Abner was at Hebron, Joab was absent on a military enterprise.  In that enterprise he had been

very successful, and he was able to appear at Hebron
with the most popular evidence of success that a general
could bring—a large amount of spoil.  No doubt Joab
was elated with his success, and was in that very
temper when a man is most disposed to resent his
being overlooked and to take more upon him than is
meet.   When he heard of David's agreement with Abner,
he was highly displeased.   First he went to the king,
and scolded him for his simplicity in believing Abner.
It was but a stratagem of Abner's to allow him to come
to Hebron, ascertain the state of David's affairs, and
take his own steps more effectively in the interest of
his opponent,   Suspicion reigned in Joab's heart; the
generosity of David's nature was not only not shared
by him, but seemed silliness itself.   His rudeness to
David is highly offensive.   He speaks to him in the
tone of a master to a servant, or in the tone of those
servants who rule their master.   " What hast thou
done ?   Behold, Abner came unto thee ; why is it that
thou hast sent him away, and he is quite gone ?   Thou
knowest Abner the son of Ner, that he came to deceive
thee, and to know thy going out and thy coming in,
and to know all that thou doest."   David is spoken to
like one guilty of inexcusable folly, as if he were
accountable to Joab, and not Joab to him.   Of the
king's answer to Joab, nothing is recorded ; but from
David's confession (ver. 39) that the sons of Zeruiah
were too strong for him, we may infer that it was not very
firm or decided, and that Joab set it utterly at nought.
For the very first thing that Joab did after seeing
the king was to send a message to Abner, most
likely in David's name, but without David's knowledge,
asking him to return.   Joab was at the gate ready for
his treacherous business, and taking Abner aside as if

for private conversation, he plunged his dagger in his breast, ostensibly in revenge for the death of his brother Asahel. There was something eminently mean and dastardly in the deed. Abner was now on the best of terms with Joab's master, and he could not have apprehended danger from the servant. If assassination be mean among civilians, it is eminently mean among soldiers. The laws of hospitality were outraged when one who had just been David's guest was assassinated in David's city. The outrage was all the greater, as was also the injury to King David and to the whole kingdom, that the crime was committed when Abner was on the eve of an important and delicate negotiation with the other tribes of Israel, since the arrangement which he hoped to bring about was likely to be broken off by the news of his shameful death. At no moment are the feelings of men less to be trifled with than when, after long and fierce alienation, they are on the point of coming together. Abner had brought the tribes of Israel to that point, but now, like a flock of birds frightened by a shot, they were certain to fly asunder. All this danger Joab set at nought, the one thought of taking revenge for the death of his brother absorbing every other, and making him, like so many other men when excited by a guilty passion, utterly regardless of every consequence provided only his revenge was satisfied.

How did David act toward Joab? Most kings would at once have put him to death, and David's subsequent action towards the murderers of Ishbosheth shows that, even in his judgment, this would have been the proper retribution on Joab for his bloody deed. But David did not feel himself strong enough to deal with Joab according to his deserts. It might have

been better for him during the rest of his life if he had
acted with more vigour now.    But instead of making
an example of Joab, he contented himself with pouring
out on him a vial of indignation, publicly washing his
hands of the nefarious transaction, and pronouncing on
its author and his family a terrible malediction.    We
cannot but shrink from the way in which David brought
in Joab's family to share his curse: "Let there not
fail from the house of Joab one that hath an issue, or
that is a leper, or that leaneth on a staff, or that falleth
on the sword, or that lacketh bread."    Yet we must
remember that according to the sentiment of those
times a man and his house were so identified that the
punishment due to the head was regarded as due to
the whole.    In our day we see a law in constant
operation which visits iniquities of the parents upon
the children with a terrible retribution.    The drunkard's
children are woeful sufferers for their parent's sin ; the
family of the felon carries a stigma for ever.    We
recognise this as a law of Providence; but we do not
act on it ourselves in inflicting punishment.    In David's
time, however, and throughout the whole Old Testament
period, punishments due to the fathers were formally
shared by their families.    When Joshua sentenced
Achan to die for his crime in stealing from the spoils of
Jericho a wedge of gold and a Babylonish garment, his
wife and children were put to death along with him.
In denouncing the curse on Joab's family as well as
himself, David therefore only recognised a law which
was universally acted on in his day.    The law may
have been a hard one, but we are not to blame David
for acting on a principle of retribution universally
acknowledged.    We are to remember, too, that David
was now acting in a public capacity, and as the chief

magistrate of the nation.   If he had put Joab to death, his act would have involved his family in many a woe; in denouncing his deeds and calling for retribution on them generation after generation, he only carried out the same principle a little further.   That Joab deserved to die for his dastardly crime, none could have denied; if David abstained from inflicting that punishment, it was only natural that he should be very emphatic in proclaiming what such a criminal might look for, in never-failing visitations on himself and his seed, when he was left to be dealt with by the God of justice.

Having thus disposed of Joab, David had next to dispose of the dead body of Abner.   He determined that every circumstance connected with Abner's funeral should manifest the sincerity of his grief at his untimely end.   In the first place, he caused him to be buried at Hebron.   We know of the tomb at Hebron where the bodies of the patriarchs lay; if it was at all legitimate to place others in that grave, we may believe that a place in it was found for Abner.   In the second place, the mourning company attended the funeral with rent clothes and girdings of sackcloth, while the king himself followed the bier, and at the grave both king and people gave way to a burst of tears.   In the third place, the king pronounced an elegy over him, short, but expressive of his sense of the unworthy death which had come to such a man:—

" Should Abner die as a fool dieth?
  Thy hands were not bound, nor thy feet put into fetters;
  As a man falleth before the children of iniquity, so didst thou fall."

Had he died the death of one taken in battle, his bound hands and his feet in fetters would have denoted that after honourable conflict he had been defeated in

the field, and that he died the death due to a public
enemy.   Instead of this, he had fallen before the children
of iniquity, before men mean enough to betray him and
murder him, while he was under the protection of the
king.   In the fourth place, he sternly refused to eat bread
till that day, so full of darkness and infamy, should
have passed away.   The public manifestations of David's
grief showed very clearly how far he was from approving
of the death of Abner.   And they had the desired
effect.   The people were pleased with the evidence
afforded of David's feelings, and the event that had
seemed likely to destroy his prospects turned out in
this way in his favour.   "The people took notice of
this, and it pleased them, as whatsoever the king did
pleased all the people."   It was another evidence of
the conquering power of goodness and forbearance.
By his generous treatment of his foes, David secured a
position in the hearts of his people, and established his
kingdom on a basis of security which he could not
have obtained by any amount of severity.   For ages
and ages, the two methods of dealing with a reluctant
people, generosity and severity, have been pitted against
each other, and always with the effect that severity
fails and generosity succeeds.   There were many who
were indignant at the clemency shown by Lord Canning
after the Indian mutiny.   They would have had him
inspire terror by acts of awful severity.   But the
peaceful career of our Indian empire and the absence
of any attempt to renew the insurrection since that time
show that the policy of clemency was the policy of
wisdom and of success.

Still another step was taken by David that shows
how painfully he was impressed by the death of Abner.
To "his servants"—that is, his cabinet or his staff—he

said in confidence, " Know ye not that there is a prince
and a great man fallen this day in Israel ? " He recognised in Abner one of those men of consummate ability
who are born to rule, or at least to render the highest
service to the actual ruler of a country by their great
influence over men. It seems very probable that he
looked to him as his own chief officer for the future.
Rebel though he had been, he seemed quite cured of
his rebellion, and now that he cordially acknowledged
David's right to the throne, he would probably have
been his right-hand man. Abner, Saul's cousin, was
probably a much older man than Joab, who was David's
nephew, and who could not have been much older than
David himself. The loss of Abner was a great personal loss especially as it threw him more into the
hands of these sons of Zeruiah, Joab and Abishai,
whose impetuous, lordly temper was too much for him
to restrain. The representation to his confidential
servants, "I am weak, and these men, the sons of
Zeruiah, are too strong for me," was an appeal to them
for cordial help in the affairs of the kingdom, in order
that Joab and his brother might not be able to carry
everything their own way. David, like many another
man, needed to say, Save me from my friends. We get
a vivid glimpse of the perplexities of kings, and of the
compensations of a humbler lot. Men in high places,
worried by the difficulties of managing their affairs and
servants, and by the endless annoyances to which their
jealousies and their self-will give rise, may find much to
envy in the simple, unembarrassed life of the humblest
of the people.

From the assassination of Abner, the real source
of the opposition that had been raised to David, the
narrative proceeds to the assassination of Ishbosheth,

the titular king. " When Saul's son heard that Abner
was dead in Hebron, his hands were feeble, and all
the Israelites were troubled." The contrast is striking
between his conduct under difficulty and that of David.
In the history of the latter, faith often faltered in times
of trouble, and the spirit of distrust found a footing in
his soul. But these occasions occurred in the course
of protracted and terrible struggles ; they were
exceptions to his usual bearing ; faith commonly bore
him up in his darkest trials. Ishbosheth, on the other
hand, seems to have had no resource, no sustaining
power whatever, under visible reverses. David's slips
were like the temporary falling back of the gallant
soldier when surprised by a sudden onslaught, or
when, fagged and weary, he is driven back by superior
numbers ; but as soon as he has recovered himself,
he dashes back undaunted to the conflict. Ishbosheth was like the soldier who throws down his arms
and rushes from the field as soon as he feels the bitter
storm of battle. With all his falls, there was something in David that showed him to be cast in a different
mould from ordinary men. He was habitually aiming
at a higher standard, and upheld by the consciousness
of a higher strength ; he was ever and anon resorting to
"the secret place of the Most High," taking hold of
Him as his covenant God, and labouring to draw down
from Him the inspiration and the strength of a nobler
life than that of the mass of the children of men.

The godless course which Ishbosheth had followed
in setting up a claim to the throne in opposition to the
Divine call of David not only lost him the distinction
he coveted, but cost him his life. He made himself
a mark for treacherous and heartless men ; and one
day, while lying in his bed at noon, was despatched by

two of his servants. The two men that murdered him seem to have been among those whom Saul enriched with the spoil of the Gibeonites. They were brothers, men of Beeroth, which was formerly one of the cities of the Gibeonites, but was now reckoned to Benjamin.

Saul appears to have attacked the Beerothites, and given their property to his favourites (comp. 1 Sam. xxii. 7 and 2 Sam. xxi. 2). A curse went with the transaction; Ishbosheth, one of Saul's sons, was murdered by two of those who were enriched by the unhallowed deed; and many years after, his bloody house had to yield up seven of his sons to justice, when a great famine showed that for this crime wrath rested on the land.

The murderers of Ishbosheth, Baanah and Rechab, mistaking the character of David as much as it had been mistaken by the Amalekite who pretended that he had slain Saul, hastened to Hebron, bearing with them the head of their victim, a ghastly evidence of the reality of the deed. This revolting trophy they carried all the way from Mahanaim to Hebron, a distance of some fifty miles. Mean and selfish themselves, they thought other men must be the same. They were among those poor creatures who are unable to rise above their own poor level in their conceptions of others. When they presented themselves before David, he showed all his former superiority to selfish, jealous feelings. He was roused indeed to the highest pitch of indignation. We can hardly conceive the astonishment and horror with which they would receive his answer, "As the Lord liveth, who hath redeemed my soul out of all adversity, when one told me saying, Behold, Saul is dead, thinking to have brought good tidings, I took hold on him and slew him in Ziklag, who thought that I would have given him a reward for his tidings. How much more when wicked men have slain a righteous person in his own house upon his bed ! Shall I not therefore require his blood at your hand, and take you away from the earth ? " Simple death was not judged a severe enough punishment for such guilt ; as they had cut off the head of Ishbosheth after killing him, so after they were slain their hands and their feet were cut off; and thereafter they were hanged over the pool in Hebron—a token of the execration in which the crime was held. Here was another evidence that deeds of violence done to his rivals, so far from finding acceptance, were detestable in the eyes of David. And here was another fulfilment of the resolution which he had made when he took possession of the throne—" I will early destroy all the wicked of the land, that I may cut off all wicked doers from the city of the Lord."

These rapid, instantaneous executions by order of David have raised painful feelings in many. Granting that the retribution was justly deserved, and granting that the rapidity of the punishment was in accord with military law, ancient and modern, and that it was necessary in order to make a due impression on the people, still it may be asked, How could David, as a pious man, hurry these sinners into the presence of their Judge without giving them any exhortation to repentance or leaving them a moment in which to ask for mercy ? The question is undoubtedly a difficult one. But the difficulty arises in a great degree from our ascribing to David and others the same knowledge of the future state and the same vivid impressions regarding it that we have ourselves. We often forget that to those who lived in the Old Testament the future life was wrapped in far greater obscurity than it is to us. That good men had no knowledge of it, we cannot allow; but certainly they knew vastly less about it than has been revealed to us. And the general effect of this was that the consciousness of a future life was much fainter even among good men then than now. They did not think about it; it was not present to their thoughts. There is no use trying to make David either a wiser or a better man than he was. There is no use trying to place him high above the level or the light of his age. If it be asked, How did David feel with reference to the future life of these men? the answer is, that probably it was not much, if at all, in his thoughts. That which was prominent in his thoughts was that they had sacrificed their lives by their atrocious wickedness, and the sooner they were punished the better. If he thought of their future, he would feel that they were in the hands of God, and that they would be judged by Him according to the tenor of their lives. It cannot be said that compassion for them mingled with David's feelings. The one prominent feeling he had was that of their guilt; for that they must suffer. And David, like other soldiers who have shed much blood, was so accustomed to the sight of violent death, that the horror which it usually excites was no longer familiar to him.

It is the Gospel of Jesus Christ that has brought life and immortality to light. So far from the future life being a dim and shadowy revelation, it is now one of the clearest doctrines of the faith. It is one of the doctrines which every earnest preacher of the Gospel is profoundly earnest in dwelling on. That death ushers us into the presence of God, that after death cometh the judgment, that every one of us is to give account of himself to God, that the final condition of

men is to be one of misery or one of life, are among the
clearest revelations of the Gospel.   And this fact invests
every man's death with profound significance in the
Christian's view.   That the condemned criminal may
have time to prepare, our courts of law invariably
interpose an interval between the sentence and the
punishment.   Would only that men were more consistent here !   If we shudder at the thought of a dying
sinner appearing in all the blackness of his guilt before
God, let us think more how we may turn sinners from
their wickedness while they live.   Let us see the
atrocious guilt of encouraging them in ways of sin that
cannot but bring on them the retribution of a righteous
God.   O ye who, careless yourselves, laugh at the
serious impressions and scruples of others ; ye who
teach those that would otherwise do better to drink and
gamble and especially to scoff ; ye who do your best
to frustrate the prayers of tender-hearted fathers and
mothers whose deepest desire is that their children
may be saved ; ye, in one word, who are missionaries
of the devil and help to people hell—would that you
pondered your awful guilt !   For "whosoever shall
cause any of the least of these to offend, it were better
for him that a millstone were hanged about his neck
and he were cast into the depths of the sea."

# CHAPTER VI.

## *DAVID KING OF ALL ISRAEL.*

### 2 SAMUEL v. 1—9.

AFTER seven and a half years of opposition,* David
was now left without a rival, and the representatives of the whole tribes came to Hebron to anoint him
king. They gave three reasons for their act, nearly all
of which, however, would have been as valid at the
death of Saul as they were at this time.

The first was that David and they were closely related—" Behold, we are thy bone and thy flesh ;" rather
an unusual reason, but in the circumstances not unnatural. For David's alliance with the Philistines had
thrown some doubt on his nationality ; it was not very
clear at that time whether he was to be regarded as a
Hebrew or as a naturalized Philistine ; but now the
doubts that had existed on that point had all disappeared ; conclusive evidence had been afforded that
David was out-and-out a Hebrew, and therefore that he
was not disqualified for the Hebrew throne.

---

* There is difficulty in adjusting all the dates. In chap. ii. 10, it is said
that Ishbosheth reigned two years. The usual explanation is that he
reigned two years before war broke out between him and David.
Another supposition is that there was an interregnum in Israel of five
and a half years, and that Ishbosheth reigned the last two years of
David's seven and a half. The accuracy of the text has been questioned,
and it has been proposed (on very slender MS. authority) to read that
Ishbosheth reigned *six* years in place of two.

This conclusion is confirmed by what they give as their second reason—his former exploits and services against their enemies. "Also, in time past, when Saul was king, thou wast he that leddest out and broughtest in Israel." In former days, David had proved himself Saul's most efficient lieutenant; he had been at the head of the armies of Israel, and his achievements in that capacity pointed to him as the fit and natural successor of Saul.

The third reason is the most conclusive—" The Lord said to thee, Thou shalt feed My people Israel, and thou shalt be a captain over Israel." It was little to the credit of the elders that this reason, which should have been the first, and which needed no other reasons to confirm it, was given by them as the last. The truth, however, is, that if they had made it their first and great reason, they would on the very face of their speech have condemned themselves. Why, if this was the command of God, had they been so long of carrying it out? Ought not effect to have been given to it at the very first, independent of all other reasons whatsoever? The elders cannot but give it a place among their reasons for offering him the throne; but it is not allowed to have its own place, and it is added to the others as if they needed to be supplemented before effect could be given to it. The elders did not show that supreme regard to the will of God which ought ever to be the first consideration in every loyal heart. It is the great offence of multitudes, even among those who make a Christian profession, that while they are willing to pay regard to God's will as one of many considerations, they are not prepared to pay supreme regard to it. It may be taken along with other considerations, but it is not allowed to be the chief con-

sideration. Religion may have a place in their life, but
not the first place. But can a service thus rendered
be acceptable to God ? Can God accept the second or
the third place in any man's regard ? Does not the
first commandment dispose of this question : " Thou
shalt have no other gods before Me " ?

" So all the elders of Israel came to the king to
Hebron ; and King David made a league with them in
Hebron before the Lord ; and they anointed David
king over Israel."

It was a happy circumstance that David was able to
neutralise the effects of the murders of Abner and
Ishbosheth, and to convince the people that he had no
share in these crimes. Notwithstanding the prejudice
against his side which in themselves they were fitted
to create in the supporters of Saul's family, they did
not cause any further opposition to his claims. The
tact of the king removed any stumbling-block that
might have arisen from these untoward events. And
thus the throne of David was at last set up, amid the
universal approval of the nation.

This was a most memorable event in David's history.
It was the fulfilment of one great instalment of God's
promises to him. It was fitted very greatly to deepen
his trust in God, as his Protector and his Friend. To
be able to look back on even one case of a Divine
promise distinctly fulfilled to us is a great help to faith
in all future time. For David to be able to look back on
that early period of his life, so crowded with trials and
sufferings, perplexities and dangers, and to mark how
God had delivered him from every one of them, and, in
spite of the fearful opposition that had been raised
against him, had at last seated him firmly on the
throne, was well fitted to advance the spirit of trust

to that place of supremacy which it gained in him. After such an overwhelming experience, it was little wonder that his trust in God became so strong, and his purpose to serve God so intense. The sorrows of death had compassed him, and the pains of Hades had taken hold on him, yet the Lord had been with him, and had most wonderfully delivered him. And in token of his deliverance he makes his vow of continual service, " O Lord, truly I am Thy servant ; I am Thy servant and the son of Thine handmaid ; Thou hast loosed my bonds. I will offer to Thee the sacrifices of praise, and will call upon the name of the Lord."

We can hardly pass from this event in David's history without recalling his typical relation to Him who in after-years was to be known as the "Son of David." The resemblance between the early history of David and that of our blessed Lord in some of its features is too obvious to need to be pointed out. Like David, Jesus spends His early years in the obscurity of a country village. Like him, He enters on His public life under a striking and convincing evidence of the Divine favour—David by conquering Goliath, Jesus by the descent of the Spirit at His baptism, and the voice from heaven which proclaimed, " This is My beloved Son, in whom I am well pleased." Like David, soon after His Divine call Jesus is led out to the wilderness, to undergo hardship and temptation ; but, unlike David, He conquers the enemy at every onset. Like David, Jesus attaches to Himself a small but valiant band of followers, whose achievements in the spiritual warfare rival the deeds of David's "worthies" in the natural. Like David, Jesus is concerned for His relatives ; David, in his extremity, commits his father and mother to the king of Moab : Jesus, on the cross, commits His mother to the beloved disciple. In the higher exercises of David's spirit, too, there is much that resembles the experiences of Christ. The convincing proof of this is, that most of the Psalms which the Christian Church has ever held to be Messianic have their foundation in the experiences of David. It is impossible not to see that in one sense there must have been a measureless distance between the experience of a sinful man like David and that of the Lord Jesus Christ. In the Divinity of His person, the atoning efficacy of His death, and the glory of His resurrection, Jesus is high above any of the sons of men. Yet there must likewise have been some marvellous similarity between Him and David, seeing that David's words of sorrow and of hope were so often accepted by Jesus to express His own emotions. Strange indeed it is that the words in which David, in the twenty-second Psalm, pours out the desolation of his spirit, were the words in which Jesus found expression for His unexampled distress upon the cross. Strange, too, that David's deliverances were so like Christ's that the same language does for both; nay, that the very words in which Jesus commended His soul to the Father, as it was passing from His body, were words which had first been used by David.

But it does not concern us at present to look so much at the general resemblances between David and our blessed Lord, as at the analogy in the fortunes of their respective kingdoms. And here the most obvious feature is the bitter opposition to their claims offered in both instances even by those who might have been expected most cordially to welcome them. Of both it might be said, "They came unto their own, but their own received them not." First, David is hunted almost to death by Saul; and then, even after Saul's death, his claims are resisted by most of the tribes. So in His lifetime Jesus encounters all the hatred and opposition of the scribes and Pharisees; and even after His resurrection, the council do their utmost to denounce His claims and frighten His followers. Against the one and the other the enemy brings to bear all the devices of hatred and opposition. When Jesus rose from the grave, we see Him personally raised high above all the efforts of His enemies; when David was acknowledged king by all Israel, he reached a corresponding elevation. And now that David is recognised as king, how do we find him employing his energies? It is to defend and bless his kingdom, to obtain for it peace and prosperity, to expel its foes, to secure to the utmost of his power the welfare of all his people. From His throne in glory, Jesus does the same. And what encouragement may not the friends and subjects of Christ's kingdom derive from the example of David! For if David, once he was established in his kingdom, spared no effort to do good to his people, if he scattered blessings among them from the stores which he was able to command, how much more may Christ be relied on to do the same! Has He not been placed far above all principality and power, and every name that is named, and been made " Head over all things for the Church which is His body"? Rejoice then, ye members of Christ's kingdom! Raise your eyes to the throne of glory, and see how God has set His King upon His holy hill of Zion! And be encouraged to tell Him of all your own needs and the troubles and needs of His Church; for has He not ascended on high, and led captivity captive, and received gifts for men? And if you have faith as a grain of mustard seed, will you not ask, and shall you not receive according to your faith? Will not God supply all your need according to His riches in glory by Christ Jesus?

From the spectacle at Hebron, when all the elders of Israel confirmed David on the throne, and entered into a solemn league with reference to the kingdom, we pass with David to the field of battle. The first enterprise to which he addressed himself was the capture of Jerusalem, or rather of the stronghold of Zion. It is not expressly stated that he consulted God before taking this step, but we can hardly suppose that he would do it without Divine direction. From the days of Moses, God had taught His people that a place would be appointed by Him where He would set His name; Jerusalem was to be that place; and it cannot be thought that when David would not even go up to Hebron without consulting the Lord, he would proceed to make Jerusalem his capital without a Divine warrant.

No doubt the place was well known to him. It had already received consecration when Melchizedek reigned in it, "king of righteousness and king of peace." In the days of Joshua its king was Adonizedek, "lord of righteousness"—a noble title, brought down from the days of Melchizedek, however unworthy the bearer of it might be of the designation, for he was the head of the confederacy against Joshua (Josh. x. 1, 3), and he ended his career by being hanged on a tree. After the slaughter of the Philistine, David had carried his head to Jerusalem, or to some place so near that it might be called by that name; very probably Nob was the place, which, according to an old tradition, was situated on the slope of Mount Olivet. Often in his wanderings, when his mind was much occupied with fortresses and defences, the image of this place would occur to him; observing how the mountains were round about Jerusalem, he would see how well it was adapted to be the metropolis of the country. But this could not be done while the stronghold of Zion was in the hands of the Jebusites, and while the Jebusites were so numerous that they might be called "the people of the land."

So impregnable was this stronghold deemed, that any attempt that David might make to get possession of it was treated with contempt. The precise circumstances of the siege are somewhat obscure; if we compare the marginal readings and the text in the Authorized Version, and still more in the Revised Version, we may see what difficulty our translators had in arriving at the meaning of the passage. The most probable supposition is that the Jebusites placed their lame and blind on the walls, to show how little artificial defence the place needed, and defied David to touch even these sorry defenders. Such defiance David could not but have regarded as he regarded the defiance of Goliath— as an insult to that mighty God in whose name and in whose strength he carried on his work. Advancing in the same strength in which he advanced against Goliath, he got possession of the stronghold. To stimulate the chivalry of his men he had promised the first place in his army to whoever, by means of the watercourse, should first get on the battlements and defeat the Jebusites. Joab was the man who made this daring and successful attempt. Reaping the promised reward, he thereby raised himself to the first place in the now united forces of the twelve tribes of Israel. After the murder of Abner, he had probably been degraded; but now, by his dash and bravery, he

established his position on a firmer basis than ever.
While he contributed by this means to the security
and glory of the kingdom, he diminished at the same
time the king's personal satisfaction, inasmuch as
David could not regard without anxiety the possession
of so much power and influence by so daring and
useful, but unscrupulous and bold-tempered, a man.

The place thus taken was called the city, and sometimes the castle, of David, and it became from this time
his residence and the capital of his kingdom.  Much
though the various sites in Jerusalem have been
debated, it is surely beyond reasonable doubt that the
fortress thus occupied was Mount Zion, the same
height which still exists in the south-western corner
of the area which came to be covered by Jerusalem.
This seems to have been the only part that the Jebusites
had fortified, and with the loss of this stronghold their
hold of other parts of Jerusalem was lost.   Henceforth,
as a people, they disappear from Jerusalem, although
individual Jebusites might still, like Araunah, hold
patches of land in the neighbourhood (2 Sam. xxiv. 16).
The captured fortress was turned by David into his
royal residence.  And seeing that a military stronghold was very inadequate for the purposes of a capital,
he began, by the building of Millo, that extension of
the city which was afterwards carried out by others on
so large a scale.

By thus taking possession of Mount Zion and com-
mencing those extensions which helped to make Jerusalem so great and celebrated a city, David introduced
two names into the sacred language of the Bible which
have ever since retained a halo, surpassing all other
names in the world.  Yet, very obviously, it was nothing
in the little hill which has borne the name of Zion for so

many centuries, nor in the physical features of the city of
Jerusalem, that has given them their remarkable distinction. Neither is it for mere historical or intellectual
associations, in the common sense of the term, that they
have attained their eminence. It would not be difficult
to find more picturesque rocks than Zion and more
striking cities than Jerusalem. It would not be difficult
to find places more memorable in art, in science, and
intellectual culture. That which gives them their unrivalled pre-eminence is their relation to God's revelation
of Himself to man. Zion was memorable because it
was God's dwelling-place, Jerusalem because it was
the city of the great King. If Jerusalem and Zion
impress our imagination even above other places, it is
because God had so much to do with them. The very
idea of God makes them great.

But they impress much more than our imagination.
We recall the unrivalled moral and spiritual forces that
were concentrated there : the goodly fellowship of the
prophets, the noble army of the martyrs, the glorious
company of the apostles, all living under the shadow
of Mount Zion, and uttering those words that have
moved the world as they received them from the mouth
of the Lord. We recall Him who claimed to be Himself
God, whose blessed lessons, and holy life, and atoning
death were so closely connected with Jerusalem, and
would alone have made it for ever memorable, even if
it had been signalized by nothing else. Unless David
was illuminated from above to a far greater degree than
we have any reason to believe, he could have little
thought, when he captured that citadel, what a marvellous chapter in the world's history he was beginning.
Century after century, millennium after millennium has
passed ; and still Zion and Jerusalem draw all eyes and

hearts, and pilgrims from the ends of the earth, as they
look even on the ruins of former days, are conscious of
a thrill which no other city in all the world can give.
Nor is that all.   When a name has to be found on earth
for the home of the blessed in heaven, it is the new
Jerusalem; when the scene of heavenly worship, vocal
with the voice of harpers harping with their harps, has
to be distinguished, it is said to be Mount Zion.   Is not
all this a striking testimony that nothing so ennobles
either places or men as the gracious fellowship of God?
View this distinction of Jerusalem and Mount Zion,
if you choose, as the result of mere natural causes.
Though the effect must be held far beyond the efficacy
of the cause, yet you have this fact: that the places
in all the world that to civilized mankind have become
far the most glorious are those with which it is
believed that God maintained a close and unexampled
connection.   View it, as it ought to be viewed, as a
supernatural result; count the fellowship of God at
Jerusalem a real fellowship, and His Spirit a living
Spirit; count the presence of Jesus Christ to have been
indeed that of God manifest in the flesh; you have now
a cause really adequate to the effect, and you have a
far more striking proof than before of the dignity and
glory which God's presence brings.   Would that every
one of you might ponder the lesson of Jerusalem and
Zion!   O ye sons of men, God has drawn nigh to you,
and He has drawn nigh to you as a God of salvation.
Hear then His message!   "For if they escaped not who
refused Him that spake on earth, much more shall not
we escape if we refuse Him that speaketh from
heaven."

# CHAPTER VII.

## *THE KINGDOM ESTABLISHED.*

### 2 SAMUEL v. 10—25.

THE events in David's reign that followed the capture of Mount Zion and the appointment of Jerusalem as the capital of the country were all of a prosperous kind. "David," we are told, "waxed greater and greater, for the Lord of hosts was with him." "And David perceived that the Lord had established him to be king over Israel, and that He had exalted his kingdom for His people Israel's sake."

In these words we find two things : a fact and an explanation. The fact is, that now the tide fairly turned in David's history, and that, instead of a sad chronicle of hardship and disappointment, the record of his reign becomes one of unmingled success, and prosperity. The fact is far from an unusual one in the history of men's lives. How often, even in the case of men who have become eminent, has the first stage of life been one of disappointment and sorrow, and the last part one of prosperity so great as to exceed the fondest dreams of youth. Effort after effort has been made by a young man to get a footing in the literary world, but his books have proved comparative failures. At last he issues one which catches in a remarkable degree the popular taste, and thereafter fame and fortune attend him, and lay their richest offerings at his feet. A similar tale is to be told of many an artist and professional man. And even persons of more ordinary gifts, who have found the battle of life awfully difficult in its earlier stages, have gradually, through diligence and perseverance, acquired an excellent position, more than fulfilling every reasonable desire for success. No man is indeed exempt from the risk of failure if he chooses a path of life for which he has no special fitness, or if he encounters a storm of un- favourable contingencies; but it is an encouraging thing for those who begin life under hard conditions, but with a brave heart and a resolute purpose to do their best, that, as a general rule, the sky clears as the day advances, and the troubles and struggles of the morning yield to success and enjoyment later in the day.

But in the present instance we have not merely a statement of the fact that the tide turned in the case of David, giving him prosperity and enlargement in every quarter, but an explanation of the fact—it was due to the gracious presence and favour of God. This by no means implies that his adversities were due to an opposite cause. God had been with him in the wilder- ness, save when he resorted to deceit and other tricks of carnal policy; but He had been with him to try him and to train him, not to crown him with prosperity. But now, the purpose of the early training being accomplished, God is with him to "grant him all his heart's desire and fulfil all his counsel." If God, indeed, had not been with him, sanctifying his early trials, He would not have been with him in the end, crowning him with loving-kindness and tender mercies. But in the time of their trials, God is with His people

more in secret, hid, at least, from the observation of the
world ; when the time comes for conspicuous blessing
and prosperity, He comes more into view in His own
gracious and bountiful character.   In the case of David,
God was not only with him, but David "perceived"
it; he was conscious of the fact.   His filial spirit
recognized the source of all his prosperity and blessing,
as it had done when he was enabled in his boyhood
to slay the lion and the bear, and in his youth to
triumph over Goliath.   Unlike many successful men,
who ascribe their success so largely to their personal
talents and ways of working, he felt that the great
factor in his success was God.   If he possessed talents
and had used them to advantage, it was God who had
given them originally, and it was God who had enabled
.iim to employ them well.   But in every man's career,
there are many other elements to be considered besides
his own abilities.   There is what the world calls "luck,"
that is to say those conditions of success which are
quite out of our control; as for instance in business the
unexpected rise or fall of markets, the occurrence of
favourable openings, the honesty or dishonesty of
partners and connections, the stability or the vicissitudes
of investments.   The difference between the successful
man of the world and the successful godly man in
these respects is, that the one speaks only of his luck,
the other sees the hand of God in ordering all such
things for his benefit.   This last was David's case.
Well did he know that the very best use he could make
of his abilities could not ensure success unless God
was present to order and direct to a prosperous issue
the ten thousand incidental influences that bore on
the outcome of his undertakings.   And when he saw
that these influences were all directed to this end, that

nothing went wrong, that all conspired steadily and harmoniously to the enlargement and establishment of his kingdom, he perceived that the Lord was with him, and was now visibly fulfilling to him that great principle of His government which He had so solemnly declared to Eli, " Them that honour Me, I will honour."

But is this way of claiming to be specially favoured and blessed by God not objectionable ?  Is it not what the world calls "cant" ?  Is it not highly offensive in any man to claim to be a favourite of Heaven ?  Is this not what hypocrites and fanatics are so fond of doing, and is it not a course which every good, humble-minded man will be careful to avoid ?

This may be a plausible way of reasoning, but one thing is certain—it has not the support of Scripture. If it be an offence publicly to recognise the special favour and blessing with which it has pleased God to visit us, David himself was the greatest offender in this respect the world has ever known.  What is the great burden of his psalms of thanksgiving ?  Is it not an acknowledgment of the special mercies and favours that God bestowed on him, especially in his times of great necessity ?  And does not the whole tenor of the Psalms and the whole tenor of Scripture prove that good men are to take especial note of all the mercies they receive from God, and are not to confine them to their own bosom, but to tell of all His gracious acts and bless His name for ever and ever ?  "They shall abundantly utter the memory of Thy great goodness, and shall sing of Thy righteousness."  That God is to be acknowledged in all our ways, that God's mercy in choosing us in Christ Jesus and blessing us with all spiritual blessings in Him is to be especially recognized, and that we are not to shrink from extolling God's

name for conferring on us favours infinitely beyond what
belong to the men of the world, are among the plainest
lessons of the word of God.

What the world is so ready to believe is, that this
cannot be done save in the spirit of the Pharisee who
thanked God that he was not as other men. And
whenever a worldly man falls foul of one who owns the
distinguishing spiritual mercies that God has bestowed
on him, it is this accusation he is sure to hurl at his
head. But this just shows the recklessness and injustice of the world. Strange indeed if God in His
word has imposed on us a duty which cannot be discharged but in company with those who say, "Stand
by thyself; come not nigh; I am holier than thou"!
The truth is, the world cannot or will not distinguish
between the Pharisee, puffed up with the conceit of his
goodness, and for this goodness of his deeming himself
the favourite of Heaven, and the humble saint, conscious
that in him dwelleth no good thing, and filled with adoring wonder at the mercy of God in making of one so
unworthy a monument of His grace. The one is as
unlike the other as light is to darkness. What good
men need to bear in mind is, that when they do make
mention of the special goodness of God to them they
should be most careful to do so in no boastful mood,
but in the spirit of a most real, and not an assumed or
formal, humility. And seeing how ready the world is
to misunderstand and misrepresent the feeling, and to
turn into a reproach what is done as a most sincere
act of gratitude to God, it becomes them to be cautious
how they introduce such topics among persons who
have no sympathy with their view. "Cast not your
pearls before swine," said our Lord, "lest they turn
again and rend you." "Come near," said the Psalmist,

" and hear, *all ye that fear God*, and I will declare what He hath done for my soul."

Midway between the two statements before us on the greatness and prosperity which God conferred on David, mention is made of his friendly relations with the king of Tyre (ver. 11). The Phœnicians were not included among the seven nations of Palestine whom the Israelites were to extirpate, so that a friendly alliance with them was not forbidden. It appears that Hiram was disposed for such an alliance, and David accepted of his friendly overtures. There is something refreshing in this peaceful episode in a history and in a time when war and violence seem to have been the normal condition of the intercourse of neighbouring nations. Tyre had a great genius for commerce; and the spirit of commerce is alien from the spirit of war. That it is always a nobler spirit cannot be said; for while commerce *ought* to rest on the idea of mutual benefit, and many of its sons honourably fulfil this condition, it often degenerates into the most atrocious selfishness, and heeds not what havoc it may inflict on others provided it derives personal gain from its undertakings. What an untold amount of sin and misery has been wrought by the opium traffic, as well as by the traffic in strong drink, when pressed by cruel avarice on barbarous nations that have so often lost all of humanity they possessed through the fire-water of the *Christian* trader! But we have no reason to believe that there was anything specially hurtful in the traffic which Tyre now began with Israel, although the intercourse of the two countries afterwards led to other results pernicious to the latter—the introduction of Phœnician idolatry and the overthrow of pure worship in the greater part of the tribes of Israel.

Meanwhile what Hiram does is to send to David cedar trees, and carpenters, and masons, by means of whom a more civilized style of dwelling is introduced; and the new city which David has commenced to build, and especially the house which is to be his own, present features of skill and beauty hitherto unknown in Israel. For, amid all his zeal for higher things, the young king of Israel does not disdain to advance his kingdom in material comforts. Of these, as of other things of the kind, he knows well that they are good if a man use them lawfully; and his effort is at once to promote the welfare of the kingdom in the amenities and comforts of life, and to deepen that profound regard for God and that exalted estimate of His favour which will prevent His people from relying for their prosperity on mere outward conditions, and encourage them ever to place their confidence in their heavenly Protector and King.

We pass by, as not requiring more comment than we have already bestowed on a parallel passage (2 Sam. iii. 2-5), the unsavoury statement that "David took to him more concubines and wives" in Jerusalem. With all his light and grace, he had not overcome the prevalent notion that the dignity and resources of a kingdom were to be measured by the number and rank of the king's wives. The moral element involved in the arrangement he does not seem to have at all apprehended; and consequently, amid all the glory and prosperity that God has given him, he thoughtlessly multiplies the evil that was to spread havoc and desolation in his house.

We proceed, therefore, to what occupies the remainder of this chapter—the narrative of his wars with the Philistines. Two campaigns against these inveterate enemies of Israel are recorded, and the decisive encounter in both cases took place in the neighbourhood of Jerusalem.

The narrative is so brief that we have difficulty in apprehending all the circumstances. The first invasion of the Philistines took place soon after David was anointed king over all Israel. It is not said whether this occurred before David possessed himself of Mount Zion, nor, considering the structure common in Hebrew narrative, does the circumstance that in the history it follows that event prove that it was subsequent to it in the order of time. On the contrary, there is an expression that seems hardly consistent with this idea. We read (ver. 17) that when David heard of the invasion he "went *down* into the hold." Now, this expression could not be used of the stronghold of Zion, for that hill is on the height of the central plateau, and invariably the Scriptures speak of " going up to Zion." If he had possession of Mount Zion, he would surely have gone to it when the Philistines took possession of the plain of Rephaim. The hold to which he went down must have been in a lower position ; indeed, " the hold " is the expression used of the place or places of protection to which David resorted when he was pursued by Saul (see 1 Sam. xxii. 4). Further, when we turn to the twenty-third chapter of this book, which records some memorable incidents of the war with the Philistines, we find (vers. 13, 14) that when the Philistines pitched in the valley of Rephaim David was in a hold near the cave of Adullam. The valley of Rephaim, or " the giants," is an extensive plain to the south-west of Jerusalem, forming a great natural entrance to the city. When we duly consider the import of these facts, we see that the campaign was very serious, and David's difficulties very great. The Philistines were encamped in force on the summit of the plateau near the natural metropolis of the country. David was encamped in a hold in the low country in the south-west, making use of that very cave of Adullam where he had taken refuge in his conflicts with Saul. This was far from a hopeful state of matters. To the eye of man, his position may have appeared very desperate. Such an emergency was a fit time for a solemn application to God for direction. " David inquired of the Lord, saying, Shall I go up to the Philistines ? Wilt Thou deliver them into mine hand ? And the Lord said unto David, Go up, for I will doubtless deliver the Philistines into thine hand." Up, accordingly, David went, attacked the Philistines and smote them at a place called Baal-perazim, somewhere most likely between Adullam and Jerusalem. The expression " The Lord hath broken forth on mine enemies before me, as the breach of waters," seems to imply that He broke the Philistine host into two, like flooded water breaking an embankment, preventing them from uniting and rallying, and sending them in two detachments into flight and confusion. Considering the superior position of the Philistines, and the great advantage they seem to have had over David in numbers also, this was a signal victory, even though it did not reduce the foe to helplessness.

For when the Philistines had got time to recover, they again came up, pitched again in the plain of Rephaim, and appeared to render unavailing the signal achievement of David at Baal-perazim. Again David inquired what he should do. The reply was somewhat different from before. David was not to go straight up to face the enemy, as he had done before. He was to " fetch a compass behind them," that is, as we understand it, to make a circuit, so as to get in the enemy's rear over against a grove of mulberry trees. That tree has not yet disappeared from the neighbourhood of Jerusalem; a mulberry tree still marks the spot in the valley of Jehoshaphat where, according to tradition, Isaiah was sawn asunder (Stanley's "Sinai and Palestine"). When he should hear "the sound of a going" (Revised Version, "the sound of a march") in the tops of the mulberry trees, then he was to bestir himself. It is difficult to conceive any natural cause that should give rise to a sound like that of a march "in the tops of the mulberry trees;" but if not a natural, it must have been a supernatural indication of some sound that would alarm the Philistines and make the moment favourable for an attack. It is probable that the presence of David and his troop in the rear of the Philistines was not suspected, the mulberry trees forming a screen between them. When David got his opportunity, he availed himself of it to great advantage; he inflicted a thorough defeat on the Philistines, and smiting them from Geba to Gazer, he appears to have all but annihilated their force. In this way, he gave the *coup de grâce* to his former allies.

We have said that it appears to have been during these campaigns against the Philistines that the incidents took place which are recorded fully in the twenty-third chapter of this book. It does not seem possible that these incidents occurred at or about the time when David was flying from Saul, at which time the cave of Adullam was one of his resorts. Neither is it likely that they occurred during the early years of David's reign, while he was yet at strife with the house of Saul. At least, it is more natural to refer them to the time when the Philistines, having heard that David had been anointed king over Israel, came up to seek David, although we do not consider it impossible that they occurred in the earlier period of his reign. The record shows how wonderfully the spirit of David had passed into his men, and what splendid deeds of courage were performed by them, often in the face of tremendous odds. We get a fine glimpse here of one of the great sources of David's popularity—his extraordinary *pluck* as we now call it, and readiness for the most daring adventures, often crowned with all but miraculous success. In all ages, men of this type have been marvellous favourites with their comrades. The annals of the British army, and still more the British navy, contain many such records. And even when we go down to pirates and freebooters, we find the odium of their mode of life in many cases remarkably softened by the splendour of their valour, by their running unheard-of risks, and sometimes by sheer daring and bravery obtaining signal advantages over the greatest odds. The achievements of David's "three mighties," as well as of his "thirty," formed a splendid instance of this kind of warfare. All that we know of them is comprised within a few lines, but when we call to mind the enthusiasm that used to be awakened all over our own country by the achievements of Nelson and his officers, or more recently by General Gordon, of China and Egypt, we can easily understand the thrilling effect which these wonderful tales of valour would have throughout all the tribes of Israel.

The personal affection for David and his heroes which would thus be formed must have been very warm, nay, even enthusiastic. In the case of David, whatever may have been true of the others, all the influence thus acquired was employed for the welfare of the nation and the glory of God. The supreme desire of his heart was that the people might give all the glory to Jehovah, and derive from these brilliant successes fresh assurances how faithful God was to His promises to Israel. Alike as a man of piety and a man of patriotism, he made this his aim. Knowing as he did what was due to God, and animated by a profound desire to render to God His due, he would have been horrified had he intercepted in his own person aught of the honour and glory which were His. But for the people's sake also, as a man of patriotism, his desire was equally strong that God should have all the glory. What were military successes however brilliant to the nation, or a reputation however eminent, compared to their enjoying the favour and friendship of God? Success—how ephemeral it was; reputation—as transient as the glow of a cloud beside the setting sun; but God's favour and gracious presence with the nation was a perpetual treasure, enlivening, healing, strengthening, guiding for evermore. "Happy is that people that is in such a case; yea, happy is that people whose God is the Lord."

# CHAPTER VIII.

2 SAMUEL vi.

THE first care of David when settled on the throne had been to obtain possession of the stronghold of Zion, on which and on the city which was to surround it he fixed as the capital of the kingdom and the dwelling-place of the God of Israel. This being done, he next set about bringing up the ark of the testimony from Kirjath-jearim, where it had been left after being restored by the Philistines in the early days of Samuel. David's first attempt to place the ark on Mount Zion failed through want of due reverence on the part of those who were transporting it; but after an interval of three months the attempt was renewed, and the sacred symbol was duly installed on Mount Zion, in the midst of the tabernacle prepared by David for its reception.

In bringing up the ark to Jerusalem, the king showed a commendable desire to interest the whole nation, as far as possible, in the solemn service. He gathered together the chosen men of Israel, thirty thousand, and went with them to bring up the ark from Baale of Judah, which must be another name for Kirjath-jearim, distant from Jerusalem about ten miles. The people, numerous as they were, grudged neither the time, the trouble, nor the expense. A handful might have sufficed for all the actual labour that was required; but thousands of the chief people were summoned to be present, and that on the principle both of rendering due honour to God, and of conferring a benefit on the people. It is not a handful of professional men only that should be called to take a part in the service of religion; Christian people generally should have an interest in the ark of God; and other things being equal, that Church which interests the greatest number' of people and attracts them to active work will not only do most for advancing God's kingdom, but will enjoy most of inward life and prosperity.

The joyful spirit in which this service was performed by David and his people is another interesting feature of the transaction. Evidently it was not looked on as a toilsome service, but as a blessed festival, adapted to cheer the heart and raise the spirits. What was the precise nature of the service? It was to bring into the heart of the nation, into the new capital of the kingdom, the ark of the covenant, that piece of sacred furniture which had been constructed nearly five hundred years before in the wilderness of Sinai, the memorial of God's holy covenant with the people, and the symbol of His gracious presence among them. In spirit it was bringing God into the very midst of the nation, and on the choicest and most prominent pedestal the country now supplied setting up a constant memento of the presence of the Holy One. Rightly understood, the service could bring joy only to spiritual hearts; it could give pleasure to none who had reason to dread the presence of God. To those who knew Him as their reconciled Father and the covenant God of the nation, it was most attractive. It was as if the sun were again shining on them after a long eclipse, or as if the father of a loved and loving family had returned after a weary absence. God enthroned on Zion, God in the midst of Jerusalem—what happier or more thrilling thought was it possible to cherish ?   God, the sun and shield of the nation, occupying for His residence the one fitting place in all the land, and sending over Jerusalem and over all the country emanations of love and grace, full of blessing for all that feared His name!   The happiness with which this service was entered on by David and his people is surely the type of the spirit in which all service to God should be rendered by those whose sins He has blotted out, and on whom He has bestowed the privileges of His children.

But the best of services may be gone about in a faulty way.   There may be some criminal neglect of God's will that, like the dead fly in the apothecary's pot of ointment, causes the perfume to send forth a stinking savour.   And so it was on this occasion. God had expressly directed that when the ark was moved from place to place it should be borne on poles on the shoulders of the Levites, and never carried in a cart, like a common piece of furniture.   But in the removal of the ark from Kirjath-jearim, this direction was entirely overlooked.   Instead of following the directions given to Moses, the example of the Philistines was copied when they sent the ark back to Bethshemesh.   The Philistines had placed it in a new cart, and the men of Israel now did the same.   What induced them to follow the example of the Philistines rather than the directions of Moses, we do not know, and can hardly conjecture.   It does not appear to have been a mere oversight.   It had something of a deliberate plan about it, as if the law given in the wilderness were now obsolete, and in so small a matter any method might be chosen that the people liked. It was substituting a heathen example for a Divine rule in the worship of God. We cannot suppose that David was guilty of deliberately setting aside the authority of God. On his part, it may have been an error of inadvertence. But that somewhere there was a serious offence is evident from the punishment with which it was visited (1 Chron. xv. 13). The jagged bridlepaths of those parts are not at all adapted for wheeled conveyances, and when the oxen stumbled, and the ark was shaken, Uzzah, who was driving the cart, put forth his hand to steady it. "The anger of God," we are told, "was kindled against Uzzah ; and God smote him there for his error; and there he died by the ark of God." His effort to steady the ark must have been made in a presumptuous way, without reverence for the sacred vessel. Only a Levite was authorized to touch it, and Uzzah was apparently a man of Judah. The punishment may seem to us hard for an offence which was ceremonial rather than moral ; but in that economy, moral truth was taught through ceremonial observances, and neglect of the one was treated as involving neglect of the other. The punishment was like the punishment of Nadab and Abihu, the sons of Aaron, for offering strange fire in their censers. It may be that both in their case, and in the case of Uzzah, there were unrecorded circumstances, unknown to us, making it clear that the ceremonial offence was not a mere accident, but that it was associated with evil personal qualities well fitted to provoke the judgment of God. The great lesson for all time is to beware of following our own devices in the worship of God when we have clear instructions in His word how we are to worship Him.

This lamentable event put a sudden end to the joyful service. It was like the bursting of a thunderstorm on an excursion party that rapidly sends every one to flight. And it is doubtful whether the spirit shown by David was altogether right. He was displeased "because the Lord had made a breach upon Uzzah, and he called the name of the place Perez-uzzah to this day. And David was afraid of the Lord that day and said, How shall the ark of the Lord come to me? So David would not remove the ark of the Lord into the city of David; but David carried it aside into the house of Obed-edom the Gittite." The narrative reads as if David resented the judgment which God had inflicted, and in a somewhat petulant spirit abandoned the enterprise because he found God too hard to please. That some such feeling should have fluttered about his heart was not to be wondered at; but surely it was a feeling to which he ought not to have given entertainment, as it certainly was one on which he ought not to have acted. If God was offended, David surely knew that He must have had good ground for being so. It became him and the people, therefore, to accept God's judgment, humble themselves before Him, and seek forgiveness for the negligent manner in which they had addressed themselves to this very solemn service. Instead of this David throws up the matter in a fit of sullen temper, as if it were impossible to please God in it, and the enterprise must there- fore be abandoned. He leaves the ark in the house of Obed-edom the Gittite, returning to Jerusalem crestfallen and displeased, altogether in a spirit most opposite to that in which he had set out.

It may happen to you that some Christian under- taking on which you have entered with great zeal and ardour, and without any surmise that you are not doing right, is not blessed, but meets with some rough shock, that places you in a very painful position. In the most disinterested spirit, you have tried perhaps to set up in some neglected district a school or a mission, and you expect all encouragement and approbation from those who are most interested in the welfare of the district. Instead of receiving approval, you find that you are regarded as an enemy and an intruder. You are attacked with unexampled rudeness, sinister aims are laid to your charge, and the purpose of your undertaking is declared to be to hurt and discourage those whom you were bound to aid. The shock is so violent and so rude that for a time you cannot understand it. On the part of man it admits of no reasonable justification whatever. But when you go into your closet, and think of the matter as permitted by God, you wonder still more why God should thwart you in your endeavour to do good. Rebellious feelings hover about your heart that if God is to treat you in this way, it were better to abandon His service altogether. But surely no such feeling is ever to find a settled place in your heart. You may be sure that the rebuff which God has permitted you to encounter is meant as a trial of your faith and humility; and if you wait on God for further light and humbly ask a true view of God's will; if, above all, you beware of retiring in sullen silence from God's active service, good may come out of the apparent evil, and you may yet find cause to bless God even for the shock that made you so uncomfortable at the time.

The Lord does not forsake His people, nor leave them for ever under a cloud. It was not long before the downcast heart of David was reassured. When the ark had been left at the house of Obed-edom, Obed-edom was not afraid to take it in. Its presence in other places had hitherto been the signal for disaster and death. Among the Philistines, in city after city, at Bethshemesh, and now at Perez-uzzah, it had spread death on every side. Obed-edom was no sufferer. Probably he was a God-fearing man, conscious of no purpose but that of honouring God. A manifest blessing rested on his house. "The God of heaven," says Bishop Hall, "pays liberally for His lodging." It is not so much God's ark in our time and country that needs a lodging, but God's servants, God's poor, sometimes persecuted fugitives flying from an oppressor, very often pious men in oreign countries labouring under infinite discouragements to serve God. The Obed-edom who takes them in will not suffer. Even should he be put to loss or inconvenience, the day of recompense draweth nigh. "I was a stranger, and ye took Me in."

Again, then, King David, encouraged by the experience of Obed-edom, goes forth in royal state to bring up the ark to Jerusalem. The error that had proved so fatal was now rectified. "David said, None ought to carry the ark of God but the Levites, for them hath the Lord chosen to carry the ark of God and to minister unto Him for ever" (1 Chron. xv. 2). In token of his humility and his conviction that every service that man renders to God is tainted and needs forgiveness, oxen and fatlings were sacrificed ere the bearers of the ark had well begun to move. The spirit of enthusiastic joy again swayed the multitude, brightened probably by the assurance that no judgment need now be dreaded, but that they might confidently look for the smile of an approving God. The feelings of the king himself were wonderfully wrought up, and he gave free expression to the joy of his heart. There are occasions of great rejoicing when all ceremony is forgotten, and no forms or appearances are suffered to stem the tide of enthusiasm as it gushes right from the heart. It was an occasion of this kind to David. The check he had sustained three months before had only dammed up his feelings, and they rolled out now with all the greater volume. His soul was stirred by the thought that the symbol of Godhead was now to be placed in his own city, close to his own dwelling; that it was to find an abiding place of rest in the heart of the kingdom, on the heights where Melchizedek had reigned, close to where he had blessed Abraham, and which God had destined as His own dwelling from the foundations of the world. Glorious memories of the past, mingling with bright anticipations of the future, recollections of the grace revealed to the fathers, and visions of the same grace streaming forth to distant ages, as generation after generation of the faithful came up here to attend the holy festivals, might well excite that tumult of emotion in David's breast before which the ordinary restraints of royalty were utterly flung aside. He sacrificed, he played, he sang, he leapt and danced before the Lord, with all his might; he made a display of enthusiasm which the cold-hearted Michal, as she could not understand it nor sympathise with it, had the folly to despise and the cruelty to ridicule. The ordinary temper of the sexes was reversed—the man was enthusiastic; the woman was cold. Little did she know of the springs of true enthusiasm in the service of God! To her faithless eye, the ark was little more than a chest of gold, and where it was kept was of little consequence; her carnal heart could not appreciate the glory that excelleth; her blind eye could see none of the visions that had overpowered the soul of her husband.

A few other circumstances are briefly noticed in connection with the close of the service, when the ark had been solemnly enshrined within the tabernacle that David had reared for it on Mount Zion.

The first is that " David offered burnt-offerings and peace-offerings before the Lord." The burnt-offering was a fresh memorial of sin, and therefore a fresh confession that even in connection with that very holy service there were sins to be confessed, atoned for, and forgiven. For there is this great difference between the service of the formalist and the service of the earnest worshipper : that while the one can see nothing faulty in his performance, the other sees a multitude of imperfections in his. Clearer light and a clearer eye, even the light thrown by the glory of God's purity on the best works of man, reveal a host of blemishes, unseen in ordinary light and by the carnal eye. Our very prayers need to be purged, our tears to be wept over, our repentances repented of. Little could the best services ever done by him avail the spiritual worshipper if it were not for the High-priest over the house of God who ever liveth to make intercession for him.

Again, we find David after the offering of the burnt-offerings and the peace-offerings " blessing the people in the name of the Lord of hosts." This was something more than merely expressing a wish or offering a prayer for their welfare. It was like the benediction with which we close our public services. The benediction is more than a prayer. The servant of the

Lord appears in the attitude of dropping on the heads
of the people the blessing which he invokes.   Not that he
or any man can convey heavenly blessings to a people
that do not by faith appropriate them and rejoice in
them.   But the act of benediction implies this : These
blessings are yours if you will only have them.   They
are provided, they are made over to you, if you will
only accept them.   The last act of public worship is a
great encouragement to faith.   When the peace of God
that passeth all understanding, or the blessing of God
the Father, Son and Holy Ghost, or the grace of the
Lord Jesus Christ, and the love of God, and the
communion of the Holy Ghost are invoked over your
heads, it is to assure you that if you will but accept of
them through Jesus Christ, these great blessings are
actually yours.   True, there is no part of our service
more frequently spoiled by formality ; but there is none
richer with true blessing to faith.   So when David
blessed the people, it was an assurance to them that
God's blessing was within their reach ; it was theirs if
they would only take it.   How strange that any hearts
should be callous under such an announcement ; that
any should fail to leap to it, as it were, and rejoice
in it, as glad tidings of great joy !

The third thing David did was to deal to every one of
Israel, both man and woman, a loaf of bread, and a
good piece of flesh, and a flagon of wine.   It was a
characteristic act, worthy of a bountiful and generous
nature like David's.   It may be that associating bodily
gratifications with Divine service is liable to abuse,
that the taste which it gratifies is not a high one, and
that it tempts some men to attend religious services for
the same reason as some followed Jesus—for the loaves
and fishes.   Yet Jesus did not abstain on some rare

occasions from feeding the multitude, though the act was liable to abuse. The example both of David and of Jesus may show us that though not habitually, yet occasionally, it is both right and fitting that religious service should be associated with a simple repast. There is nothing in Scripture to warrant the practice, adopted in some missions in very poor districts, of feeding the people habitually when they come up for religious service, and there is much in the argument that such a practice degrades religion and obscures the glory of the blessings which Divine service is designed to bring to the poor. But occasionally the rigid rule may be somewhat relaxed, and thus a sort of symbolical proof afforded that godliness is profitable unto all things, having promise of the life that now is and of that which is to come.

The last thing recorded of David is, that he returned to bless his house. The cares of the State and the public duties of the day were not allowed to interfere with his domestic duty. Whatever may have been his ordinary practice, on this occasion at least he was specially concerned for his household, and desirous that in a special sense they should share the blessing. It is plain from this that, amid all the imperfections of his motley household, he could not allow his children to grow up ignorant of God, thus dealing a rebuke to all who, outdoing the very heathen in heathenism, have houses without an altar and without a God. It is painful to find that the spirit of the king was not shared by every member of his family. It was when he was returning to this duty that Michal met him and addressed to him these insulting words: "How glorious was the king of Israel to-day, who uncovered himself to-day in the eyes of the handmaids of his servants, as one of the vain fellows shamefully uncovers himself." On the mind of David himself, this ebullition had no effect but to confirm him in his feeling, and reiterate his conviction that his enthusiasm reflected on him not shame but glory. But a woman of Michal's character could not but act like an icicle on the spiritual life of the household. She belonged to a class that cannot tolerate enthusiasm in religion. In any other cause, enthusiasm may be excused, perhaps extolled and admired : in the painter, the musician, the traveller, even the child of pleasure ; the only persons whose enthusiasm is unbearable are those who are enthusiastic in their regard for their Saviour, and in the answer they give to the question, " What shall I render to the Lord for all His benefits toward me ? " There are, doubtless, times to be calm, and times to be enthusiastic ; but can it be right to give all our coldness to Christ and all our enthusiasm to the world ?

# CHAPTER IX.

## *PROPOSAL TO BUILD A TEMPLE.*

### 2 SAMUEL vii.

THE spirit of David was essentially active and fond
of work. He was one of those who are ever
pressing on, not content to keep things as they are,
moving personally towards improvement, and urging
others to do the same. Even in Eastern countries, with
their proverbial stillness and conservatism, such men
are sometimes found, but they are far more common
elsewhere. Great undertakings do not frighten them ;
they have spirit enough for a lifetime of effort, they
never seem weary of pushing on. When they look on
the disorders of the world they are not content with
the languid utterance, "Something must be done;"
they consider what it is possible for them to do, and
gird themselves to the doing of it.

For some time David seems to have found ample
scope for his active energies in subduing the Philistines
and other hostile tribes that were yet mingled with the
Israelites, and that had long given them much annoyance. His friendship with Hiram of Tyre probably
gave a new impulse to his mind, and led him to
project many improvements in Jerusalem and elsewhere.
When all his enemies were quieted, and he sat in his
house, he began to consider to what work of internal

improvement he would now give his attention. Having recently removed the Ark, and placed it in a tabernacle on Mount Zion, constructed probably in accordance with the instructions given to Moses in the wilderness, he did not at first contemplate the erection of any other kind of building for the service of God. It was while he sat in his new and elegant house that the idea came into his mind that it was not seemly that he should be lodged in so substantial a home, while the Ark of God dwelt between curtains. Curtains might have been suitable, nay, necessary, in the wilderness, where the Ark had constantly to be moved about; and even in the land of Israel, while the nation was comparatively unsettled, curtains might still have been best; but now that a permanent resting-place had been found for the Ark, was it right that there should be such a contrast between the dwelling-place of David and the dwelling-place of God? It was the very argument that was afterwards used by Haggai and Zechariah after the return from captivity, to rouse the languid zeal of their countrymen for the re-erection of the house of God. " Is it time for you, O ye, to dwell in your ceiled houses and this house lie waste? "

A generous heart, even though it be a godless one, is uncomfortable when surrounded by elegance and luxury, while starvation and misery prevail in its neighbourhood. We see in our day the working of this feeling in those cases, unhappily too few, where men and women born to gold and grandeur feel wretched unless they are doing something to equalise the conditions of life by helping those who are born to rags and wretchedness. To the feelings of the godly a disreputable place of worship, contrasting meanly with the taste and elegance of the hall, or even the villa, is a pain and a reproach. There is not much need at the present day for urging the unseemliness of such a contrast, for the tendency of our time is toward handsome church buildings, and in many cases towards extravagance in the way of embellishment. What we have more need to look at is the disproportion of the sums paid by rich men, and even by men who can hardly be called rich, in gratifying their own tastes and in extending the kingdom of Christ. We are far from blaming those who, having great wealth, spend large sums from year to year on yachts, on equipages, on picture galleries, on jewellery and costly furnishings. Wealth which remunerates honest and wholesome labour is not all selfishly thrown away. But it is somewhat strange that we hear so seldom of rich Christian men devoting their superfluous wealth to maintaining a mission station with a whole staff of labourers, or to the rearing of colleges, or hospitals, or Christian institutions, which might provide on a large scale for Christian activity in ways that might be wonderfully useful. It is in this direction that there is most need to press the example of David. When shall this new enlargement of Christian activity take place ? Or when shall men learn that the pleasure of spreading the blessings of the Gospel by the equipment and main-tenance of a foreign missionary or mission station far exceeds anything to be derived from refinements and luxuries of which they themselves are the object and the centre ?

When the thought of building a temple occurred to David, he conferred on the subject with the prophet Nathan. The Scripture narrative is so brief that it gives us no information about Nathan, except in con-nection with two or three events in which he had a

share.   Apparently he was a prophet of Jerusalem, on
intimate terms with David, and perhaps attached to his
court.   When first consulted on the subject by the
king, he gave him a most encouraging answer, but
without having taken any special steps to ascertain the
mind of God.   He presumed that as the undertaking
was itself so good, and as David generally was so
manifestly under Divine guidance, nothing was to be
said but that he should go on.   " Nathan said to the
king, Go, do all that is in thine heart, for the Lord is
with thee."   That same night, however, a message came
to Nathan that gave a new complexion to the proposal.
He was instructed to remind David, first, that God had
never complained of His tabernacle-dwelling from the
day when He brought up the children of Israel to that
hour, and had never given a hint that He desired a
house of cedar.   Further, he was commissioned to
convey to David the assurance of God's continued
interest and favour towards him—of that interest
which began by taking him from the sheepfold to make
him king over Israel, and which had been shown con-
tinuously in the success which had been given him in
all his enterprises, and the great name he had acquired,
entitling him to rank with the great men of the earth.
Towards the nation of Israel, too, God was actuated by
the same feeling of affectionate interest ; they would be
planted, set firm in a place of their own, delivered from
the thraldom of enemies, and allowed to prosper and
expand in peace and comfort.   Still further—and this
was a very special blessing—Nathan was to inform
David that, unlike Saul, he was not to be the only one
of his race to occupy the throne; his son would reign
after he was gathered to his fathers, the kingdom would
be established in his hands, and the throne of his

kingdom would be established for ever. To this favoured son of his would be entrusted the honour of building the temple, God would be his Father, and he would be God's son. If he should fall into sin, he would be chastised for his sin, but not destroyed. The Divine mercy would not depart from him as it had departed from Saul. The kernel of the message was in these gracious concluding words—"Thine house and thy kingdom shall be established for ever before thee; thy throne shall be established for ever."

Here, certainly, was a very remarkable message, containing both elements of refusal and elements of encouragement. The proposal which David had made to build a temple was declined. The time for a change, though drawing near, had not yet arrived. The curtain-canopied tabernacle had been designed by God to wean His people from those sensuous ideas of worship to which the magnificent temples of Egypt had accustomed them, and to give them the true idea of a spiritual service, though not without the visible emblem of a present God. The time had not yet arrived for changing this simple arrangement. God could impart His blessing in the humble tent as well as in the stately temple. As long as it was God's pleasure to dwell in the tabernacle, so long might David expect that His grace would be imparted there. So we may say, that so long as it is manifestly God's pleasure that a body of His worshippers shall occupy a humble tabernacle, so long may they expect that He will shine forth there, imparting that fulness of grace and blessing which is the true and only glory of any place of worship.

But the message through Nathan contained also elements of encouragement, chiefly with reference to David's offspring, and to the stability and permanence

of his throne. To appreciate the value of this promise
for the future, we must bear in mind the great in-
security of new dynasties in Eastern countries, and the
fearful tragedies that were often perpetrated to get rid
of the old king's family, and prepare the way for some
ambitious and unscrupulous usurper.

We hardly need to recall the tragic end of Saul, the
base murder of Ishbosheth, or the painful deaths of
Asahel and Abner. We have but to think of what
happened in the sister kingdom of the ten tribes, from
the death of the son of its first king, Jeroboam, on to
its final extinction. What an awful record the history
of that kingdom presents of conspiracies, murders, and
massacres! How miserable a distinction it was to be
of the seed royal in those days! It only made one
the more conspicuous a mark for the poisoned cup or
the assassin's dagger. It associated with the highest
families of the realm horrors and butcheries of which
the poorest had no cause even to dream. Any one
who had been raised to a throne could not but sicken at
the thought of the atrocities which his very elevation
might one day bring upon his children. A new king
could hardly enjoy his dignity but by steeling his heart
against every feeling of parental love.

And, moreover, these constant changes of the royal
family were very hurtful to the kingdom at large. They
divided it into sections that raged against each other
with terrible fury. For of all wars civil wars are the
worst for the fierceness of the passions they evoke, and
the horrors which they inflict. Scotland and England
too have had too much experience of these conflicts in
other days. Many generations have elapsed since they
were ended, but we have many memorials still of the
desolation which they spread, while our progress and

prosperity, ever since they passed away, show us clearly of what a multitude of mercies they robbed the land.

To David, therefore, it was an unspeakable comfort to be assured that his dynasty would be a stable dynasty; that his son would reign after him; that a succession of princes would follow with unquestioned right to the throne; and that if his son, or his son's son, should commit sins deserving of chastisement, that chastisement would not be withheld, but it would not be fatal, it would bring the needed correction, and thus the throne would be secure for ever. A father naturally desires peace and prosperity for his children, and if he extends his view down the generations, the desire is strong that it may be well with them and with their seed for ever. But no father, in ordinary circumstances, can flatter himself that his posterity shall escape their share of the current troubles and calamities of life. David, but for this assurance, must have looked forward to his posterity encountering their share of those nameless horrors to which royal children were often born. It was an unspeakable privilege to learn, as he did now, that his dynasty would be alike permanent and secure; that, as a rule, his children would not be exposed to the atrocities of Oriental successions; that they would be under the special care and protection of God; that their faults would be corrected without their being destroyed; and that this state of blessing would continue for ages and ages to come.

The emotions roused in David by this communication were alike delightful and exuberant. He takes no notice of the disappointment—of his not being permitted to build the temple. Any regret that this might occasion is swallowed up by his delight in the store of blessing actually promised. And here we may see a remarkable instance of God's way of dealing with His people's prayers. Virtually, if not formally, David had asked of God to permit him to build a temple to His name. That petition, bearing though it did very directly on God's glory, is not vouchsafed. God does not accord that privilege to David. But in refusing him that request, He makes over to him mercies of far higher reach and importance. He refuses his immediate request only to grant to him far above all that he was able to ask or think. And how often does God do so! How often, when His people are worrying and perplexing themselves about their prayers not being answered, is God answering them in a far richer way! Glimpses of this we see occasionally, but the full revelation of it remains for the future. You pray to the degree of agony for the preservation of a beloved life; it is not granted; God appears deaf to your cry; a year or two after, things happen that would have broken your friend's heart or driven reason from its throne; you understand now why God did not fulfil your petition. Oh for the spirit of trust that shall never charge God foolishly! Oh for the faith that does not make haste, but waits patiently for the Lord,—waits for the explanation that shall come in the end, at the revelation of Jesus Christ!

It is a striking scene that is presented to us when "David went in, and sat before the Lord." It is the only instance in Scripture in which any one is said to have taken the attitude of sitting while pouring his heart out to God. Yet the nature of the communion was in keeping with the attitude. David was like a child sitting down beside his father, to think over some wonderfully kind expression of his intentions to him, and pour out his full heart into his ear. We may observe in the address of David how pervaded it is by the tone of wonder. This, indeed, is its great characteristic. He expresses wonder at the past, at God's selecting one obscure in family and obscure in person; he wonders at the present: How is it Thou hast brought me thus far? and still more he wonders at the future, the provision made for the stability of his house in all time coming. "And is this the manner of man, O Lord God?"* All true religious feeling is pervaded by an element of wonder; it is this element that warms and elevates it. In David's case it kindles intense adoration and gratitude, with reference both to God's dealings with himself and His dealings with Israel. "What one nation in the earth is like Thy people, even like Israel, whom God went to redeem for a people to Himself, and to make Him a name, and to do for you great things and terrible, for Thy land, before Thy people, which Thou redeemedst to Thee from Egypt, from the nations and their gods?" This wonder at past goodness, moreover, begets great confidence for the future. And David warmly and gratefully expresses this confidence, and looks forward with exulting feelings to the blessings reserved for him and his house. And finally he falls into the attitude of supplication, and prays that it may all come to pass. Not that he doubts God's word; the tone of the whole prayer is the tone of gratitude for the past and confidence in the future.

---

* The expression is very obscure, whether we take the affirmative form of the Revised Version or the interrogative form of the Authorised Version. " And this, too, after the manner of men, O Lord God ! " (R.V.) We must choose between these opposite meanings. We prefer the interrogative form of the A.V. David's wonder being the more excited that God's ways were here so much above man's.

But he feels it right to take up the attitude of a suppliant, to show, as we believe, that it must all come of God's free and infinite mercy; that not one of all the good things which God had promised could be claimed as a right, for the least and the greatest were due alike to the rich grace of a sovereign God. " Therefore now let it please Thee to bless the house of Thy servant, that it may continue for ever before Thee; for Thou, O Lord God, hast spoken it, and with Thy blessing let the house of Thy servant be blessed for ever." Appropriate ending for a remarkable prayer! appropriate, too, not for David only, but for every Christian praying for his country, and for every Christian father praying for his family! " With Thy blessing," bestowed alike in mercy and in chastisement, in what Thou givest and in what Thou withholdest, but making all things work together for eternal good— " With Thy blessing let the house of Thy servant be blessed for ever."

We seem to see in this prayer the very best of David —much intensity of feeling, great humility, wondering gratitude, holy intimacy and trust, and supreme satisfaction in the blessing of God. We see him walking in the very light of God's countenance, and supremely happy. We see Jacob's ladder between earth and heaven, and the angels of God ascending and descending on it. Moreover, we see the infinite privilege which is involved in having God for our Father, and in being able to realise that He is full of most fatherly feelings to us. The joy of David in this act of fellowship with God was the purest of which human beings are capable. It was indeed a joy unspeakable and full of glory. Oh that men would but acquaint themselves with God and be at peace! Let it be our aim to cherish as warm sentiments of trust in God, and to look forward to the future with equal satisfaction and delight.

A very important question arises in connection with this chapter, to which we have not yet adverted, but which we cannot pass by. In that promise of God respecting the stability of David's throne and the perpetual duration of his dynasty, was there any reference to the Messiah, any reference to the spiritual kingdom of which alone it could be said with truth that it was to last for ever? The answer to this question is very plain, because some of the words addressed by God to David are quoted in the New Testament as having a Messianic reference. "To which of the angels said He at any time, I will be to him a Father, and he shall be to Me a son?" (Heb. i. 5). If we consider, too, how David's dynasty really came to an end as a reigning family some five hundred years after, we see that the language addressed to him was not exhausted by the fortunes of his family. In the Divine mind the prophecy reached forward to the time of Christ, and only in Christ was it fully verified. And it seems plain from some words of St. Peter on the day of Pentecost that David understood this. He knew that "God had sworn to him that of the fruit of his loins, according to the flesh, He would raise up Christ to sit on His throne" (Acts ii. 30). From the very exalted emotions which the promise raised in his breast, and the enthusiasm with which he poured forth his thanksgivings for it, we infer that David saw in it far more than a promise that for generations to come his house would enjoy a royal dignity. He must have concluded that the great hope of Israel was to be fulfilled in connection with his race. God's words implied, that it was in His line the promise to Abraham was to be fulfilled—" In thee and in thy seed shall all the nations of the earth be blessed." He saw Christ's day afar off and was glad. To us who look back on that day the reasons for gladness and gratitude are far stronger than they were even to him. Then let us prize the glorious fact that the Son of David has come, even the Son of God, who hath given us understanding that we may know Him that is true. And while we prize the truth, let us embrace the privilege; let us become one with Him in whom we too become sons of God, and with whom we may cherish the hope of reigning for ever as kings and priests, when He comes to gather His redeemed that they may sit with Him on the throne of His glory.

# CHAPTER X.

## 2 SAMUEL viii. 1—14.

THE transitions of the Bible, like those of actual life, are often singularly abrupt; that which now hurries us from the scene of elevated communion with God to the confused noise and deadly struggles of the battle-field is peculiarly startling. We are called to contemplate David in a remarkable light, as a professional warrior, a man of the sword, a man of blood; wielding the weapons of destruction with all the decision and effect of the most daring commanders. That the sweet singer of Israel, from whose tender heart those blessed words poured out to which the troubled soul turns for composure and peace, should have been so familiar with the horrors of the battle-field, is indeed a surprise. We can only say that he was led to regard all this rough work as indispensable to the very existence of his kingdom, and to the fulfilment of the great ends for which Israel had been called. Painful and miserable though it was in itself, it was necessary for the accomplishment of greater good. The bloodthirsty spirit of these hostile nations would have swallowed up the kingdom of Israel, and left no trace of it remaining. The promise to Abraham, "In thee and in thy seed shall all the families of the earth be blessed," would have ceased to have any basis for its fulfilment. Painful though it was to deal death and destruction on every side, it would have been worse to see the nation of Israel destroyed, and the foundation of the world's greatest blessings swept for ever away.

The "rest from all his enemies round about," referred to in the first verse of the seventh chapter, seems to refer to the nearer enemies of the kingdom, while the wars mentioned in the present chapter were mostly with enemies more remote. The most important of the wars now to be considered was directed against the occupants of that large territory lying between Palestine and the Euphrates which God had promised to Abraham, although no command had been given to dispossess the inhabitants, and therefore it could be held only in tributary subjection. In some respects, David was the successor of Joshua as well as of Moses. He had to continue Joshua's work of conquest, as well as Moses' work of political arrangement and administration. The nations against whom he had now to go forth were most of them warlike and powerful; some of them were banded together in leagues against him, rendering his enterprise very perilous, and such as could have been undertaken by no one who had not an immovable trust in God. The twentieth Psalm seems to express the feelings with which the godly part of the nation would regard him as he went forth to these distant and perilous enterprises :—

> The Lord answer thee in the day of trouble;
> The name of the God of Jacob set thee up on high;
> Send thee help from the sanctuary,
> And strengthen thee out of Zion;
> Remember all thy offerings,
> And accept thy burnt-sacrifice;　　[Selah
> Grant thee thy heart's desire,

And fulfil all thy counsel.
We will triumph in thy salvation,
And in the name of our God we will set up our banners :
The Lord fulfil all thy petitions.
Now know I that the Lord saveth His anointed ;
He will answer him from His holy heaven
With the saving strength of His right hand.
Some trust in chariots, and some in horses,
But we will make mention of the name of the **Lord our God.**
They are bowed down and fallen ;
But we are risen, and stand upright.
Save, Lord ;
Let the King answer us when we call.

It is an instructive fact that the history of these wars is given so shortly. A single verse is all that is given to most of the campaigns. This brevity shows very clearly that another spirit than that which moulded ordinary histories guided the composition of this book. It would be beyond human nature to resist the temptation to describe great battles, the story of which is usually read with such breathless interest, and which gratify the pride of the people and reflect glory on the nation. It is not the object of Divine revelation to furnish either brief annals or full details of wars and other national events, except in so far as they have a spiritual bearing—a bearing on the relation between God and the people. From first to last the purpose of the Bible is simply to unfold the dispensation of grace,—God's progress in revelation of His method of making an end of sin, and bringing in everlasting righteousness.

We shall briefly notice what is said regarding the different undertakings.

1. The first campaign was against the Philistines. Not even their disastrous discomfiture near the plain of Rephaim had taught submission to that restless

people.    On this occasion David carried the war into
their own country, and took some of their towns,
establishing garrisons there, as the Philistines had done
formerly in the land of Israel.    There is some obscurity
in the words which describe one of his conquests.
According to the Authorised Version, " He took
Metheg-ammah out of the hand of the Philistines."
The Revised Version renders, " He took the bridle of the
mother city out of the hand of the Philistines."    The
parallel passage in 1 Chron. xviii. 1 has it, " He took
Gath and her towns out of the hand of the Philistines."
This last rendering is quite plain ; the other passage
must be explained in its light.    Gath, the city of King
Achish, to which David had fled twice for refuge, now
fell into his hands.    The loss of Gath must have been
a great humiliation to the Philistines ; not even Samson
had ever inflicted on them such a blow.    And the
policy that led David (it could hardly have been without
painful feelings) to possess himself of Gath turned
out successful ; the aggressive spirit of the Philistines
was now fairly subdued, and Israel finally delivered
from the attacks of a neighbour that had kept them for
many generations in constant discomfort.

2. His next campaign was against Moab.    As David
himself had at one time taken refuge in Gath, so he had
committed his father and mother to the custody of the
king of Moab (1 Sam. xxii. 3, 4).    Jewish writers have
a tradition that after a time the king put his parents to
death, and that this was the origin of the war which he
carried on against them.    That David had received from
them some strong provocation, and deemed it necessary
to inflict a crushing blow for the security of that part
of his kingdom, it seems hardly possible to doubt.
Ingratitude was none of his failings, nor would he

who was so grateful to the men of Jabesh-gilead for burying Saul and his sons have been severe on Moab if Moab had acted the part of a true friend in caring for his father and mother. When we read of the severity practised on the army of Moab, we are shocked. And yet it is recorded rather as a token of forbearance than a mark of severity. How came it that the Moabite army was so completely in David's power? Usually, as we have seen, when an army was defeated it was pursued by the victors, and in the course of the flight a terrible slaughter ensued. But the Moabite army had come into David's power comparatively whole. This could only have been through some successful piece of generalship, by which David had shut them up in a position where resistance was impossible. Many an Eastern conqueror would have put the whole army to the sword; David with a measuring line measured two-thirds for destruction and a full third for preservation. Thus the Moabites in the south-east were subdued as thoroughly as the Philistines in the south-west, and brought tribute to the conqueror, in token of their subjection. The explanation of some commentators that it was not the army, but the fortresses, of Moab that David dealt with is too strained to be for a moment entertained. It proceeds on a desire to make David superior to his age, on unwillingness to believe, what, however, lies on the very surface of the story, that in the main features of his warlike policy he fell in with the maxims and spirit of the time.

3. The third of his campaigns was against Hadad-ezer, the son of Rehob, king of Zobah. It is said in the chapter before us that the encounter with this prince took place " as he went to recover his border at the

river Euphrates;" in the parallel passage of 1 Chronicles
it is "as he went to stablish his dominion by the river
Euphrates." The natural interpretation is, that David
was on his way to establish his dominion by the river
Euphrates, when this Hadadezer came out to oppose
him. The terms of the covenant of God with Abraham
assigned to him the land "from the river of Egypt to
the great river, the river Euphrates" (Gen. xv. 18), and
when the territory was again defined to Joshua, its
boundary was "from the wilderness and this Lebanon
even unto the great river, the river Euphrates." Under
the provisions of this covenant, as made by Him whose
is the earth and the fulness thereof, David held himself
entitled to fix the boundary of his dominion by the
banks of the river. In what particular form he designed to do this, we are not informed; but whatever
may have been his purpose, Hadadezer set himself to
defeat it. The encounter with Hadadezer could not
but have been serious to David, for his enemy had a
great force of military chariots and horsemen against
whom he could oppose no force of the same kind. Nevertheless, David's victory was complete; and in dealing
with that very force in which he himself was utterly
deficient, he was quite triumphant; for he took from
his opponent a thousand and seven hundred horsemen,
as well as twenty thousand footmen. There must have
been some remarkable stroke of genius in this achievement, for nothing is more apt to embarrass and baffle a
commonplace general than the presence of an opposing
force to which his army affords no counterpart.

4. But though David had defeated Hadadezer, not
far, as we suppose, from the base of Mount Hermon,
his path to the Euphrates was by no means clear.
Another body of Syrians, the Syrians of Damascus,

having come from that city to help Hadadezer, seem to have been too late for this purpose, and to have encountered David alone. This, too, was a very serious enterprise for David; for though we are not informed whether, like Hadadezer, they had arms which the king of Israel could not match, it is certain that the army of so rich and civilized a state as Syria of Damascus would possess all the advantages that wealth and experience could bestow. But in his battle with them, David was again completely victorious. The slaughter was very great—two-and-twenty thousand men. This immense figure illustrates our remark a little while ago: that the slaughter of defeated and retreating armies was usually prodigious. So entire was the humiliation of this proud and ancient kingdom, that " the Syrians became servants to David, and brought presents," thus acknowledging his suzerainty over them. Between the precious things that were thus offered to King David and the spoil which he took from captured cities, he brought to Jerusalem an untold mass of wealth, which he afterwards dedicated for the building of the Temple.

5. In one case, the campaign was a peaceful one. " When Toi, king of Hamath, heard that David had smitten all the host of Hadadezer, then Toi sent Joram his son unto King David to salute him and to bless him, because he had fought against Hadadezer and had smitten him, for Hadadezer had wars with Toi." The kingdom of Toi lay in the valley between the two parallel ranges of Lebanon and anti-Lebanon, and it too was within the promised boundary, which extended to " the entering in of Hamath." Accordingly, the son of Toi brought with him vessels of silver, and vessels of gold, and vessels of brass; these also did King David dedicate to the Lord. The fame of David as a warrior

was now such, at least in these northern regions, that
further resistance seemed out of the question.  Submission was the only course when the conqueror was
evidently supported by the might of Heaven.

6. In the south, however, there seems to have been
more of a spirit of opposition.  No particulars of the
campaign against the Edomites are given; but it is
stated that David put garrisons in Edom; "throughout
all Edom put he garrisons, and all the Edomites
became servants to David."  The placing of garrisons
through all their country shows how obstinate these
Edomites were, and how certain to have returned to
fresh acts of hostility had they not been held in
restraint by these garrisons.   From the introduction
to Psalm lx. it would appear that the insurrection of
Edom took place while David was in the north contending with the two bodies of Syrians that opposed
him—the Syrians of Zobah and those of Damascus.
It would appear that Joab was detached from the
army in Syria in order that he might deal with the
Edomites.   In the introduction to the Psalm, twelve
thousand of the Edomites are said to have fallen in
the Valley of Salt.   In the passage now before us,
it is said that eighteen thousand Syrians fell in that
valley.   The Valley of Salt is in the territory of
Edom.   It may be that a detachment of Syrian troops
was sent to aid the Edomites, and that both sustained
a terrible slaughter.   Or it may be that, as in Hebrew
the words for Syria and Edom are very similar (ארם
and אדם), the one word may by accident have been
substituted for the other.

7. Mention is also made of the Ammonites, the
Amalekites, and the Philistines as having been subdued
by David.   Probably in the case of the Philistines and

the Amalekites the reference is to the previous campaign already recorded, while the Ammonite campaign may be the one of which we have the record afterwards. But the reference to these campaigns is accompanied with no particulars.

Twice in the course of this chapter we read that "the Lord gave David victory whithersoever he went." It does not appear, however, that the victory was always purchased with ease, or the situation of David and his armies free from serious dangers. The sixtieth Psalm, the title of which ascribes it to this period, makes very plain allusion to a time of extraordinary trouble and disaster in connection with one of these campaigns. "O God, Thou hast cast us off; Thou hast scattered us ; Thou hast been displeased: oh turn Thyself to us again." It is probable that when David first encountered the Syrians he was put to great straits, his difficulty being aggravated by his distance from home and the want of suitable supplies. If the Edomites, taking advantage of his difficulty, chose the time to make an attack on the southern border of the kingdom, and if the king was obliged to diminish his own force by sending Joab against Edom, with part of his men, his position must have been trying indeed. But David did not let go his trust in God; courage and confidence came to him by prayer, and he was able to say, "Through God we shall do valiantly; for He it is that shall tread down all our enemies."

The effect of these victories must have been very striking. In the Song of the Bow, David had celebrated the public services of Saul, who had "clothed the daughters of Israel in scarlet, with other delights, who had put on ornaments of gold on their apparel"; but

all that Saul had done for the kingdom was now
thrown into the shade by the achievements of David.
With all his bravery, Saul had never been able to
subdue his enemies, far less to extend the limits of
the kingdom.   David accomplished both ; and it is the
secret of the difference that is expressed in the words,
"The Lord gave victory to David whithersoever he
went." It is one of the great lessons of the Old
Testament that the godly man can and does perform
his duty better than any other man, because the Lord
is with him : that whether he be steward of a house,
or keeper of a prison, or ruler of a kingdom, like
Joseph; or a judge and lawgiver, like Moses; or a
warrior, like Samson, or Gideon, or Jephthah; or a
king, like David, or Jehoshaphat, or Josiah ; or a prime
minister, like Daniel, his godliness helps him to do
his duty as no other man can do his.   This is especially
a prominent lesson in the book of Psalms; it is in-
scribed on its very portals ; for the godly man, as
the very first Psalm tells us, "shall be like a tree
planted by the rivers of water, that bringeth forth his
fruit in his season ; his leaf also shall not wither, and
whatsoever he doeth shall prosper."

In these warlike expeditions, King David foreshadowed the spiritual conquests of the Son of David,
who went forth "conquering and to conquer,"
staggered for a moment, as in Gethsemane, by the
rude shock of confederate enemies, but through prayer
regaining his confidence in God, and triumphing
in the hour and power of darkness.   That noble
effusion of fire and feeling, the sixty-eighth Psalm,
seems to have been written in connection with these
wars.   The soul of the Psalmist is stirred to its depths ;
the majestic goings of Jehovah, recently witnessed

by the nation, have roused his most earnest feelings, and he strains every nerve to produce a like feeling in the people. The recent exploits of the king are ranked with His doings when He marched before His people through the wilderness, and Mount Sinai shook before Him. Great delight is expressed in God's having taken up His abode on His holy hill, in the exaltation of His people in connection with that step, and likewise in looking forward to the future and anticipating the peaceful triumphs when " princes should come out of Egypt, and Ethiopia stretch forth her arms to God." Benevolent and missionary longings mingle with the emotions of the conqueror and the feelings of the patriot.

" Sing unto the Lord, ye kingdoms of the earth ;
Oh, sing praises unto the Lord,
To Him that rideth upon the heaven of heavens that are of old.
Lo, He uttereth His voice, and that a mighty voice."

It is interesting to see how in this extension of his influence among heathen nations, the Psalmist began to cherish and express these missionary longings, and to call on the nations to sing praises unto the Lord. It has been remarked that, in the ordinary course of Providence, the Bible follows the sword, that the seed of the Gospel falls into furrows that have been prepared by war. Of this missionary spirit we find many evidences in the Psalms. It was delightful to the Psalmist to think of the spiritual blessings that were to spread even beyond the limits of the great empire that now owned the sway of the king of Israel. Mount Zion was to become the birth-place of the nations ; from Egypt and Babylonia, from Philistia, Tyre, and Ethiopia, additions were to be made to her citizens (Ps. ixxxvii.). " The people shall be gathered together, and the nations, to serve the Lord" (Ps. cii. 22). "All the ends of the earth shall remember and turn to the Lord, and all the kindreds of the nations shall worship before Him" (Ps. xxii. 27). "All nations whom Thou hast made shall come and worship before Thee, O Lord; and they shall glorify Thy name" (Ps. lxxxvi. 9). "Make a joyful noise unto the Lord, all ye lands. Enter into His gates with thanksgiving, and into His courts with praise" (Ps. c. 1, 4).

Alas, the era of wars has not yet passed away. Even Christian nations have been woefully slow to apply the Christian precept, "Inasmuch as lieth in you, live peaceably with all men." But let us at least make an earnest endeavour that if there must be war, its course may be followed up by the heralds of mercy, and that wherever there may occur "the battle of the warrior, and garments rolled in blood," there also it may speedily be proclaimed, "Unto us a Child is born, unto us a Son is given, and the government is on His shoulders: and His name is called Wonderful, Counsellor, Mighty God, the Everlasting Father, Prince of Peace" (Isa. ix. 6).

# CHAPTER XI.

2 SAMUEL viii. 15—18.

IF the records of David's warlike expeditions are brief, still more so are the notices of his work of peace. How he fulfilled his royal functions when there was no war to draw him from home, and to engross the attention both of the king and his officers of state, is told us here in the very briefest terms, barely affording even the outline of a picture. Yet it is certain that the activity of David's character, his profound interest in the welfare of his people, and his remarkable talent for administration, led in this department to very conspicuous and remarkable results. Some of the Psalms afford glimpses both of the principles on which he acted, and the results at which he aimed, that are fitted to be of much use in filling up the bare skeleton now before us. In this point of view, the subject may become interesting and instructive, as undoubtedly it is highly important. For we must remember that it was with reference to the spirit in which he was to rule that David was called the man after God's heart, and that he formed such a contrast to his predecessor. And further we are to bear in mind that in respect of the moral and spiritual qualities of his reign David had for his Successor the Lord Jesus Christ. "The Lord God will give unto Him the throne of His servant David," said the angel Gabriel to Mary, "and He shall reign over the house of Judah for ever, and of His kingdom there shall be no end." It becomes us to make the most of what is told us of the peaceful administration of David's kingdom, in order to understand the grounds on which our Lord is said to have occupied His throne.

The first statement in the verses before us is comprehensive and suggestive : "And David reigned over all Israel ; and David executed judgment and justice unto all his people." The first thing pointed out to us here is the catholicity of his kingly government, embracing *all* Israel, *all* people. He did not bestow his attention on one favoured section of the people, to the neglect or careless oversight of the rest. He did not, for example, seek the prosperity of his own tribe, Judah, to the neglect of the other eleven. In a word, there was no favouritism in his reign. This is not to say that he did not like some of his subjects better than the rest. There is every reason to believe that he liked the tribe of Judah best. But whatever preferences of this kind he may have had—and he would not have been man if he had had none—they did not limit or restrict his royal interest ; they did not prevent him from seeking the welfare of every portion of the land, of every section of the people. Just as, in the days when he was a shepherd, there were probably some of his sheep and lambs for which he had a special affection, yet that did not prevent him from studying the welfare of the whole flock and of every animal in it with most conscientious care ; so was it with his people. The least interesting of them were sacred in his eyes. They were part of his charge, and they were to be studied and cared for in the same manner as the rest. In this he reflected that universality of God's care on which we find the Psalmist dwelling with such complacency: "The Lord is good to all; and His tender mercies are over all His works. The eyes of all wait upon Thee; and Thou givest them their meat in due season. Thou openest Thine hand, and satisfiest the desire of every living thing." And may we not add that this quality of David's rule foreshadowed the catholicity of Christ's kingdom and His glorious readiness to bestow blessing on every side? "Come unto Me, all ye that labour and are heavy-laden, and I will give you rest." "On the last, that great day of the feast, Jesus stood and cried, If any man thirst, let him come unto Me and drink." "Where there is neither Jew nor Greek, circumcision nor uncircumcision, bond nor free; but Christ is all and in all." "Ye are all one in Christ Jesus."

In the next place, we have much to learn from the statement that the most prominent thing that David did was to "execute judgment and justice to the people." That was the solid foundation on which all his benefits rested. And these words are not words of form or words of course. For it is never said that Saul did anything of the kind. There is nothing to show that Saul was really interested in the welfare of the people, or that he took any pains to secure that just and orderly administration on which the prosperity of his kingdom depended. And most certainly they are not words that could have been used of the ordinary government of Oriental kings. Tyranny, injustice, oppression, robbery of the poor by the rich, government by favourites more cruel and unprincipled than their masters, imprisonments, fines, conspiracies, and assassinations, were the usual features of Eastern government. And to a great extent they are features of the

government of Syria and other Eastern countries even
at the present day.   It is in vivid contrast to all these
things that it is said, " David executed judgment and
justice."   Perhaps there is no need for assigning a
separate meaning to each of these words ; they may be
regarded as just a forcible combination to denote the
all-pervading justice which was the foundation of the
whole government.   He was just in the laws which he
laid down, and just in the decisions which he gave.
He was inaccessible to bribes, proof against the influence of the rich and powerful, and deaf in such
matters to every plea of expediency ; he regarded
nothing but the scales of justice.   What confidence and
comfort an administration of this kind brought may in
some measure be inferred from the extraordinary satisfaction of many an Eastern people at this day when the
administration of justice is committed even to foreigners,
if their one aim will be to deal justly with all.   On this
foundation, as on solid rock, a ruler may go on to
devise many things for the welfare of his people.   But
apart from this any scheme of general improvement
which may be devised is sure to be a failure, and all
the money and wisdom and practical ability that may
be expended upon it will only share the fate of the
numberless cart-loads of solid material in the " Pilgrim's
Progress " that were cast into the Slough of Despond.

   This idea of equal justice to all, and especially to those
who had no helper, was a very beautiful one in David's
eyes.   It gathered round it those bright and happy
features which in the seventy-second Psalm are associated with the administration of another King.   " Give
the king Thy judgments, O God, and Thy righteousness
to the king's son.   He shall judge Thy people with
righteousness, and Thy poor with judgment."   The

beauty of a just government is seen most clearly in its treatment of the poor. It is the poor who suffer most from unrighteous rulers. Their feebleness makes them easier victims. Their poverty prevents them from dealing in golden bribes. If they have little individually wherewith to enrich the oppressor, their numbers make up for the small share of each. Very beautiful, therefore, is the government of the king who " shall judge the poor of the people, who shall save the children of the needy, and shall break in pieces the oppressor." The thought is one on which the Psalmist dwells with great delight. " He shall deliver the needy when he crieth, the poor also, and him that hath no helper. He shall spare the poor and needy, and shall save the souls of the needy. He shall redeem their soul from deceit and violence, and precious shall their blood be in his sight." So far from need and poverty repelling him, they rather attract him. His interest and his sympathy are moved by the cry of the destitute. He would fain lighten the burdens that weigh them down so heavily, and give them a better chance in the struggle of life. He would do something to elevate their life above the level of mere hewers of wood and drawers of water. He recognises fully the brotherhood of man.

And in all this we find the features of that higher government of David's Son which shows so richly His most gracious nature. The cry of sorrow and need, as it rose from this dark world, did not repel, but rather attracted, Him. Though the woes of man sprang from his own misdeeds, He gave Himself to bear them and carry their guilt away. All were in the lowest depths of spiritual poverty, but for that reason His hand was the more freely offered for their help. The one condition on which that help was given was, that they should own their poverty, and acknowledge Him as their Benefactor, and accept all as a free gift at His hands.

But more than that, the condition of the poor in the natural sense was very interesting to Jesus. It was with that class He threw in His lot. It was among them He lived ; it was their sorrows and trials He knew by personal experience ; it was their welfare for which He laboured most. Always accessible to every class, most respectful to the rich, and ever ready to bestow His blessings wherever they were prized, yet it was true of Christ that " He spared the poor and needy and saved the souls of the needy." And in a temporal point of view, one of the most striking effects of Christ's religion is, that it has so benefited, and tends still more to benefit, the poor. Slavery and tyranny are among its most detested things. Regard for man as man is one of its highest principles. It detects the spark of Divinity in every human soul, grievously overlaid with the scum and filth of the world ; and it seeks to cleanse and brighten it, till it shine forth in clear and heavenly lustre. It is a most Christian thought that the gems in the kingdom of God are not to be found merely where respectability and culture disguise the true spiritual condition of humanity, but even among those who outwardly are lost and disreputable. Not the least honourable of the reproachful terms applied to Jesus was—" the Friend of publicans and sinners."

We are not to think of David, however, as being satisfied if he merely secured justice to the poor and succeeded in lightening their yoke. His ulterior aim was to fill his kingdom with active, useful, honourable citizens. This is plain from the beautiful language of some of the Psalms. Both for old and young, he had a beautiful ideal. " The righteous shall flourish as the palm tree; he shall grow like a cedar in Lebanon. Those that be planted in the house of the Lord shall flourish in the courts of our God. They shall still bring forth fruit in old age; they shall be fat and flourishing" (Ps. xcii. 12-14). And so for the young his desire was— "That our sons may be as plants, grown up in their youth; that our daughters may be as corner-stones, polished after the similitude of a palace." Moral beauty, and especially the beauty of active and useful lives, was the great object of his desire. Can anything be better or more enlightened as a royal policy than that which we thus see to have been David's—in the first place, a policy of universal justice; in the second place, of special regard for those who on the one hand are most liable to oppression and on the other are most in need of help and encouragement; and in the third place, a policy whose aim is to promote excellence of character, and to foster in the young those graces and virtues which wear longest, which preserve the freshness and enjoyment of life to the end, and which crown their possessors, even in old age, with the respect and the affection of all ?

The remaining notices of David's administration in the passage before us are simply to the effect that the government consisted of various departments, and that each department had an officer at its head.

1. There was the military department, at the head of which was Joab, or rather he was over "the host"— the great muster of the people for military purposes. A more select body, "the Cherethites and the Pelethites," seems to have formed a bodyguard for the king, or a band of household troops, and was under a separate commander. The troops forming "the host" were

divided into twelve courses of twenty-four thousand each, regularly officered, and for one month of the year the officers of one of the courses, and probably the people, or some of them, attended on the king at Jerusalem (1 Chron. xxvii. 1). Of the most distinguished of his soldiers who excelled in feats of personal valour, David seems to have formed a legion of honour, conspicuous among whom were the thirty honourable, and the three who excelled in honour (2 Sam. xxiii. 28). It is certain that whatever extra power could be given by careful organization to the fighting force of the country, the army of Israel under David possessed it in the fullest degree.

2. There was the civil department, at the head of which were Jehoshaphat the recorder and Seraiah the scribe or secretary. While these were in attendance on David at Jerusalem, they did not supersede the ordinary home rule of the tribes of Israel. Each tribe had still its prince or ruler, and continued, under a general superintendence from the king, to conduct its local affairs (1 Chron. xxvii. 16-22). The supreme council of the nation continued to assemble on occasions of great national importance (1 Chron. xxviii. 1), and though its influence could not have been so great as it was before the institution of royalty, it continued an integral element of the constitution, and in the time of Rehoboam, through its influence and organization (1 Kings xii. 3, 16), the kingdom of the ten tribes was set up, almost without a struggle (1 Chron. xxiii. 4). This home-rule system, besides interesting the people greatly in the prosperity of the country, was a great check against the abuse of the royal authority; and it is a proof that the confidence of Rehoboam in the stability of his government, confirmed perhaps by a

superstit ous view of that promise to David, must have
been an absolute infatuation, the product of utter inexperience on his part, and of the most foolish counsel
ever tendered by professional advisers.

3. Ecclesiastical administration. The capture of Jerusalem and its erection into the capital of the kingdom
made a great change in ecclesiastical arrangements.
For some time before it would have been hard to tell
where the ecclesiastical capital was to be found. Shiloh
had been stripped of its glory when Ichabod received his
name, and the Philistine armies destroyed the place.
Nob had shared a similar fate at the hands of Saul.
The old tabernacle erected by Moses in the wilderness
was at Gibeon (1 Chron. xxi. 29), and remained there
even after the removal of the ark to Zion (1 Kings iii. 4).
At Hebron, too, there must have been a shrine while
David reigned there. But from the time when David
brought up the ark to Jerusalem, that city became the
greatest centre of the national worship. There the
services enjoined by the law of Moses were celebrated ;
it became the scene of the great festivals of Passover,
Pentecost, and Tabernacles.

We are told that the heads of the ecclesiastical
department were Zadok the son of Ahitub and Ahimelech the son of Abiathar. These represented the elder
and the younger branches of the priesthood. Zadok
was the lineal descendant of Eleazar, Aaron's son
(1 Chron. vi. 12), and was therefore the constitutional
successor to the high-priesthood. Ahimelech the son
of Abiathar represented the family of Eli, who seems to
have been raised to the high-priesthood cut of order,
perhaps in consequence of the illness or incompetence
of the legitimate high-priest. It is of some interest to
note the fact that under David two men were at the

head of the priesthood, much as it was in the days of
our Lord, when Annas and Caiaphas are each called
the high-priest. The ordinary priests were divided
into four-and-twenty courses, and each course served
in its turn for a limited period, an arrangement which
still prevailed in the days of Zacharias, the father of
John the Baptist. A systematic arrangement of the
Levites was likewise made ; some were allocated to the
service of the Temple, some were porters, some were
singers, and some were officers and judges. Of the
six thousand who filled the last-named office, " chief
fathers " as they were called, nearly a half were allocated
among the tribes east of the Jordan, as being far from
the centre, and more in need of oversight. It is probable that this large body of Levites were not limited
to strictly judicial duties, but that they performed important functions in other respects, perhaps as teachers,
physicians, and registrars. It is not said that Samuel's
schools of the prophets received any special attention,
but the deep interest that David must have taken in
Samuel's work, and his early acquaintance with its
effects, leave little room to doubt that these institutions
were carefully fostered, and owed to David some share
of the vitality which they continued to exhibit in the
days of Elijah and Elisha. It is very probable that
the prophets Gad and Nathan were connected with
these institutions.

It is scarcely possible to say how far these careful
ecclesiastical arrangements were instrumental in foster-
ing the spirit of genuine piety. But there is too much
reason to fear that even in David's time that element
was very deficient. The bursts of religious enthusiasm that occasionally rolled over the country were no
sure indications of piety in a people easily roused to

temporary gushes of feeling, but deficient in stability. There often breathes in David's psalms a sense of loneliness, a feeling of his being a stranger on the earth, that seems to show that he wanted congenial company, that the atmosphere was not of the godly quality he must have wished. The bloody Joab was his chief general, and at a subsequent period the godless Ahithophel was his chief counsellor. It is even probable that the intense piety of David brought him many secret enemies. The world has no favour for men, be they kings or priests, that repudiate all compromise in religion, and insist on God being regarded with supreme and absolute honour. Where religion interferes with their natural inclinations and lays them under inviolable obligations to have regard to the will of God, they rebel in their hearts against it, and they hate those who consistently uphold its claims. The nation of Israel appears to have been pervaded by an undercurrent of dislike to the eminent holiness of David, which, though kept in check by his distinguished services and successes, at last burst out with terrific violence in the rebellion of Absalom. That villainous movement would not have had the vast support it received, especially in Jerusalem, if even the people of Judah had been saturated with the spirit of genuine piety. We cannot think much of the piety of a people that rose up against the sweet singer of Israel and the great benefactor of the nation, and that seemed to anticipate the cry, " Not this man, but Barabbas."

The systematic administration of his kingdom by King David was the fruit of a remarkable faculty of orderly arrangement that belonged to most of the great men of Israel. We see it in Abraham, in his prompt and successful marshalling of his servants to

pursue and attack the kings of the East when they
carried off Lot ; we see it in Joseph, first collecting and
then distributing the stores of food in Egypt ; in Moses,
conducting that marvellous host in order and safety
through the wilderness ; and, in later times, in Ezra
and Nehemiah, reducing the chaos which they found at
Jerusalem to a state of order and prosperity which
seemed to verify the vision of the dry bones.   We see
it in the Son of David, in the orderly way in which all
His arrangements were made : the sending forth of the
twelve Apostles and the seventy disciples, the arranging
of the multitude when He fed the five thousand, and
the careful gathering up of the fragments "that nothing
be lost."   In the spiritual kingdom, a corresponding
order is demanded, and times of peace and rest in the
Church are times when this development is specially to
be studied.   Spiritual order, spiritual harmony : God
in His own place, and self, with all its powers and
interests, as well as our brethren, our neighbours, and
the world, all in their's—this is the great requisite in
the individual heart.   The development of this holy
order in the *individual* soul; the development of *family*
graces, the due Christian ordering of homes ; the
development of *public* graces—patriotism, freedom,
godliness, in the State, and in the Church of the spirit
that seeks the instruction of the ignorant, the recovery
of the erring, the comforting of the wretched, and the
advancement everywhere of the cause of Christ—in
a word, the increase of spiritual wealth—these very
specially are objects to which in all times, but especially
in quiet times, all hearts and energies should be turned.
What can be more honourable, what can be more
blessed, than to help in advancing these ?   More life,
more grace, more prayer, more progress, more mis-

sionary ardour, more self-denying love, more spiritual beauty—what higher objects can the Christian minister aim at? And how better can the Christian king or the Christian statesman fulfil and honour his office than by using his influence, so far as he legitimately may, in furthering the virtues and habits characteristic of men that fear God while they honour the king?

# CHAPTER XII.

## DAVID AND MEPHIBOSHETH.

### 2 SAMUEL ix.

THE busy life which King David was now leading did not prevent memory from occasionally running back to his early days and bringing before him the friends of his youth. Among these remembrances of the past, his frien'ship and his covenant with Jonathan were sure to hold a conspicuous place. On one of these occasions the thought occurred to him that possibly some descendant of Jonathan might still be living. He had been so completely severed from his friend during the last years of his life, and the unfortunate attempt on the part of Ishbosheth had made personal intercourse so much more difficult, that he seems not to have been aware of the exact state of Jonathan's family. It is evident that the survival of any descendant of his friend was not publicly known, and probably the friends of the youth who was discovered had thought it best to keep his existence quiet, being of those who would give David no credit for higher principles than were current between rival dynasties. Even Michal, Jonathan's sister, does not seem to have known that a son of his survived. It became necessary, therefore, to make a public inquiry of his officers and attendants. "Is there yet any that is left of the house of Saul, that I may show him kindness for Jonathan's sake ? " It was not essential that he should be a child of Jonathan's; any descendant of Saul's would have been taken for Jonathan's sake.

It is a proof that the bloody wars in which he had been engaged had not destroyed the tenderness of his heart, that the very chapter which follows the account of his battles opens with a yearning of affection—a longing for an outlet to feelings of kindness. It is instructive, too, to find the proof of love to his neighbour succeeding the remarkable evidence of supreme regard to the honour of God recently given in the proposal to build a temple. This period of David's life was its golden era, and it is difficult to understand how the man that was so remarkable at this time for his regard for God and his interest in his neighbour should soon afterwards have been betrayed into a course of conduct that showed him most grievously forgetful of both.

This proceeding of David's in making inquiry for a fit object of beneficence may afford us a lesson as to the true course of enlightened kindness. Doubtless David had numberless persons applying for a share of his bounty; yet he makes inquiry for a new channel in which it may flow. The most clamorous persons are seldom the most deserving, and if a bountiful man simply recognises, however generously, even the best of the cases that press themselves on his notice, he will not be satisfied with the result; he will feel that his bounty has rather been frittered away on miscellaneous undertakings, than that it has achieved any solid and satisfying result. It is easy for a rich man to fling a pittance to some wretched-looking creature that whines out a tale of horror in his ear; but this may be done only to relieve his own feelings, and harm instead of good may be the result. Enlightened benevolence aims at something higher than the mere relief of passing distress. Benevolent men ought not to lie at the mercy either of the poor who ask their charity, or of the philanthropic Christians who appeal for support to their schemes. Pains must be taken to find out the deserving, to find out those who have the strongest claim. Even the open-handed, whose purse is always at hand, and who are ready for every good work, may be neglecting some case or class of cases which have far stronger claims on them than those which are so assiduously pressed on their notice.

And hence we may see that it is right and fitting, especially in those to whom Providence has given much, to cast over in their minds, from time to time, the state of their obligations, and think whether among old friends, or poor relations, or faithful but needy servants of God, there may not be some who have a claim on their bounty. There are other debts besides money debts it becomes you to look after. In youth, perhaps, you received much kindness from friends and relatives which at the time you could not repay; but now the tables are turned; you are prosperous, they or their families are needy. And these cases are apt to slip out of mind. It is not always hard-heartedness that makes the prosperous forget the less fortunate; it is often utter thoughtlessness. It is the neglect of that rule which has such a powerful though silent effect when it is carried out—Put yourself in their place. Imagine how you would feel, strained and worried to sleeplessness through narrow means, and seeing old friends rolling in wealth, who might, with little or no inconvenience, lighten the burden that is crushing you so painfully. It is a strange thing that

this counsel should be more needed by the rich than
by the poor.   Thoughtlessness regarding his neighbours is not a poor man's vice.   The empty house is
remembered, even though it costs a sacrifice to send
it a little of his own scanty supplies.   Few men are
so hardened as not to feel the obligation to show
kindness when that obligation is brought before them.
What we urge is, that no one should lie at the mercy
of others for bringing his obligations before him.   Let
him think for himself; and especially let him cast his
eye round his own horizon, and consider whether
there be not some representatives of old friends or
old relations to whom kindness ought to be shown.

To return to the narrative.   The history of
Mephibosheth, Jonathan's son, had been a sad one.
When Israel was defeated by the Philistines on Mount
Gilboa, and Saul and Jonathan were slain, he was but
an infant; and his nurse, terror-stricken at the news
of the disaster, in her haste to escape had let him fall,
and caused an injury which made him lame for life.
What the manner of his upbringing was, we are not
told.   When David found him, he was living with
Machir, the son of Ammiel, of Lo-debar, on the other
side of the Jordan, in the same region where his
uncle Ishbosheth had tried to set up his kingdom.
Mephibosheth became known to David through Ziba,
a servant of Saul's, a man of more substance than
principle, as his conduct showed at a later period
of his life.   Ziba, we are told, had fifteen sons and
twenty servants.   He seems to have contrived to make
himself comfortable notwithstanding the wreck of his
master's fortunes, more comfortable than Mephibosheth, who was living in another man's house.

There seems to have been a surmise among David's

people that this Ziba could tell something of Jonathan's family; but evidently he was not very ready to do so; for it was only to David himself that when sent for he gave the information, and that after David had emphatically stated his motive—not to do harm, but to show kindness for Jonathan's sake. The existence of Mephibosheth being thus made known, he is sent for and brought into David's presence. And we cannot but be sorry for him when we mark his abject bearing in the presence of the king. When he was come unto David, "he fell on his face and did reverence." And when David explained his intentions, "he bowed himself and said, What is thy servant, that thou shouldest look on such a dead dog as I am?" Naturally of a timid nature, and weakened in nerve by the accident of his infancy, he must have grown up under great disadvantages. His lameness excluded him from sharing in any youthful game or manly exercise, and therefore threw him into the company of the women who, like him, tarried at home. What he had heard of David had not come through a friendly channel, had come through the partisans of Saul, and was not likely to be very favourable. He was too young to remember the generous conduct of David in reference to his father and grandfather; and those who were about him probably did not care to say much about it.

Accustomed to think that his wisest course was to conceal from David his very existence, and looking on him with the dread with which the family of former kings regarded the reigning monarch, he must have come into his presence with a strange mixture of feeling. He had a profound sense of the greatness which David had achieved and the honour implied in his countenance and fellowship. But there was no need for his humbling himself so low. There was no need for his calling himself a dog, a dead dog,—the most humiliating image it was possible to find. We should have thought him more worthy of his father if, recognizing the high position which David had attained by the grace of God, he had gracefully thanked him for the regard shown to his father's memory, and shown more of the self-respect which was due to Jonathan's son. In his subsequent conduct, in the days of David's calamity, Mephibosheth gave evidence of the same disinterested spirit which had shone so beautifully in Jonathan, but his noble qualities were like a light twinkling among ruins or a jewel glistening in a wreck.

This shattered condition both of mind and body, however, commended him all the more to the friendly regard of David. Had he shown himself a high-minded, ambitious youth, David might have been embarrassed how to act towards him. Finding him modest and respectful, he had no difficulty in the case. The kindness which he showed him was twofold. In the first place, he restored to him all the land that had belonged to his grandfather ; and in the second place, he made him an inmate of his own house, with a place at his table, the same as if he had been one of his own sons. And that he might not be embarrassed with having the land to care for, he committed the charge of it to Ziba, who was to bring to Mephibosheth the produce or its value.

Every arrangement was thus made that could conduce to his comfort. His being a cripple did not deprive him of the honour of a place at the royal table, little though he could contribute to the lustre of the palace. For David bestowed his favours not on the

principle of trying to reflect lustre on himself or his
house, but on the principle of doing good to those who
had a claim on his consideration.  The lameness and
consequent awkwardness, that would have made many
a king ashamed of such an inmate of his palace only
recommended him the more to David.  Regard for
outward appearances was swallowed up by a higher
regard—regard for what was right and true.

It might be thought by some that such an incident
as this was hardly worthy of a place in the sacred
record; but the truth is, that David seldom showed
more of the true spirit of God than he did on this
occasion.  The feeling that led him to seek out any
stray member of the house in order to show kindness
to him was the counterpart of that feeling that has led
God from the very beginning to seek the children of
men, and that led Jesus to seek and to save that which
was lost.  For that is truly the attitude in which God
has ever placed Himself towards our fallen race.  The
sight to be seen in this world has not been that of men
seeking after God, but that of God seeking after men.
All day long He has been stretching forth His hands,
and inviting the children of men to taste and see that
He is gracious.  If we ask for the principle that unifies
all parts of the Bible, it is this gracious attitude of God
towards those who have forfeited His favour.  The
Bible presents to us the sight of God's Spirit striving
with men, persevering in the thankless work long
after He has been resisted, and ceasing only when all
hope of success through further pleading is gone.

There were times when this process was prosecuted
with more than common ardour ; and at last there came
a time when the Divine pleadings reached a climax, and
God, who at sundry times and in divers manners spake

to the fathers by the prophets, spake to them at last by
His own Son.   And what was the life of Jesus Christ
but a constant appeal to men, in God's name, to accept
the kindness which God was eager to show them ?
Was not His invitation to all that laboured and were
heavy laden, " Come unto Me, and I will give you rest "?
Did He not represent the Father as a householder,
making a marriage feast for his son, sending forth his
servants to bid the guests to the wedding, and when
the natural guests refused, bidding them go to the high-
ways and the hedges, and fetch the lame and the blind
and any outcast they could find, because he longed to
see guests of some kind enjoying the good things he
had provided ?   The great crime of the ancient Jews
was rejecting Him who had come in the name of the
Lord to bless them.    Their crowning condemnation
was, not that they had failed to keep the Ten Commandments, though that was true ; not that they had
spent their lives in pleasing themselves instead of
pleasing God, though that also was true ; but that they
had rejected God's unspeakable gift, and requited the
Eternal Son, when He came from heaven to bless them,
with the cursed death of the cross.   But even after they
had committed that act of unprecedented wickedness,
God's face would not be wholly turned away from them.
The very attitude in which Jesus died, with His hands
outstretched on the tree, would still represent the attitude
of the Divine heart towards the very murderers of His
Son.   " I, if I be lifted up, will draw all men toward
Me."   " Unto you first, God, having raised up His Son
Jesus, hath sent Him to bless you, in turning away
every one of you from his iniquities."   " Repent ye,
therefore, and be converted, that your sins may be
blotted out."

Here, my friends, is the most glorious feature of
the Christian religion.  Happy those of you who have
apprehended this attitude of your most gracious Father,
who have believed in His love, and who have accepted
His grace !  For not only has God received you back
into His family, and given you a name and a place in
His temple better than that of sons and daughters, but
He has restored to you your lost inheritance.  " If
children, then heirs, heirs of God and joint heirs with
Jesus Christ."  Nay, more, He has not only restored to
you your lost inheritance, but He has conferred on you
an inheritance more glorious than that of which sin
deprived you.  " Blessed be the God and Father of our
Lord Jesus Christ, who according to His abundant
mercy hath begotten us again unto a lively hope through
the resurrection of Jesus Christ from the dead, to an
inheritance incorruptible, and undefiled, and that fadeth
not away, reserved in heaven for you, who are kept by
the power of God through faith unto salvation, ready
to be revealed in the last day."

But if the grace of God in thus stretching out His
hands to sinful men and offering them all the blessings
of salvation is very wonderful, it makes the case of
those all the more terrible, all the more hopeless, who
treat His invitations with indifference, and turn their
backs on an inheritance the glory of which they do not
see.  How men should be so infatuated as to do this it
were hard to understand, if we had not ample evidence
of it in the godless tendencies of our natural hearts.
Still more mysterious is it to understand how God
should fail to carry His point in the case of those to
whom He stretches out His hands.  But of all considerations there is none more fitted to astonish and
alarm the careless than that they are capable of refusing

all the appeals of Divine love, and rejecting all the
bounty of Divine grace.   If this be persevered in, what
a rude awakening you will have in the world to come,
when in all the bitterness of remorse you will think
on the glories that were once within your reach, but
with which you trifled when you had the chance!
How foolish would Mephibosheth have been if he had
disbelieved in David's kindness and rejected his offer!
But David was sincere, and Mephibosheth believed in
his sincerity.   May we not, must we not, believe that
God is sincere?   If a purpose of kindness could arise
in a human heart, how much more in the Divine heart,
how much more in the heart of Him the very essence
of whose nature is conveyed to us in the words of the
beloved disciple—" God is love"!

There is yet another application to be made of this
passage in David's history.   We have seen how it
exemplifies the duty incumbent on us all to consider
whether kindness is not due from us to the friends or
the relatives of those who have been helpful to ourselves.   This remark is not applicable merely to temporal obligations, but also, and indeed emphatically, to
spiritual.   We should consider ourselves in debt to
those who have conferred spiritual benefits upon us.
Should a descendant of Luther or Calvin, of Latimer
or Cranmer or Knox, appear among us in need of
kindness, what true Protestant would not feel that for
what he owed to the fathers it was his duty to show
kindness to the children?   But farther back even than
this was a race of men to whom the Christian world
lies under still deeper obligations.   It was the race
of David himself, to which had belonged " Moses and
Aaron among His priests, Samuel with them that called
on His name," and, in after-times, Isaiah and Jeremiah,

Ezekiel and Daniel ; Peter, and James, and John, and
Paul ; and, outshining them all, like the sun of heaven,
Jesus of Nazareth, the Saviour of men.  With what
models of lofty piety has that race furnished every
succeeding generation !  From the study of their holy
lives, their soaring faith, their burning zeal, what
blessing has been derived in the past, and what an
impulse will yet go forth to the very end of time !  No
wonder though the Apostle had great sorrow and continual heaviness in his heart when he thought of the
faithless state of the people, " to whom pertaineth the
adoption, and the glory, and the covenants, and the
giving of the law, and the service of God " !  Yet none
are more in need of your friendly remembrance at this
day than the descendants of these men.  It becomes
you to ask, " Is there yet any that is left of their house
to whom we may show kindness for Jesus' sake ? "  For
God has not finally cast them off, and Jesus has not
ceased to care for those who were His brethren according to the flesh.  If there were no other motive to
induce us to seek the good of the Jews, this consideration should surely prevail.  Ill did the world requite
its obligation during the long ages when all manner of
contumely and injustice was heaped upon the Hebrew
race, as if Jesus had never prayed, " Father, forgive
them ; they know not what they do."  Their treatment
by the Gentiles has been so harsh that, even when
better feelings prevail, they are slow, like Mephibosheth,
—to believe that we mean them well.  They may have
done much to repel our kindness, and they may appear
to be hopelessly encrusted with unbelief in Him whom
we present as the Saviour.  But charity never faileth ;
and in reference to them as to other objects of philanthropic effort, the exhortation holds good, " Let us not

be weary in well-doing; for in due season we shall reap if we faint not."

Such kindness to those who are in need is not only a duty of religion, but tends greatly to commend it. Neglect of those who have claims on us, while objects more directly religious are eagerly prosecuted, is not pleasing to God, whether the neglect take place in our lives or in the destination of our substance at death. "Give, and it shall be given unto you : good measure, pressed down and shaken together and running over, shall men give into your bosom. For with the same measure that ye mete withal, it shall be measured to you again."

# CHAPTER XIII.

## *DAVID AND HANUN.*

### 2 SAMUEL x.

POWERFUL though David had proved himself in every direction in the art of war, his heart was inclined to peace. A king who had been victorious over so many foes had no occasion to be afraid of a people like the Ammonites. It could not have been from fear therefore that, when Nahash the king of the Ammonites died, David resolved to send a friendly message to his son. Not the least doubt can be thrown on the statement of the history that what moved him to do this was a grateful remembrance of the kindness which he had at one time received from the late king. The position which he had gained as a warrior would naturally have made Hanun more afraid of David than David could be of Hanun. The king of Israel could not have failed to know this, and it might naturally occur to him that it would be a kindly act to the young king of Ammon to send him a message that showed that he might thoroughly rely on his friendly intentions. The message to Hanun was another emanation of a kindly heart. If there was anything of policy in it, it was the policy of one who felt that so many things are continually occurring to set nations against one another as to make it most desirable to improve every opportunity of drawing them closer together.

It is a happy thing for any country when its rulers and men of influence are ever on the watch for opportunities to strengthen the spirit of friendship. It is a happy thing in the Church when the leaders of different sections are more disposed to measures that conciliate and heal than to measures that alienate and divide. In family life, and wherever men of different views and different tempers meet, this peace-loving spirit is of great price. Men that like fighting, and that are ever disposed to taunt, to irritate, to divide, are the nuisances of society. Men that deal in the soft answer, in the message of kindness, and in the prayer of love, deserve the respect and gratitude of all.

It is a remarkable thing that, of all the nations that were settled in the neighbourhood of the Israelites, the only one that seemed desirous to live on friendly terms with them was that of Tyre. Even those who were related to them by blood,—Edomites, Midianites, Moabites, Ammonites,—were never cordial, and often at open hostility. Though their rights had been carefully respected by the Israelites on their march from Sinai to Palestine, no feeling of cordial friendship was established with any of them. None of them were impressed even so much as Balaam had been, when in language so beautiful he blessed the people whom God had blessed. None of them threw in their lot with Israel, in recognition of their exalted spiritual privileges, as Hobab and his people had done near Mount Sinai. Individuals, like Ruth the Moabitess, had learned to recognise the claims of Israel's God and the privileges of the covenant, but no entire nation had ever shown even an inclination to such a course. These neighbouring nations continued therefore to be fitting symbols of that world-power which has so generally

been found in antagonism to the people of God. Israel
while they continued faithful to God were like the lily
among thorns; and Israel's king, like Him whom he
typified, was called to rule in the midst of his enemies.
The friendship of the surrounding world cannot be the
ordinary lot of the faithful servant, otherwise the Apostle
would not have struck such a loud note of warning.
" Ye adulterers and adulteresses, know ye not that the
friendship of the world is enmity wi h God ?   Whosoever, therefore, would be the friend of the world is the
enemy of God."

Between the Ammonites and the Israelites collisions
had occurred on two former occasions, on both of
which the Ammonites appear to have been the
aggressors.   The former of these was in the days
of Jephthah.   The defeat of the Ammonites at that
time was very thorough, and probably unexpected, and,
like other defeats of the same kind, it no doubt left
feelings of bitter hatred rankling in the breasts of
the defeated party.   The second was the collision at
Jabesh-gilead at the beginning of the reign of Saul.
The king of the Ammonites showed great ferocity and
cruelty on that occasion.   When the men of Jabesh,
brought to bay, begged terms of peace, the bitter
answer was returned that it would be granted only on
condition that every man's right eye should be put out.
It was then that Saul showed such courage and
promptitude.   In the briefest space he was at Jabesh-
gilead in defence of his people, and by his successful
tactics inflicted on the Ammonites a tearible defeat,
killing a great multitude and scattering the remainder,
so that not any two of them were left together.   Men
do not like to have a prize plucked from their hands
when they are on the eve of enjoying it.   After such

a defeat, Nahash could not have very friendly feelings
to Saul. And when Saul proclaimed David his enemy,
Nahash would naturally incline to David's side. There
is no record of the occasion on which he showed
kindness to him, but in all likelihood it was at the
time when he was in the wilderness, hiding from Saul.
If, when David was near the head of the Dead Sea, and
therefore not very far from the land of the Ammonites,
or from places where they had influence, Nahash sent
him any supplies for his men, the gift would be very
opportune, and there could be no reason why David
should not accept of it. Anyhow, the act of kindness,
whatever it was, made a strong impression on his
heart. It was long, long ago when it happened, but
love has a long memory, and the remembrance of it
was still pleasant to David. And now the king of
Israel purposes to repay to the son the debt he had
incurred to the father. Up to this point it is a pretty
picture ; and it is a great disappointment when we
find the transaction miscarry, and a negotiation which
began in all the warmth and sincerity of friendship
terminate in the wild work of war.

The fault of this miscarriage, however, was glaringly
on the other side. Hanun was a young king, and it
would only have been in accordance with the frank
and unsuspecting spirit of youth had he received
David's communication with cordial pleasure, and
returned to it an answer in the same spirit in which
it was sent. But his counsellors were of another mind.
They persuaded their master that the pretext of
comforting him on the death of his father was a hollow
one, and that David desired nothing but to spy out the
city and the country, with a view to bring them under
his dominion. It is hard to suppose that they really

believed this. It was they, not David, that wished a pretext for going to war. And having got something that by evil ingenuity might be perverted to this purpose, they determined to treat it so that it should be impossible for David to avoid the conflict. Hanun appears to have been a weak prince, and to have yielded to their counsels. Our difficulty is to understand how sane men could have acted in such a way. The determination to provoke war, and the insolence of their way of doing it, appear so like the freaks of a madman, that we cannot comprehend how reasonable men should in cold blood have even dreamt of such proceedings. Perhaps at this early period they had an understanding with those Syrians that afterwards came to their aid, and thought that on the strength of this they could afford to be insolent. The combined force which they could bring into the field would be such as to make even David tremble.

It is hardly necessary to say a word to bring out the outrageous character of their conduct. First, there was the repulse of David's kindness. It was not even declined with civility; it was repelled with scorn. It is always a serious thing to reject overtures of kindness. Even the friendly salutations of dumb animals are entitled to a friendly return, and the man that returns the caresses of his dog with a kick and a curse is a greater brute than the animal that he treats so unworthily. Kindness is too rare a gem to be trampled under foot. Even though it should be mistaken kindness, though the form it takes should prove an embarrassment rather than a help, a good man will appreciate the motive that prompted it, and will be careful not to hurt the feelings of those who, though they have blundered, meant him well. None are more liable to make mistakes than young children in their little efforts to please ; meaning to be kind, they sometimes only give trouble  The parent that gives way to irritation, and meets this with a volley of scolding, deals cruelly with the best and tenderest part of the, child's nature. There are few things more deserving to be attended to through life than the habit not only of appreciating little kindnesses, but showing that you appreciate them. How much more sweetly might the current run in social life if this were universally attended to!

But Hanun not only repelled David's kindness, but charged him with meanness, and virtually flung in his face a challenge to war.  To represent his apparent kindness as a mean cover of a hostile purpose was an act which Hanun might think little of, but which was fitted to wound David to the quick.  Unscrupulous natures have a great advantage over others in the charges they may bring.  In a street collision a man in dirty clothing is much more powerful for mischief than one in clean raiment.  Rough, unscrupulous men are restrained by no delicacy from bringing atrocious charges against those to whom these charges are supremely odious.  They have little sense of the sin of them, and they toss them about without scruple.  Such poisoned arrows inflict great pain, not because the charges are just, but because it is horrible to refined natures even to hear them.  There are two things that make some men very sensitive—the refinement of grace, and the refinement of the spirit of courtesy. The refinement of grace makes all sin odious, and makes a charge of gross sin very serious.  The refinement of courtesy creates great regard to the feelings of others, and a strong desire not to wound them unnecessarily.  In circles where real courtesy prevails, accu-

sations against others are commonly couched in very
gentle language. Rough natures ridicule this spirit,
and pride themselves on their honesty in calling a
spade a spade. Evidently Hanun belonged to the
rough, unscrupulous school. Either he did not know
how it would make David writhe to be accused of the
alleged meanness, or, if he did know, he enjoyed the
spectacle. It gratified his insolent nature to see the
pious king of Israel posing before all the people of
Ammon as a sneak and a liar, and to hear the laugh of
scorn and hatred resounding on every side.

To these offences Hanun added yet another—scornful treatment of David's ambassadors. In the eyes of
all civilized nations the persons of ambassadors were
held sacred, and any affront or injury to them was
counted an odious crime. Very often men of eminent
position, venerable age, and unblemished character
were chosen for this function, and it is quite likely that
David's ambassadors to Hanun were of this class.
When therefore these men were treated with contumely—half their beards, which were in a manner
sacred, shorn away, their garments mutilated, and their
persons exposed—no grosser insult could have been inflicted. When the king and his princes were the authors
of this treatment, it must have been greatly enjoyed
by the mass of the people, whose coarse glee over the
dishonoured ambassadors of the great King David one
can easily imagine. It is a painful moment when true
worth and nobility lie at the mercy of insolence and
coarseness, and have to bear their bitter revilings.
Such things may happen in public controversy in a
country where the utmost liberty of speech is allowed,
and when men of ruffian mould find contumely and
insult their handiest weapons. In times of religious

persecution the most frightful charges have been hurled
at the heads of godly men and women, whose real crime
is to have striven to the utmost to obey God.   Oh, how
much need there is of patience to bear insult as well
as injury !   And insult will sometimes rouse the temper
that injury does not ruffle.   Oh for the spirit of Christ,
who, when He was reviled, reviled not again !

The Ammonites did not wait for a formal declaration
of war by David.   Nor did they flatter themselves,
when they came to their senses, that against one who
had gained such renown as a warrior they could stand
alone.   Their insult to King David turned out a costly
affair.   To get assistance they had to give gold.   The
parallel passage in Chronicles gives a thousand talents
of silver as the cost of the first bargain with the
Syrians.   These Syrian mercenaries came from various
districts—Beth-rehob, Zoba, Beth-maacah, and Tob.
Some of these had already been subdued by David ; in
other cases there was apparently no previous collision.
But all of them no doubt smarted under the defeats
which David had inflicted either on them or on their
neighbours, and when a large subsidy was allotted to
them to begin with, in addition to whatever booty might
fall to their share if David should be subdued, it is no
great wonder that an immense addition was made to
the forces of the Ammonites.   It became in fact a very
formidable opposition ; all the more that they were very
abundantly supplied with chariots and horsemen, of
which arm David had scarcely any.   He met them first
by sending out Joab and "all the host" of the mighty
men.   The whole resources of his army were forwarded.
And when Joab came to the spot, he found that he had
a double enemy to face.   The Ammonite army came
out from the city to encounter him, while the Syrian

army were encamped in the country, ready to place him between two fires when the battle began. To guard against this, Joab divided his force into two. The Syrian host was the more formidable body; therefore Joab went in person against it, at the head of a select body of troops chosen from the general army. The command of the remainder was given to his brother Abishai, who was left to deal with the Ammonites. If either section found its opponent too much for it, aid was to be given by the other. No fault can be found either with the arrangements made by Joab for the encounter or the spirit in which he entered on the fight. "Be of good courage," he said to his men, "and let us play the men for our people, and for the cities of our God; and the Lord do that which seemeth to Him good." It was just such an exhortation as David himself might have given. Some were trusting in chariots and some in horses, but they were remembering the name of the Lord their God. The first movement was made by Joab and his part of the army against the Syrians; it was completely successful; the Syrians fled before him, chariots and horsemen and all. When the Ammonite army saw the fate of the Syrians they did not even hazard a conflict, but wheeled about and made for the city. Thus ended their first proud effort to sustain and complete the humiliation of King David. The hired troops on which they had leaned so much turned out utterly untrustworthy; and the wretched Ammonites found themselves *minus* their thousand talents, without victory, and without honour.

But their allies the Syrians were not disposed to yield without another conflict. Determined to do his utmost, Hadarezer, king of the Syrians of Zobah, sent across the Euphrates, and prevailed on their neighbours

there to join them in the effort to crush the power of
David. That a very large number of these Mesopota-
mian Syrians responded to the invitation of Hadarezer
is apparent from the number of the slain (ver. 18).
The matter assumed so serious an aspect that David
himself was now constrained to take the field, at the
head of "all Israel." The Syrian troops were commanded by Shobach, who appears to have been a
distinguished general. It must have been a death-
struggle between the Syrian power and the power of
David. But again the victory was with the Israelites,
and among the slain were the men of seven hundred
chariots, and forty thousand horsemen (1 Chron. xix. 18,
" footmen "), along with Shobach, captain of the Syrian
host. It must have been a most decisive victory, for
after it took place all the states that had been tributary
to Hadarezer transferred their allegiance to David.
The Syrian power was completely broken ; all help
was withdrawn from the Ammonites, who were now
left to bear the brunt of their quarrel alone. Single-
handed, they had to look for the onset of the army
which had so remarkably prevailed against all the
power of Syria, and to answer to King David for the
outrage they had perpetrated on his ambassadors.
Very different must their feelings have been now from
the time when they began to negotiate with Syria, and
when, doubtless, they looked forward so confidently to
the coming defeat and humiliation of King David.

It requires but a very little consideration to see that
the wars which are so briefly recorded in this chapter
must have been most serious and perilous undertakings.
The record of them is so short, so unimpassioned, so
simple, that many readers are disposed to think very
little of them. But when we pause to think what it

was for the king of Israel to meet, on foreign soil, confederates so numerous, so powerful, and so familiar with warfare, we cannot but see that these were tremendous wars. They were fitted to try the faith as well as the courage of David and his people to the very utmost. In seeking dates for those psalms that picture a multitude of foes closing on the writer, and that record the exercises of his heart, from the insinuations of fear at the beginning to the triumph of trust and peace at the end, we commonly think only of two events in David's life,—the persecution of Saul and the insurrection of Absalom. But the Psalmist himself could probably have enumerated a dozen occasions when' his danger and his need were as great as they were then. He must have passed through the same experience on these occasions as on the other two; and the language of the Psalms may often have as direct reference to the former as to the latter. We may understand, too, how the destruction of enemies became so prominent a petition in his prayers. What can a general desire and pray for, when he sees a hostile army, like a great engine of destruction, ready to dash against all that he holds dear, but that the engine may be shivered, deprived of all power of doing mischief —in other words, that the army may be destroyed? The imprecations in the Book of Psalms against his enemies must be viewed in this light. The military habit of the Psalmist's mind made him think only of the destruction of those who, in opposing him, opposed the cause of God. It ought not to be imputed as a crime to David that he did not rise high above a soldier's feelings ; that he did not view things from the point of view of Christianity ; that he was not a thousand years in advance of his age. The one outlet from the frightful danger which these Syrian hordes brought to him and his people was that they should be destroyed. Our blessed Lord gave men another view when He said, " The Son of man is come not to destroy men's lives, but to save them." He familiarised us with other modes of conquest. When He appeared to Saul on the way to Damascus, and turned the persecutor into the chief of apostles, He showed that there are other ways than that of destruction for delivering His Church from its enemies. " I send thee to open their eyes, and to turn them from darkness to light, and from the power of Satan unto God." This commission to Saul gives us reason for praying, with reference to the most clever and destructive of the enemies of His Church, that by His Spirit He would meet them too, and turn them into other men. And not until this line of petition has been exhausted can we fall back in prayer on David's method. Only when their repentance and conversion have become hopeless are we entitled to pray God to destroy the grievous wolves that work such havoc in His flock.

# CHAPTER XIV.

## *DAVID AND URIAH.*

### 2 SAMUEL xi.

HOW ardently would most, if not all readers, of the life of David have wished that it had ended before this chapter! Its golden era has passed away, and what remains is little else than a chequered tale of crime and punishment. On former occasions, under the influence of strong and long-continued temptations, we have seen his faith give way and a spirit of dissimulation appear; but these were like spots on the sun, not greatly obscuring his general radiance. What we now encounter is not like a spot, but a horrid eclipse; it is not like a mere swelling of the face, but a bloated tumour that distorts the countenance and drains the body of its life-blood. To human wisdom it would have seemed far better had David's life ended now, so that no cause might have been given for the everlasting current of jeer and joke with which his fall has supplied the infidel. Often, when a great and good man is cut off in the midst of his days and of his usefulness, we are disposed to question the wisdom of the dispensation; but when we find ourselves disposed to wonder whether this might not have been better in the case of David, we may surely acquiesce in the ways of God.

If the composition of the Bible had been in human hands it would never have contained such a chapter as this. There is something quite remarkable in the fearless way in which it unveils the guilt of David; it is set forth in its nakedness, without the slightest attempt either to palliate or to excuse it; and the only statement in the whole record designed to characterise it is the quiet but terrible words with which the chapter ends—" But the thing that David had done displeased the Lord." In the fearless march of providence we see many a proof of the courage of God. It is God alone that could have the fortitude to place in the Holy Book this foul story of sin and shame. He only could deliberately encounter the scorn which it has drawn down from every generation of ungodly men, the only wise God, who sees the end from the beginning, who can rise high above all the fears and objections of short-sighted men, and who can quiet every feeling of uneasiness on the part of His children with the sublime words, " Be still, and know that I am God."

The truth is, that though David's reputation would have been brighter had he died at this point of his career, the moral of his life, so to speak, would have been less complete. There was evidently a sensual element in his nature, as there is in so many men of warm, emotional temperament; and he does not appear to have been alive to the danger involved in it. It led him the more readily to avail himself of the toleration of polygamy, and to increase from time to time the number of his wives. Thus provision was made for the gratification of a disorderly lust, which, if he had lived like Abraham or Isaac, would have been kept back from all lawless excesses. And when evil desire has large scope for its exercise, instead of being satisfied it becomes more greedy and more lawless. Now, this painful chapter of David's history is designed to show us what the final effect of this was in his case—what came ultimately of this habit of pampering the lust of the flesh. And verily, if any have ever been inclined to envy David's liberty, and think it hard that such a law of restraint binds them while he was permitted to do as he pleased, let them study in the latter part of his history the effects of this unhallowed indulgence; let them see his home robbed of its peace and joy, his heart lacerated by the misconduct of his children, his throne seized by his son, while he has to fly from his own Jerusalem; let them see him obliged to take the field against Absalom, and hear the air rent by his cries of anguish when Absalom is slain; let them think how even his deathbed was disturbed by the noise of revolt, and how legacies of blood had to be bequeathed to his successor almost with his dying breath,—and surely it will be seen that the license which bore such wretched fruits is not to be envied, and that, after all, the way even of royal transgressors is hard.

But a fall so violent as that of David does not occur all at once. It is generally preceded by a period of spiritual declension, and in all likelihood there was such an experience on his part. Nor is it very difficult to find the cause. For many years back David had enjoyed a most remarkable run of prosperity. His army had been victorious in every encounter; his power was recognized by many neighbouring states; immense riches flowed from every quarter to his capital; it seemed as if nothing could go wrong with him. When everything prospers to a man's hand, it is a short step to the conclusion that he can do nothing wrong. How many great men in the world have been spoiled

by success, and by unlimited, or even very great power !
In how many hearts has the fallacy obtained a footing,
that ordinary laws were not made for them, and that
they did not need to regard them ! David was no
exception ; he came to think of his will as the great
directing force within his kingdom, the earthly consideration that should regulate all.

Then there was the absence of that very powerful
stimulus, the pressure of distress around him, which
had driven him formerly so close to God. His enemies
had been defeated in every quarter, with the single
exception of the Ammonites, a foe that could give him
no anxiety ; and he ceased to have a vivid sense of his
reliance on God as his Shield. The pressure of trouble
and anxiety that had made his prayers so earnest was
now removed, and probably he had become somewhat
remiss and formal in prayer. We little know how
much influence our surroundings have on our spiritual
life till some great change takes place in them ; and
then, perhaps, we come to see that the atmosphere of
trial and difficulty which oppressed us so greatly was
really the occasion to us of our highest strength and
our greatest blessings.

And further, there was the fact that David was idle,
at least without active occupation. Though it was
the time for kings to go forth to battle, and though his
presence with his army at Rabbah would have been a
great help and encouragement to his soldiers, he was
not there. He seems to have thought it not worth his
while. Now that the Syrians had been defeated, there
could be no difficulty with the Ammonites. At evening-
tide he arose from off his bed and walked on the roof
of his house. He was in that idle, listless mood in
which one is most readily attracted by temptation, and

in which the lust of the flesh has its greatest power.
And, as it has been remarked, "oft the sight of means
to do ill makes ill deeds done." If any scruples arose
in his conscience they were not regarded. To brush
aside objections to anything on which he had set his
heart was a process to which, in his great undertakings,
he had been well accustomed; unhappily, he applies
this rule when it is not applicable, and with the whole
force of his nature rushes into temptation.

Never was there a case which showed more emphatically the dreadful chain of guilt to which a first act,
apparently insignificant, may give rise. His first sin
was allowing himself to be arrested to sinful intents
by the beauty of Bathsheba. Had he, like Job, made a
covenant with his eyes; had he resolved that when the
idea of sin sought entrance into the imagination it should
be sternly refused admission; had he, in a word, nipped
the temptation in the bud, he would have been saved a
world of agony and sin. But instead of repelling the
idea he cherishes it. He makes inquiry concerning
the woman. He brings her to his house. He uses his
royal position and influence to break down the objections
which she would have raised. He forgets what is due
to the faithful soldier, who, employed in his service, is
unable to guard the purity of his home. He forgets the
solemn testimony of the law, which denounces death to
both parties as the penalty of the sin. This is the first
act of the tragedy.

Then follow his vain endeavours to conceal his crime,
frustrated by the high self-control of Uriah. Yes,
though David gets him intoxicated he cannot make a
tool of him. Strange that this Hittite, this member of
one of the seven nations of Canaan, whose inheritance
was not a blessing but a curse, shows himself a paragon

in that self-command, the utter absence of which, in the favoured king of Israel, has plunged him so deeply in the mire. Thus ends the second act of the tragedy.

But the next is far the most awful. Uriah must be got rid of, not, however, openly, but by a cunning stratagem that shall make it seem as if his death were the result of the ordinary fortune of war. And to compass this David must take Joab into his confidence. To Joab, therefore, he writes a letter, indicating what is to be done to get rid of Uriah. Could David have descended to a lower depth? It was bad enough to compass the death of Uriah; it was mean enough to make him the bearer of the letter that gave directions for his death; but surely the climax of meanness and guilt was the writing of that letter. Do you remember, David, how shocked you were when Joab slew Abner? Do you remember your consternation at the thought that you might be held to approve of the murder? Do you remember how often you have wished that Joab were not so rough a man, that he had more gentleness, more piety, more concern for bloodshedding? And here are you making this Joab your confidant in sin, and your partner in murder, justifying all the wild work his sword has ever done, and causing him to believe that, in spite of all his holy pretensions David is just such a man as himself.

Surely it was a horrible sin—aggravated, too, in many ways. It was committed by the head of the nation, who was bound not only to discountenance sin in every form, but especially to protect the families and preserve the rights of the brave men who were exposing their lives in his service. And that head of the nation had been signally favoured by God, and had been exalted in room of one whose selfishness and godlessness had caused him to be deposed from his dignity. Then there was the profession made by David of zeal for God's service and His law, his great enthusiasm in bringing up the ark to Jerusalem, his desire to build a temple, the character he had gained as a writer of sacred songs, and indeed as the great champion of religion in the nation. Further, there was the mature age at which he had now arrived, a period of life at which sobriety in the indulgence of the appetites is so justly and reasonably expected. And finally, there was the excellent character and the faithful services of Uriah, entitling him to the high rewards of his sovereign, rather than the cruel fate which David measured out to him— his home rifled and his life taken away.

How then, it may be asked, can the conduct of David be accounted for? The answer is simple enough—on the ground of original sin. Like the rest of us, he was born with proclivities to evil—to irregular desires craving unlawful indulgence. When divine grace takes possession of the heart it does not annihilate sinful tendencies, but overcomes them. It brings considerations to bear on the understanding, the conscience, and the heart, that incline and enable one to resist the solicitations of evil, and to yield one's self to the law of God. It turns this into a habit of the life. It gives one a sense of great peace and happiness in resisting the motions of sin, and doing the will of God. It makes it the deliberate purpose and desire of one's heart to be holy; it inspires one with the prayer, "Oh that my ways were directed to keep Thy statutes! Then shall I not be ashamed, when I have respect unto all Thy commandments."

But, meanwhile, the cravings of the old nature are not wholly destroyed. "The flesh lusteth against the spirit, and the spirit lusteth against the flesh." It is as if two armies were in collision. The Christian who naturally has a tendency to sensuality may feel the craving for sinful gratification even when the general bent of his nature is in favour of full compliance with the will of God. In some natures, especially strong natures, both the old man and the new possess unusual vehemence; the rebellious energisings of the old are held in check by the still more resolute vigour of the new; but if it so happen that the opposition of the new man to the old is relaxed or abated, then the outbreak of corruption will probably be on a fearful scale. Thus it was in David's nature. The sensual craving, the law of sin in his members, was strong; but the law of grace, inclining him to give himself up to the will of God, was stronger, and usually kept him right. There was an extraordinary activity and energy of character about him; he never did things slowly, tremblingly, timidly; the wellsprings of life were full, and gushed out in copious currents; in whatever direction they might flow, they were sure to flow with power. But at this time the energy of the new nature was suffering a sad abatement; the considerations that should have led him to conform to God's law had lost much of their usual power. Fellowship with the Fountain of life was interrupted; the old nature found itself free from its habitual restraint, and its stream came out with the vehemence of a liberated torrent. It would be quite unfair to judge David on this occasion as if he had been one of those feeble creatures who, as they seldom rise to the heights of excellence, seldom sink to the depths of daring sin.

We make these remarks simply to account for a fact, and by no means to excuse a crime. Men are liable to ask, when they read of such sins done by good men,

Were they really good men? Can that be genuine
goodness which leaves a man liable to do such deeds of
wickedness? If so, wherein are your so-called good
men better than other men? We reply, They are
better than other men in this,—and David was better
than other men in this,—that the deepest and most
deliberate desire of their hearts is to do as God requires,
and to be holy as God is holy. This is their habitual
aim and desire; and in this they are in the main successful. If this be not one's habitual aim, and if in this
he do not habitually succeed, he can have no real claim
to be counted a good man. Such is the doctrine of the
Apostle in the seventh chapter of the Romans. Any
one who reads that chapter in connection with the narrative of David's fall can have little doubt that it is the
experience of the new man that the Apostle is describ-
ing. The habitual attitude of the heart is given in the
striking words, "I delight in the law of God after the
inward man." I see how good God's law is; how
excellent is the stringent restraint it lays on all that is
loose and irregular, how beautiful the life which is cast
in its mould. But for all that, I feel in me the motions
of desire for unlawful gratifications, I feel a craving
for the pleasures of sin. "I see another law in my
members, warring against the law of my mind, and
bringing me into captivity to the law of sin which is
in my members." But how does the Apostle treat this
feeling? Does he say, "I am a human creature, and,
having these desires, I may and I must gratify them"?
Far from it! He deplores the fact, and he cries for
deliverance. "O wretched man that I am, who shall
deliver me from the body of this death?" And his
only hope of deliverance is in Him whom he calls his
Saviour. "I thank God through Jesus Christ our

Lord." In the case of David, the law of sin in his members prevailed for the time over the new law, the law of his mind, and it plunged him into a state which might well have led him too to say, " O wretched man that I am ! who shall deliver me ? "

And now we begin to understand why this supremely horrible transaction should be given in the Bible, and given at such length. It bears the character of a beacon, warning the mariner against some of the most deceitful and perilous rocks that are to be found in all the sea of life. First of all, it shows the danger of interrupting, however briefly, the duty of watching and praying, lest you enter into temptation. It is at your peril to discontinue earnest daily communion with God, especially when the evils are removed that first drove you to seek His aid. An hour's sleep may leave Samson at the mercy of Delilah, and when he awakes his strength is gone. Further, it affords a sad proof of the danger of dallying with sin even in thought. Admit sin within the precincts of the imagination, and there is the utmost danger of its ultimately mastering the soul. The outposts of the spiritual garrison should be so placed as to protect even the thoughts, and the moment the enemy is discovered there the alarm should be given and the fight begun. It is a serious moment when the young man admits a polluted thought to his heart, and pursues it even in reverie. The door is opened to a dangerous brood. And everything that excites sensual feeling, be it songs, jests, pictures, books of a lascivious character, all tends to enslave and pollute the soul, till at length it is saturated with impurity, and cannot escape the wretched thraldom. And further, this narrative shows us what moral havoc and ruin may be wrought by the toleration and gratification of a single sinful desire. You may contend vigorously against ninety-and-nine forms of sin, but if you yield to the hundredth the consequences will be deadly. You may fling away a whole box of matches, but if you retain one it is quite sufficient to set fire to your house. A single soldier finding his way into a garrison may open the gates to the whole besieging army. One sin leads on to another and another, especially if the first be a sin which it is desirable to conceal. Falsehood and cunning, and even treachery, are employed to promote concealment; unprincipled accomplices are called in; the failure of one contrivance leads to other contrivances more sinful and more desperate. If there is a being on earth more to be pitied than another it is the man who has got into this labyrinth. What a contrast his perplexed feverish agitation to the calm peace of the straightforward Christian! "He that walketh uprightly walketh surely; but he that perverteth his way shall be known."

Never let any one read this chapter of 2 Samuel without paying the profoundest regard to its closing words— "But the thing that David had done displeased the Lord." In that "but" lies a whole world of meaning.

# CHAPTER XV.

## *DAVID AND NATHAN.*

### 2 SAMUEL xii. 1-12; 26-31.

IT is often the method of the writers of Scripture, when the stream of public history has been broken by a private or personal incident, to complete at once the incident, and then go back to the principal history, resuming it at the point at which it was interrupted. In this way it sometimes happens (as we have already seen) that earlier events are recorded at a later part of the narrative than the natural order would imply. In the course of the narrative of David's war with Ammon, the incident of his sin with Bathsheba presents itself. In accordance with the method referred to, that incident is recorded straight on to its very close, including the birth of Bathsheba's second son, which must have occurred at least two years later. That being concluded, the history of the war with Ammon is resumed at the point at which it was broken off. We are not to suppose, as many have done, that the events recorded in the concluding verses of this chapter (vv. 26-31) happened later than those recorded immediately before. This would imply that the siege of Rabbah lasted for two or three years—a supposition hardly to be entertained; for Joab was besieging it when David first saw Bathsheba, and there is no reason to suppose that a people like the Ammonites would be able to hold the mere outworks of the city for two or three whole years against such an army as David's and such a commander as Joab.  It seems far more likely that Joab's first success against Rabbah was gained soon after the death of Uriah, and that his message to David to come and take the citadel in person was sent not long after the message that announced Uriah's death.

In that case the order of events would be as follows : After the death of Uriah, Joab prepares for an assault on Rabbah.   Meanwhile, at Jerusalem, Bathsheba goes through the form of mourning for her husband, and when the usual days of mourning are over David hastily sends for her and makes her his wife.  Next comes a message from Joab that he has succeeded in taking the city of waters, and that only the citadel remains to be taken, for which purpose he urges David to come himself with additional forces, and thereby gain the honour of conquering the place.   It rather surprises one to find Joab declining an honour for himself, as it also surprises us to find David going to reap what another had sowed.   David, however, goes with "all the people," and is successful, and after disposing of the Ammonites he returns to Jerusalem.   Soon after Bathsheba's child is born ; then Nathan goes to David and gives him the message that lays him in the dust. This is not only the most natural order for the events, but it agrees best with the spirit of the narrative.   The cruelties practised by David on the Ammonites send a thrill of horror through us as we read them.   No doubt they deserved a severe chastisement; the original offence was an outrage on every right feeling, an outrage on the law of nations, a gratuitous and contemptuous insult; and in bringing these vast Syrian armies into the field they had subjected even the victorious Israelites to grievous suffering and loss, in toil, in money, and in lives.

Attempts have been made to explain away the severities inflicted on the Ammonites, but it is impossible to explain away a plain historical narrative. It was the manner of victorious warriors in those countries to steel their hearts against all compassion toward captive foes, and David, kind-hearted though he was, did the same. And if it be said that surely his religion, if it were religion of the right kind, ought to have made him more compassionate, we reply that at this period his religion was in a state of collapse. When his religion was in a healthy and active state, it showed itself in the first place by his regard for the honour of God, for whose ark he provided a resting-place, and in whose honour he proposed to build a temple. Love to God was accompanied by love to man, exhibited in his efforts to show kindness to the house of Saul for the sake of Jonathan, and to Hanun for the sake of Nahash. But now the picture is reversed; he falls into a cold state of heart toward God, and in connection with that declension we mark a more than usually severe punishment inflicted on his enemies. Just as the leaves first become yellow and finally drop from the tree in autumn, when the juices that fed them begin to fail, so the kindly actions that had marked the better periods of his life first fail, then turn to deeds of cruelty when that Holy Spirit, who is the fountain of all goodness, being resisted and grieved by him, withholds His living power.

In the whole transaction at Rabbah David shows poorly. It is not like him to be roused to an enterprise by an appeal to his love of fame; he might have left Joab to complete the conquest and enjoy the honour which his sword had substantially won. It is not like him to go through the ceremony of being crowned with the crown of the king of Ammon, as if it were a great thing to have so precious a diadem on his head. Above all, it is not like him to show so terrible a spirit in disposing of his prisoners of war. But all this is quite likely to have happened if he had not yet come to repentance for his sin. When a man's conscience is ill at ease, his temper is commonly irritable. Unhappy in his inmost soul, he is in the temper that most easily becomes savage when provoked. No one can imagine that David's conscience was at rest. He must have had that restless feeling which every good man experiences after doing a wrong act, before coming to a clear apprehension of it; he must have been eager to escape from himself, and Joab's request to him to come to Rabbah and end the war must have been very opportune. In the excitement of war he would escape for a time the pursuit of his conscience; but he would be restless and irritable, and disposed to drive out of his way, in the most unceremonious manner, whoever or whatever should cross his path.

We now return with him to Jerusalem. He had added another to his long list of illustrious victories, and he had carried to the capital another vast store of spoil. The public attention would be thoroughly occupied with these brilliant events; and a king entering his capital at the head of his victorious troops, and followed by waggons laden with public treasure, need not fear a harsh construction on his private actions. The fate of Uriah might excite little notice; the affair of Bathsheba would soon blow over. The brilliant victory that had terminated the war seemed at the same time to have extricated the king from a personal scandal. David might flatter himself that all would now be peace and quiet, and that the waters of oblivion would gather over that ugly business of Uriah.

"But the thing that David had done displeased the Lord."

"And the Lord sent Nathan unto David."

Slowly, sadly, silently the prophet bends his steps to the palace.  Anxiously and painfully he prepares himself for the most distressing task a prophet of the Lord ever had to go through.  He has to convey God's reproof to the king ; he has to reprove one from whom, doubtless, he has received many an impulse towards all that is high and holy.  Very happily he clothes his message in the Eastern garb of parable.  He puts his parable in such life-like form that the king has no suspicion of its real character.  The rich robber that spared his own flocks and herds to feed the traveller, and stole the poor man's ewe lamb, is a real flesh-and-blood criminal to him.  And the deed is so dastardly, its heartlessness is so atrocious, that it is not enough to enforce against such a wretch the ordinary law of fourfold restitution ; in the exercise of his high prerogative the king pronounces a sentence of death upon the ruffian, and confirms it with the solemnity of an oath—" The man that hath done this thing shall surely die."  The flash of indignation is yet in his eye, the flush of resentment is still on his brow, when the prophet with calm voice and piercing eye utters the solemn words, "Thou art the man !"  Thou, great king of Israel, art the robber, the ruffian, condemned by thine own voice to the death of the worst malefactor! " Thus saith the Lord God of Israel, I anointed thee king over Israel, and I delivered thee out of the hand of Saul; and I gave thee thy master's house, and thy

master's wives into thy bosom, and gave thee the house
of Israel and of Judah ; and if that had been too little
I would moreover have given thee such and such things.
Wherefore hast thou despised the commandment of the
Lord, to do evil in His sight ?   Thou hast killed Uriah
the Hittite with the sword, and hast slain him with the
sword of the children of Ammon."

It is not difficult to fancy the look of the king as
the prophet delivered his message—how at first when
he said, " Thou art the man," he would gaze at him
eagerly and wistfully, like one at a loss to divine his
meaning ; and then, as the prophet proceeded to apply
his parable, how, conscience-stricken, his expression
would change to one of horror and agony ; how the
deeds of the last twelve months would glare in all their
infamous baseness upon him, and outraged Justice, with
a hundred glittering swords, would seem all impatient
to devour him.

It is no mere imagination that, in a moment, the
mind may be so quickened as to embrace the actions
of a long period ; and that with equal suddenness the
moral aspect of them may be completely changed.
There are moments when the powers of the mind as
well as those of the body are so stimulated as to become
capable of exertions undreamt of before.   The dumb
prince, in ancient history, who all his life had never
spoken a word, but found the power of speech when he
saw a sword raised to cut down his father, showed how
danger could stimulate the organs of the body.   The
sudden change in David's feeling now, like the sudden
change in Saul's on the way to Damascus, showed
what electric rapidity may be communicated to the
operations of the soul.   It showed too what unseen
and irresistible agencies of conviction and condemnation

the great Judge can bring into play when it is His will to do so. As the steam hammer may be so adjusted as either to break a nutshell without injuring the kernel, or crush a block of quartz to powder, so the Spirit of God can range, in His effects on the conscience, between the mildest feeling of uneasiness and the bitterest agony of remorse. "When He is come," said our blessed Lord, "He shall reprove the world of sin." How helpless men are under His operation ! How utterly was David prostrated ! How were the multitudes brought down on the day of Pentecost ! Is there any petition we more need to press than that the Spirit be poured out to convince of sin, whether as it regards ourselves or the world ? Is it not true that the great want of the Church the want of is a sense of sin, so that confession and humiliation are become rare, and our very theology is emasculated, because, where there is little sense of sin, there can be little appreciation of redemption ? And is not a sense of sin that which would bring a careless world to itself, and make it deal earnestly with God's gracious offers ? How striking is the effect ascribed by the prophet Zechariah to that pouring of the spirit of grace and supplication upon the house of David and the inhabitants of Jerusalem, when " they shall look on Him whom they have pierced, and shall mourn for Him as one mourneth for an only son, and shall be in bitterness for Him as one that is in bitterness for his firstborn." Would that our whole hearts went out in those invocations of the Spirit which we often sing, but alas ! so very tamely—

"Come, Holy Spirit, come,
    Let Thy bright beams arise ;
  Dispel the darkness from our minds,
    And open all our eyes.

" Convince us of our sin,
Lead us to Jesus' blood,
And kindle in our breast the flame
Of never-dying love."

We cannot pass from this aspect of David's case without marking the terrible power of self-deception. Nothing blinds men so much to the real character of a sin as the fact that it is their own. Let it be presented to them in the light of another man's sin, and they are shocked. It is easy for one's self-love to weave a veil of fair embroidery, and cast it over those deeds about which one is somewhat uncomfortable. It is easy to devise for ourselves this excuse and that, and lay stress on one excuse and another that may lessen the appearance of criminality. But nothing is more to be deprecated, nothing more to be deplored, than success in that very process. Happy for you if a Nathan is sent to you in time to tear to rags your elaborate embroidery, and lay bare the essential vileness of your deed! Happy for you if your conscience is made to assert its authority, and cry to you, with its awful voice, " Thou art the man !" For if you live and die in your fool's paradise, excusing every sin, and saying peace, peace, when there is no peace, there is nothing for you but the rude awakening of the day of judgment, when the hail shall sweep away the refuge of lies !

After Nathan had exposed the sin of David he proceeded to declare his sentence. It was not a sentence of death, in the ordinary sense of the term, but it was a sentence of death in a sense even more difficult to bear. It consisted of three things—first, the sword should never depart from his house ; second, out of his own house evil should be raised against him, and a dishonoured harem should show the nature and extent of the humiliation that would come upon him; and thirdly, a public exposure should thus be made of his sin, so that he would stand in the pillory of Divine rebuke, and in the shame which it entailed, before all Israel, and before the sun.   When David confessed his sin, Nathan told him that the Lord had graciously forgiven it, but at the same time a special chastisement was to mark how concerned God was for the fact that by his sin he had caused the enemy to blaspheme—the child born of Bathsheba was to die.

Reserving this last part of the sentence and David's bearing in connection with it for future consideration, let us give attention to the first portion of his retribution.   " The sword shall never depart from thy house." Here we find a great principle in the moral government of God,—correspondence between an offence and its retribution.   Of this many instances occur in the Old Testament.   Jacob deceived his father; he was deceived by his own sons.   Lot made a worldly choice; in the world's ruin he was overwhelmed.   So David having slain Uriah with the sword, the sword was never to depart from him.   He had robbed Uriah of his wife; his neighbour's would in like manner rob and dishonour him.   He had disturbed the purity of the family relation; his own house was to become a den of pollution.   He had mingled deceit and treachery with his actions; deceit and treachery would be practised towards him. What a sad and ominous prospect !   Men naturally look for peace in old age; the evening of life is expected to be calm.   But for him there was to be no calm; and his trial was to fall on the tenderest part of his nature.   He had a strong affection for his children; in that very feeling he was to be wounded, and that, too, all his life long.   Oh let not any suppose that, because God's children are saved by His mercy from eternal punishment, it is a light thing for them to despise the commandments of the Lord! "Thine own wickedness shall correct thee, and thy backslidings shall reprove thee; know therefore and see that it is an evil thing and bitter that thou hast forsaken the Lord thy God, and that thy fear is not in Me, saith the Lord of hosts."

Pre-eminent in its bitterness was that part of David's retribution which made his own house the source from which his bitterest trials and humiliations should arise. For the most part, it is in extreme cases only that parents have to encounter this trial. It is only in the wickedest households, and in households for the most part where the passions are roused to madness by drink, that the hand of the child is raised against his father to wound and dishonour him. It was a terrible humiliation to the king of Israel to have to bear this doom, and especially to that king of Israel who in many ways bore so close a resemblance to the promised Seed, who was indeed to be the progenitor of that Seed, so that when Messiah came He should be called "the Son of David." Alas! the glory of this distinction was to be sadly tarnished. "Son of David" was to be a very equivocal title, according to the character of the individual who should bear it. In one case it would denote the very climax of honour; in another, the depth of humiliation. Yes, that household of David's would reek with foul lusts and unnatural crimes. From the bosom of that home where, under other circumstances, it would have been so natural to look for model children, pure, affectionate, and dutiful, there would come forth monsters of lust and monsters of ambition, whose deeds of infamy would hardly find

a parallel in the annals of the nation ! In the breasts
of some of these royal children the devil would find
a seat where he might plan and execute the most
unnatural crimes. And that city of Jerusalem, which
he had rescued from the Jebusites, consecrated as
God's dwelling-place, and built and adorned with the
spoils which the king had taken in many a well-
fought field, would turn against him in his old age,
and force him to fly wherever a refuge could be found
as homeless, and nearly as destitute, as in the days
of his youth when he fled from Saul !

And lastly, his retribution was to be public. He had
done his part secretly, but God would do His part
openly. There was not a man or woman in all Israel
but would see these judgments coming on a king who
had outraged his royal position and his royal preroga-
tives. How could he ever go in and out happily among
them again ? How could he be sure, when he met any
of them, that they were not thinking of his crime, and
condemning him in their hearts ? How could he meet
the hardly suppressed scowl of every Hittite, that would
recall his treatment of their faithful kinsman ? What
a burden would he carry ever after, he that used to
wear such a frank and honest and kindly look, that was
so affable to all that sought his counsel, and so tender-
hearted to all that were in trouble ! And what outlet
could he find out of all this misery ? There was but
one he could think of. If only God would forgive him ;
if He, whose mercy was in the heavens, would but
receive him again of His infinite condescension into His
fellowship, and vouchsafe to him that grace which was
not the fruit of man's deserving, but, as its very name
implied, of God's unbounded goodness, then might his
soul return again to its quiet rest, though life could never

be to him what it was before.   And this, as we shall presently see, is what he set himself very earnestly to seek, and what of God's mercy he was permitted to find.   O sinner, if thou hast strayed like a lost sheep, and plunged into the very depths of sin, know that all is not lost with thee!   There is one way yet open to peace, if not to joy.   Amid the ten thousand times ten thousand voices that condemn thee, there is one voice of love that comes from heaven and says, "Return unto Me, and I will return unto you, saith the Lord."

# CHAPTER XVI.

## PENITENCE AND CHASTISEMENT.

### 2 SAMUEL xii. 13—25.

WHEN Nathan ended his message, plainly and strongly though he had spoken, David indicated no irritation, made no complaint against the prophet, but simply and humbly confessed—" I have sinned." It is so common for men to be offended when a servant of God remonstrates with them, and to impute their interference to an unworthy motive, and to the desire of some one to hurt and humiliate them, that it is refreshing to find a great king receiving the rebuke of the Lord's servant in a spirit of profound humility and frank confession. Very different was the experience of John the Baptist when he remonstrated with Herod. Very different was the experience of the famous Chrysostom when he rebuked the emperor and empress for conduct unworthy of Christians. Very different has been the experience of many a faithful minister in a humbler sphere, when, constrained by a sense of duty, he has gone to some man of influence in his flock, and spoken seriously to him of sins which bring a reproach on the name of Christ. Often it has cost the faithful man days and nights of pain; girding himself for the duty has been like preparing for martyrdom; and it has been really martyrdom when he has had to bear the long malignant enmity of the man whom he rebuked. However vile the conduct of David may have been, it is one thing in his favour that he receives his rebuke with perfect humility and submission; he makes no attempt to palliate his conduct either before God or man; but sums up his whole feeling in these expressive words, " I have sinned against the Lord."

To this frank acknowledgment Nathan replied that the Lord had put away his sin, so that he would not undergo the punishment of death. It was his own judgment that the miscreant who had stolen the ewe lamb should die, and as that proved to be himself, it indicated the punishment that was due to him. That punishment, however, the Lord, in the exercise of His clemency, had been pleased to remit. But a palpable proof of His displeasure was to be given in another way—the child of Bathsheba was to die. It was to become, as it were, the scapegoat for its father. In those times father and child were counted so much one that the offence of the one was often visited on both. When Achan stole the spoil at Jericho, not only he himself, but his whole family, shared his sentence of death. In this case of David the father was to escape, but the child was to die. It may seem hard, and barely just. But death to the child, though in form a punishment, might prove to be great gain. It might mean transference to a higher and brighter state of existence. It might mean escape from a life full of sorrows and perils to the world where there is no more pain, nor sorrow, nor death, because the former things are passed away.

We cannot pass from the consideration of David's great penitence for his sin without dwelling a little more on some of its features. It is in the fifty-first

Psalm that the working of his soul is best unfolded to us. No doubt it has been strongly urged by certain modern critics that that psalm is not David's at all; that it belongs to some other period, as the last verse but one indicates, when the walls of Jerusalem were in ruins; —most likely the period of the Captivity.  But even if we should have to say of the last two verses that they must have been added at another time, we cannot but hold the psalm to be the outpouring of David's soul, and not the expression of the penitence of the nation at large.  If ever psalm was the expression of the feelings of an individual it is this one.  And if ever psalm was appropriate to King David it is this one. For the one thing which is uppermost in the soul of the writer is his personal relation to God.  The one thing that he values, and for which all other things are counted but dung, is friendly intercourse with God. This sin no doubt has had many other atrocious effects , but the terrible thing is that it has broken the link that bound him to God, it has cut off all the blessed things that come by that channel, it has made him an outcast from Him whose lovingkindness is better than life.  Without God's favour life is but misery.  He can do no good to man; he can do no service to God.  It is a rare thing even for good men to have such a profound sense of the blessedness of God's favour. David was one of those who had it in the profoundest degree; and as the fifty-first Psalm is full of it, as it forms the very soul of its pleadings, we cannot doubt that it was a psalm of David.

The humiliation of the Psalmist before God is very profound, very thorough.  His case is one for simple mercy; he has not the shadow of a plea in self-defence. His sin is in every aspect atrocious.  It is the product of one so vile that he may be said to have been shapen in iniquity and conceived in sin. The aspect of it as sin against God is so overwhelming that it absorbs the other aspect—the sin against man. Not but that he has sinned against man too, but it is the sin against God that is so awful, so overwhelming.

Yet, if his sin abounds, the Psalmist feels that God's grace abounds much more. He has the highest sense of the excellence and the multitude of God's loving-kindnesses. Man can never make himself so odious as to be beyond the Divine compassion. He can never become so guilty as to be beyond the Divine forgiveness. "Blot out my transgressions," sobs David, knowing that it can be done. "Purge me with hyssop," he cries, "and I *shall* be clean ; wash me, and I shall be whiter than the snow. Create in me a clean heart, and renew a right spirit within me."

But this is not all ; it is far from all. He pleads most plaintively for the restoration of God's friendship. "Cast me not away from Thy presence, and take not Thy Holy Spirit from me,"—for that would be hell; "Restore unto me the joy of Thy salvation, and uphold me with Thy free Spirit,"—for that is heaven. And, with the renewed sense of God's love and grace, there would come a renewed power to serve God and be useful to men. "Then will I teach transgressors Thy ways; and sinners shall be converted unto Thee. O Lord, open Thou my lips ; and my mouth shall show forth Thy praise." Deprive me not for ever of Thy friendship, for then life would be but darkness and anguish ; depose me not for ever from Thy ministry, continue to me yet the honour and the privilege of converting sinners unto Thee. Of the sacrifices of the law it was needless to think, as if they were adequate to purge away so overwhelming a sin. "Thou desirest not sacrifice, else I would give it: Thou delightest not in burnt-offering. The sacrifices of God are a broken spirit : a broken and a contrite heart, O God, Thou wilt not despise."

With all his consciousness of sin, David has yet a profound faith in God's mercy, and he is forgiven. But as we have seen, the Divine displeasure against him is to be openly manifested in another form, because, in addition to his personal sin, he has given occasion to the enemies of the Lord to blaspheme.

This is an aggravation of guilt which only God's children can commit. And it is an aggravation of a most distressing kind, enough surely to warn off every Christian from vile self-indulgence. The blasphemy to which David had given occasion was that which denies the reality of God's work in the souls of His people. It denies that they are better than others. They only make more pretence, but that pretence is hollow, if not hypocritical. There is no such thing as a special work of the Holy Ghost in them, and therefore there is no reason why any one should seek to be converted, or why he should implore the special grace of the Spirit of God. Alas ! how true it is that when any one who occupies a con-spicuous place in the Church of God breaks down, such sneers are sure to be discharged on every side ! What a keen eye the world has for the inconsisten-cies of Christians ! With what remorseless severity does it come down on them when they fall into these inconsistencies ! Sins that would hardly be thought of if committed by others,—what a serious aspect they assume when committed by them ! Had it been Nebuchadnezzar, for example, that treated Uriah as

David did, who would have thought of it a second time ? What else could you expect of Nebuchadnezzar ? Let a Christian society or any other Christian body be guilty of a scandal, how do the worldly newspapers fasten on it like treasure-trove, and exult over their humbled victim, like Red Indians dancing their war dances and flourishing their tomahawks over some miserable prisoner. The scorn is very bitter, and sometimes it is very unjust ; yet perhaps it has on the whole a wholesome effect, just because it stimulates vigilance and carefulness on the part of the Church. But the worst of the case is, that on the part of un-believers it stimulates that blasphemy which is alike dishonouring to God and pernicious to man. Virtually this blasphemy denies the whole work of the Holy Spirit in the hearts of men. It denies the reality of any supernatural agency of the Spirit in one more than in all. And denying the work of the Spirit, it makes men careless about the Spirit ; it neutralises the solemn words of Christ, " Ye must be born again." It throws back the kingdom of God, and it turns back many a pilgrim who had been thinking seriously of beginning the journey to the heavenly city, because he is now uncertain whether such a city exists at all.

Hardly has Nathan left the king's house when the child begins to sicken, and the sickness becomes very great. We should have expected that David would be concerned and distressed, but hardly to the degree which his distress attained. In the intensity of his anxiety and grief there is something remarkable. A new-born infant could scarcely have taken that myste-rious hold on a father's heart which a little time is commonly required to develop, but which, once it is there, makes the loss even of a little child a grievous blow, and leaves the heart sick and sore for many a day. But there is something in an infant's agony which unmans the strongest heart, especially when it comes in convulsive fits that no skill can allay. And should one, in addition, be tortured with the conviction that the child was suffering on one's own account, one's distress might well be overpowering. And this was David's feeling. His sin was ever before him. As he saw that suffering infant he must have felt as if the stripes that should have fallen on him were tearing the poor babe's tender frame, and crushing him with undeserved suffering. Even in ordinary cases, it is a mysterious thing to see an infant in mortal agony. It is solemnizing to think that the one member of the family who has committed no actual sin should be the first to reap the deadly wages of sin. It leads us to think of mankind as one tree of many branches; and when the wintry frost begins to prevail it is the youngest and tenderest branchlets that first droop and die. Oh! how careful should those in mature years be, and especially parents, lest by their sins they bring down a retribution which shall fall first on their children, and perhaps the youngest and most innocent of all! Yet how often do we see the children suffering for the sins of their parents, and suffering in a way which, in this life at least, admits of no right remedy! In that "bitter cry of outcast London," which fell some years ago on the ears of the country, by far the most distressing note was the cry of infants abandoned by drunken parents before they could well walk, or living with them in hovels where blows and curses came in place of food and clothing and kindness—children brought up without aught of the sunshine of love, every tender feeling nipped and shrivelled in the very bud by the frost of bitter, brutal cruelty. And if in ordinary families children are not made to suffer so palpably for their parents' sins, yet suffer they do in many ways sufficiently serious. Wherever there is a bad example, wherever there is a laxity of principle, wherever God is dishonoured, the sin reacts upon the children. Their moral texture is relaxed; they learn to trifle with sin, and, trifling with sin, to disbelieve in the retribution for sin. And where conscience has not been altogether destroyed in the parent, and remorse for sin begins to prevail, and retribution to come, it is not what he has to suffer in his own person that he feels most deeply, but what has to be borne and suffered by his children. Does any one ask why God has constituted society so that the innocent are thus implicated in the sin of the guilty? The answer is, that this arises not from God's constitution, but from man's perversion of it. Why, we may ask, do men subvert God's moral order? Why do they break down His fences and embankments, and, contrary to the Divine plan, let ruinous streams pour their destructive waters into their homes and enclosures? If the human race had preserved from the beginning the constitution which God gave them, obeyed His law both individually and as a social body, such things would not have been. But reckless man, in his eagerness to have his own way, disregards the Divine arrangement, and plunges himself and his family into the depths of woe.

There is something even beyond this, however, that arrests our notice in the behaviour of David. Though Nathan had said that the child would die, he set himself most earnestly, by prayer and fasting, to get God to spare him. Was this not a strange proceeding? It could be justified only on the supposition that the

Divine judgment was modified by an unexpressed condition that, if David should humble himself in true
repentance, it would not have to be inflicted.   Anyhow,
we see him throwing his whole soul into these exercises :
engaging in them so earnestly that he took no regular
food, and in place of the royal bed he was content to
lie upon the earth.   His earnestness in this was well
fitted to show the difference between a religious service
gone through with becoming reverence, because it is
the proper thing to do, and the service of one who has
a definite end in view, who seeks a definite blessing,
and who wrestles with God to obtain it.   But David
had no valid ground for expecting that, even if he
should repent, God would avert the judgment from the
child ; indeed, the reason assigned for it showed the
contrary—because he had given occasion to the
enemies of the Lord to blaspheme.

And so, after a very weary and dismal week, the
child died.   But instead of abandoning himself to a
tumult of distress when this event took place, he altogether changed his demeanour.   His spirit became calm,
" he arose from the earth, and washed, and anointed
himself, and changed his apparel, and he came into the
house of the Lord and worshipped ; then he came to
his own house, and when he required, they set bread
before him, and he did eat."   It seemed to his servants
a strange proceeding.   The answer of David showed
that there was a rational purpose in it.   So long as he
thought it possible that the child's life might be spared,
he not only continued to pray to that effect, but he did
everything to prevent his attention from being turned
to anything else, he did everything to concentrate his
soul on that one object, and to let it appear to God
how thoroughly it occupied his mind.   The death of

the child showed that it was not God's will to grant
his petition, notwithstanding his deep repentance and
earnest prayer and fasting.   All suspense was now at
an end, and, therefore, all reason for continuing to fast
and pray.   For David to abandon himself to the
wailings of aggravated grief at this moment would have
been highly wrong.   It would have been to quarrel
with the will of God.   It would have been to challenge
God's right to view the child as one with its father, and
treat it accordingly.

And there was yet another reason.   If his heart still
yearned on the child, the re-union was not impossible,
though it could not take place in this life.   " I shall go
to him, but he shall not return unto me."   The glimpse
of the future expressed in these words is touching and
beautiful.   The relation between David and that little
child is not ended.   Though the mortal remains shall
soon crumble, father and child are not yet done with one
another.   But their meeting is not to be in this world.
Meet again they certainly shall, but " I shall go to him,
and he shall not return to me."

And this glimpse of the future relation of parent and
child, separated here by the hand of death, has ever
proved most comforting to bereaved Christian hearts.
Very touching and very comforting it is to light on this
bright view of the future at so early a period of Old
Testament history.   Words cannot express the desolation of heart which such bereavements cause.   When
Rachel is weeping for her children she cannot be
comforted if she thinks they are not.   But a new light
breaks on her desolate heart when she is assured that
she may go to them, though they shall not return to
her.   Blessed, truly, are the dead who die in the Lord,
and, however painful the stroke that removed them,

blessed are their surviving friends. Ye shall go to them, though they shall not return to you. How you are to recognise them, how you are to commune with them, in what place they shall be, in what condition of consciousness, you cannot tell ; but " you shall go to them ; " the separation shall be but temporary, and who can conceive the joy of re-union, re-union nevei to be broken by separation for evermore ?

One other fact we must notice ere passing from the record of David's confession and chastisement,—the moral courage which he showed in delivering the fifty-first Psalm to the chief musician, and thus helping to keep alive in his own generation and for all time coming the memory of his trespass. Most men would have thought how the ugly transaction might most effectually be buried, and would have tried to put their best face on it before their people. Not so David. He was willing that his people and all posterity should see him the atrocious transgressor he was—let them think of him as they pleased. He saw that this everlasting exposure of his vileness was essential towards extracting from the miserable transaction such salutary lessons as it might be capable of yielding. With a wonderful effort of magnanimity, he resolved to place himself in the pillory of public shame, to expose his memory to all the foul treatment which the scoffers and libertines of every after-age might think fit to heap on it. It is unjust to David, when unbelievers rail against him for his sin in the matter of Uriah, to overlook the fact that the first public record of the transaction came from his own pen, and was delivered to the chief musician, for public use. Infidels may scoff, but this narrative will be a standing proof that the foolishness of God is wiser than men. The view given to God's servants of the weakness and deceitfulness of their hearts; the warning against dallying with the first movements of sin; the sight of the misery which follows in its wake; the encouragement which the convicted sinner has to humble himself before God; the impulse given to penitential feeling; the hope of mercy awakened in the breasts of the despairing; the softer, humbler, holier walk when pardon has been got and peace restored,— such lessons as these, afforded in every age by this narrative, will render it to thoughtful hearts a constant ground for magnifying God. " O the depth of the riches both of the wisdom and knowledge of God! how unsearchable are His judgments, and His ways past finding out!"

# CHAPTER XVII.

## ABSALOM AND AMNON.

2 SAMUEL xiii. 1—37.

A LIVING sorrow, says the proverb, is worse than a dead. The dead sorrow had been very grievous to David ; what the living sorrow, of which this chapter tells us, must have been, we cannot conceive. It is his own disorderly lusts, reappearing in his sons, that are the source of this new tragedy. It is often useful for parents to ask whether they would like to see their children doing what they allow in themselves ; and in many cases the answer is an emphatic "No." David is now doomed to see his children following his own evil example, only with added circumstances of atrocity. Adultery and murder had been introduced by him into the palace ; when he is done with them they remain to be handled by his sons.

It is a very repulsive picture of sensuality that this chapter presents. One would suppose that Amnon and Absalom had been accustomed to the wild orgies of pagan idolatry. Nathan had rebuked David because he had given occasion to the enemies of the Lord to blaspheme. He had afforded them a pretext for denying the work of the Holy Spirit in regeneration and sanctification, and for affirming that so-called holy men were just like the rest of mankind. This in God's eyes was a grievous offence. Amnon and Absalom are now guilty of the same offence in another form, because they afford a pretext for ungodly men to say that the families of holy men are no better—perhaps that they are worse —than other families.   But as David himself in the matter of Uriah is an exception to the ordinary lives of godly men, so his home is an exception to the ordinary tone and spirit of religious households.   Happily we are met with a very different ideal when we look behind the scenes into the better class of Christian homes, whether high or low.   It is a beautiful picture of the Christian home, according to the Christian ideal, we find, for example, in Milton's *Comus*—pure brothers, admiring a dear sister's purity, and jealous lest, alone in the world, she should fall in the way of any of those bloated monsters that would drag an angel into their filthy sty.   Commend us to those homes where brothers and sisters, sharing many a game, and with still greater intimacy pouring into each other's ears their inner thoughts and feelings, never utter a jest, or word, or allusion with the slightest taint of indelicacy, and love and honour each other with all the higher affection that none of them has ever been near the haunts of pollution.   It is easy to ridicule innocence, to scoff at young men who " flee youthful lusts ; " yet who will say that the youth who is steeped in fashionable sensuality is worthy to be the brother and companion of pure-minded maidens, or that his breath will not contaminate the atmosphere of their home ?   What easy victories Belial gains over many !   How easily he persuades them that vice is manly, that impurity is grand, that the pig's sty is a delightful place to lie down in !   How easily he induces them to lay snares for female chastity, and put the devil's mask on woman's soul !   But " God is not mocked ; whatsoever a man

soweth, that shall he also reap; for he that soweth to
the flesh shall of the flesh reap corruption, while he
that soweth to the Spirit shall of the Spirit reap life
everlasting."

In Scripture some men have very short biographies;
Amnon is one of these. And, like Cain, all that is recorded of him has the mark of infamy. We can easily
understand that it was a great disaster to him to be
a king's son. To have his position in life determined
and all his wants supplied without an effort on his part;
to be surrounded by such plenty that the wholesome
necessity of denying himself was unknown, and whatever he fancied was at once obtained; to be so accustomed to indulge his legitimate feelings that when
illegitimate desires rose up it seemed but natural that
they too should be gratified; thus to be led on in the
evil ways of sensual pleasure till his appetite became at
once bloated and irrepressible; to be surrounded by
parasites and flatterers, that would make a point of
never crossing him nor uttering a disagreeable word,
but constantly encouraging his tastes,—all this was
extremely dangerous. And when his father had set
him the example, it was hardly possible he would avoid
the snare. There is every reason to believe that before
he is presented to us in this chapter he was already
steeped in sensuality. It was his misfortune to have a
friend, Jonadab, the son of Shimeah, David's brother,
"a very subtil man," who at heart must have been as
great a profligate as himself. For if Jonadab had been
anything but a profligate, Amnon would never have
confided to him his odious desire with reference to his
half-sister, and Jonadab would never have given him
the advice that he did. What a blessing to Amnon, at
this stage of the tragedy, would have been the faithful

advice of an honest friend—one who would have had
the courage to declare the infamy of his proposal, and
who would have so placed it in the light of truth that
it would have shocked and horrified even Amnon himself! In reality, the friend was more guilty than the
culprit. The one was blinded by passion; the other
was self-possessed and cool. The cool man encourages
the heated; the sober man urges on the intoxicated.
O ye sons of wealth and profligacy, it is sad enough
that you are often so tempted by the lusts that rise up
in your own bosoms, but it is worse to be exposed to
the friendship of wretches who never study your real
good, but encourage you to indulge the vilest of your
appetites, and smooth for you the way to hell !

The plan which Jonadab proposes for Amnon to
obtain the object of his desire is founded on a stratagem
which he is to practise on his father. He is to pretend
sickness, and under this pretext to get matters arranged
by his father as he would like. To practise deceit on a
father was a thing not unknown even among the founders
of the nation; Jacob and Jacob's sons had resorted to
it alike. But it had been handed down with the mark
of disgrace attached to it by God Himself. In spite of
this it was counted both by Jonadab and Amnon a
suitable weapon for their purpose. And so, as every
one knows, it is counted not only a suitable, but a
smart and laughable, device, in stage plays without
number, and by the class of persons whose morality
is reflected by the popular stage. Who so suitable a
person to be made a fool of as " the governor " ? Who
so little to be pitied when he becomes the dupe of
his children's cunning ? " Honour thy father and thy
mother," was once proclaimed in thunder from Sinai,
and not only men's hearts trembled, but the very earth

shook at the voice. But these were old times and old-fashioned people. Treat your father and mother as useful and convenient tools, inasmuch as they have control of the purse, of which you are often in want. But as they are not likely to approve of the objects for which you would spend their money ; as they are sure, on the other hand, to disapprove of them strongly, exercise your ingenuity in hoodwinking them as to your doings, and if your stratagem succeed, enjoy your chuckle at the blindness and simplicity of the poor old fools ! If this be the course that commends itself to any son or daughter, it indicates a heart so perverted that it would be most difficult to bring it to any sense of sin. All we would say is, See what kind of comrades you have in this policy of deceiving parents. See this royal blackguard, Amnon, and his villainous adviser Jonadab, resorting to the very same method for hoodwinking King David ; see them making use of this piece of machinery to compass an act of the grossest villainy that ever was heard of ; and say whether you hold the device to be commended by their example, and whether you feel honoured in treading a course that has been marked before you by such footprints.

If anything more was needed to show the accomplished villainy of Amnon, it is his treatment of Tamar after he has violently compassed her ruin. It is the story so often repeated even at this day,—the ruined victim flung aside in dishonour, and left unpitied to her shame. There is no trace of any compunction on the part of Amnon at the moral murder he has committed, at the life he has ruined ; no pity for the once blithe and happy maiden whom he has doomed to humiliation and woe. She has served his purpose, king's daughter though she is ; let her crawl into the earth like a poor worm to live or to die, in want or in misery; it is nothing to him. The only thing about her that he cares for is, that she may never again trouble him with her existence, or disturb the easy flow of his life. We think of those men of the olden time as utter barbarians who confined their foes in dismal dungeons, making their lives a continual torture, and denying them the slightest solace to the miseries of captivity. But what shall we say of those, high-born and wealthy men, it may be, who doom their cast-off victims to an existence of wretchedness and degradation which has no gleam of enjoyment, compared with which the silence and loneliness of a prison would be a luxury? Can the selfishness of sin exhibit itself anywhere or anyhow more terribly? What kind of heart can be left to the seducer, so hardened as to smother the faintest touch of pity for the woman he has made wretched for ever; so savage as to drive from him with the roughest execrations the poor confiding creature without whom he used to vow, in the days of her unsuspecting innocence, that he knew not how to live!

In a single word, our attention is now turned to the father of both Amnon and Tamar. "When King David heard of all these things, he was very wroth." Little wonder! But was this all? Was no punishment found for Amnon? Was he allowed to remain in the palace, the oldest son of the king, with nothing to mark his father's displeasure, nothing to neutralise his influence with the other royal children, nothing to prevent the repetition of his wickedness? Tamar, of course, was a woman. Was it for this reason that nothing was done to punish her destroyer? It does not appear that his position was in any way changed. We cannot but be indignant at the inactivity of David. Yet when we think of the past, we need not be surprised. David was too much implicated in the same sins to be able to inflict suitable punishment for them. It is those whose hands are clean that can rebuke the offender. Let others try to administer reproof—their own hearts condemn them, and they shrink from the task. Even the king of Israel must wink at the offences of his son.

But if David winked, Absalom did nothing of the kind. Such treatment of his full sister, if the king chose to let it alone, could not be let alone by the proud, indignant brother. He nursed his wrath, and watched for his opportunity. Nothing short of the death of Amnon would suffice him. And that death must be compassed not in open fight but by assassination. At last, after two full years, his opportunity came. A sheepshearing at Baal-hazor gave occasion for a feast, to which the king and all his sons should be asked. His father excused himself on the ground of the expense. Absalom was most unwilling to receive the excuse, reckoning probably that the king's presence would more completely ward off any suspicion of his purpose, and utterly heedless of the anguish his father would have felt when he found that, while asked professedly to a feast, it was really to the murder of his eldest son. David, however, refuses firmly, but he gives Absalom his blessing. Whether this was meant in the sense in which Isaac blessed Jacob, or whether it was merely an ordinary occasion of commending Absalom to the grace of God, it was a touching act, and it might have arrested the arm that was preparing to deal such a fatal blow to Amnon. On the contrary, Absalom only availed himself of his father's expression of kindly feeling to beg that he would allow Amnon to be present. And he succeeded so well that permission was given, not to Amnon only, but to all the king's sons. To Absalom's farm at Baal-hazor accordingly they went, and we may be sure that nothing would be spared to make the banquet worthy of a royal family. And now, while the wine is flowing freely, and the buzz of jovial talk fills the apartment, and all power of action on the part of Amnon is arrested by the stupefying influence of wine, the signal is given for his murder. See how closely Absalom treads in the footsteps of his father when he summons intoxi-cating drink to his aid, as David did to Uriah, when trying to make a screen of him for his own guilt. Yes, from the beginning, drink, or some other stupefying agent, has been the ready ally of the worst criminals, either preparing the victim for the slaughter or madden-ing the murderer for the deed. But wherever it has been present it has only made the tragedy more awful and the aspect of the crime more hideous. Give a wide berth, ye servants of God, to an agent with which the devil has ever placed himself in such close and deadly alliance !

It is not easy to paint the blackness of the crime of Absalom. We have nothing to say for Amnon, who seems to have been a man singularly vile ; but there is something very appalling in his being murdered by the order of his brother, something very cold-blooded in Absalom's appeal to the assassins not to flinch from their task, something very revolting in the flagrant violation of the laws of hospitality, and something not less daring in the deed being done in the midst of the feast, and in the presence of the guests. When Shake-speare would paint the murder of a royal guest, the deed is done in the dead of night, with no living eye to witness it, with no living arm at hand capable of arresting the murderous weapon. But here is a murderer of his guest who does not scruple to have the deed done in broad daylight in presence of all his guests, in presence of all the brothers of his victim, while the walls resound to the voice of mirth, and each face is radiant with festive excitement. Out from some place of concealment rush the assassins with their deadly weapons; next moment the life-blood of Amnon spurts on the table, and his lifeless body falls heavily to the ground. Before the excitement and horror of the assembled guests has subsided Absalom has made his escape, and before any step can be taken to pursue him he is beyond reach in Geshur in Syria.

Meanwhile an exaggerated report of the tragedy reaches King David's ears,—Absalom has slain all the king's sons, and there is not one of them left. Evil, at the bottom of his heart, must have been David's opinion of him when he believed the story, even in this exaggerated form. "The king arose and rent his clothes, and lay on the earth; and all his servants stood round with their clothes rent." Nor was it till Jonadab, his cousin, assured him that only Amnon could be dead, that the terrible impression of a wholesale massacre was removed from his mind. But who can fancy what the circumstances must have been, when it became a relief to David to know that Absalom had murdered but one of his brothers? Jonadab evidently thought that David did not need to be much surprised, inasmuch as this murder was a foregone conclusion with Absalom; it had been determined on ever since the day when Amnon forced Tamar. Here is a new light on the character of Jonadab. He knew that Absalom had determined that Amnon should die. It was no surprise to him

to hear that this purpose was carried out with effect.
Why did he not warn Amnon? Could it be that he
had been bribed over to the side of Absalom? He
knew the real state of the case before the king's sons
arrived. For when they did appear he appealed to
David whether his statement, previously given, was
not correct.

And now the first part of the retribution denounced
by Nathan begins to be fulfilled, and fulfilled very
fearfully,—"the sword shall never depart from thy
house." Ancient history abounds in frightful stories,
stories of murder, incest, and revenge, the materials,
real or fabulous, from which were formed the tragedies
of the great Greek dramatists. But nothing in their
dramas is more tragic than the crime of Amnon, the
incest of Tamar, and the revenge of Absalom. What
David's feelings must have been we can hardly conceive.
What must he have felt as he thought of the death of
Amnon, slain by his brother's command, in his brother's
house, at his brother's table, and hurried to God's judgment while his brain was reeling with intoxication !
What a pang must have been shot by the recollection
how David had once tried, for his own base ends, to
intoxicate Uriah as Absalom had intoxicated Amnon !
It does not appear that David's grief over Amnon was
of the passionate kind that he showed afterwards when
Absalom was slain ; but, though quieter, it must have
been very bitter. How could he but be filled with
anguish when he thought of his son, hurried, while
drunk, by his brother's act, into the presence of God, to
answer for the worse than murder of his sister, and for
all the crimes and sins of an ill-spent life ! What hope
could he entertain for the welfare of his soul ? What
balm could he find for such a wound ?

And it was not Amnon only he had to think of. These three of his children, Amnon, Tamar, Absalom, in one sense or another, were now total wrecks. From these three branches of his family tree no fruit could ever come. Nor could the dead now bury its dead. Neither the remembrance nor the effect of the past could ever be wiped out. It baffles us to think how David was able to carry such grief. "David mourned for his son every day." It was only the lapse of time that could blunt the edge of his distress.

But surely there must have been terrible faults in David's upbringing of his family before such results as these could come. Undoubtedly there were. First of all, there was the number of his wives. This could not fail to be a source of much jealousy and discord among them and their children, especially when he himself was absent, as he must often have been, for long periods at a time. Then there was his own example, so unguarded, so unhallowed, at a point where the utmost care and vigilance had need to be shown. Thirdly, there seems to have been an excessive tenderness of feeling towards his children, and towards some of them in particular. He could not bear to disappoint; his feelings got the better of his judgment; when the child insisted the father weakly gave way. He wanted the firmness and the faithfulness of Abraham, of whom God had said, "I know him that he will *command* his children and his household after him, and they shall keep the way of the Lord to do justice and judgment." Perhaps, too, busy and often much pressed as he was with affairs of state, occupied with foreign wars, with internal improvements, and the daily administration of justice, he looked on his house as a place of simple relaxation and enjoyment, and forgot that there, too, he had a solemn charge and most important duty. Thus it was that David failed in his domestic management. It is easy to spy out his defects, and easy to condemn him. But let each of you who have a family to bring up look to himself. You have not all David's difficulties, but you may have some of them. The precept and the promise is, "Train up a child in the way he should go, and when he is old he will not depart from it." It is not difficult to know the way he should go—the difficulty lies in the words, "Train up." To train up is not to force, nor is it merely to lay down the law, or to enforce the law. It is to get the whole nature of the child to move freely in the direction wished. To do this needs on the part of the parent a combination of firmness and love, of patience and decision, of consistent example and sympathetic encouragement. But it needs also, on the part of God, and therefore to be asked in earnest, believing prayer, that wondrous power which touches the springs of the heart, and draws it to Him and to His ways. Only by this combination of parental faithfulness and Divine grace can we look for the blessed result, " when he is old he will not depart from it."

# CHAPTER XVIII.

## ABSALOM BANISHED AND BROUGHT BACK

2 SAMUEL xiii. 38, 39; xiv.

GESHUR, to which Absalom fled after the murder of Amnon, accompanied in all likelihood by the men who had slain him, was a small kingdom in Syria, lying between Mount Hermon and Damascus. Maacah, Absalom's mother, was the daughter of Talmai, king of Geshur, so that Absalom was there among his own relations. There is no reason to believe that Talmai and his people had renounced the idolatrous worship that prevailed in Syria. For David to ally himself in marriage with an idolatrous people was not in accordance with the law. In law, Absalom must have been a Hebrew, circumcised the eighth day; but in spirit he would probably have no little sympathy with his mother's religion. His utter alienation in heart from his father; the unconcern with which he sought to drive from the throne the man who had been so solemnly called to it by God; the vow which he pretended to have taken, when away in Syria, that if he were invited back to Jerusalem he would "serve the Lord," all point to a man infected in no small degree with the spirit, if not addicted to the practice, of idolatry. And the tenor of his life, so full of cold-blooded wickedness, exemplified well the influence of idolatry, which bred neither fear of God nor love of man.

We have seen that Amnon had not that profound hold on David's heart which Absalom had; and therefore it is little wonder that when time had subdued the keen sensation of horror, the king " was comforted concerning Amnon, seeing he was dead." There was no great blank left in his heart, no irrepressible craving of the soul for the return of the departed. But it was otherwise in the case of Absalom,—" the king's heart was towards him." David was in a painful dilemma, placed between two opposite impulses, the judicial and the paternal; the judicial calling for the punishment of Absalom, the paternal craving his restoration. Absalom in the most flagrant way had broken a law older even than the Sinai legislation, for it had been given to Noah after the flood—" Whoso sheddeth man's blood, by man shall his blood be shed." But the deep affection of David for Absalom not only caused him to shrink from executing that law, but made him most desirous to have him near him again, pardoned, penitent as he no doubt hoped, and enjoying all the rights and privileges of the king's son. The first part of the chapter now before us records the manner in which David, in great weakness, sacrificed the judicial to the paternal, sacrificed his judgment to his feelings, and the welfare of the kingdom for the gratification of his affection. For it was too evident that Absalom was not a fit man to succeed David on the throne. If Saul was unfit to rule over God's people, and as God's vicegerent, much more was Absalom. Not only was he not the right kind of man, but, as his actions had showed, he was the very opposite. By his own wicked deed he was now an outlaw and an exile; he was out of sight and likely to pass out of mind; and it was most undesirable that any step should be taken to bring him back among the people, and give him every chance of the succession. Yet in spite of all this the king in his secret heart desired to get Absalom back. And Joab, not studying the welfare of the kingdom, but having regard only to the strong wishes of the king and of the heir-apparent, devised a scheme for fulfilling their desire.

That collision of the paternal and the judicial, which David removed by sacrificing the judicial, brings to our mind a discord of the same kind on a much greater scale, which received a solution of a very different kind. The sin of man created the same difficulty in the government of God. The judicial spirit, demanding man's punishment, came into collision with the paternal, desiring his happiness. How were they to be reconciled? This is the great question on which the priests of the world, when unacquainted with Divine revelation, have perplexed themselves since the world began. When we study the world's religions, we see very clearly that it has never been held satisfactory to solve the problem as David solved his difficulty, by simply sacrificing the judicial. The human conscience refuses to accept of such a settlement. It demands that some satisfaction shall be made to that law of which the Divine Judge is the administrator. It cannot bear to see God abandoning His judgment-seat in order that He may show indiscriminate mercy. Fantastic and foolish in the last degree, grim and repulsive too, in many cases, have been the devices by which it has been sought to supply the necessary satisfaction. The awful sacrifices of Moloch, the mutilations of Juggernaut, the penances of popery, are most repulsive solutions, while they all testify to the intuitive conviction of mankind that something in the form of atonement is indispensable. But if these solutions repel us, not less satisfactory is the opposite view, now so current, that nothing in the shape of sin-offering is necessary, that no consideration needs to be taken of the judicial, that the infinite clemency of God is adequate to deal with the case, and that a true belief in His most loving fatherhood is all that is required for the forgiveness and acceptance of His erring children. In reality this is no solution at all ; it is just David's method of sacrificing the judicial ; it satisfies no healthy conscience, it brings solid peace to no troubled soul. The true and only solution, by which due regard is shown both to the judicial and the paternal, is that which is so fully unfolded and enforced in the Epistles of St. Paul. " God was in Christ reconciling the world unto Himself, not imputing unto men their trespasses. . . . For He hath made Him to be sin for us, who knew no sin, that we might be made the righteousness of God in Him."

Returning to the narrative, we have next to examine the stratagem of Joab, designed to commit the king unwittingly to the recall of Absalom. The idea of the method may quite possibly have been derived from Nathan's parable of the ewe lamb. The design was to get the king to give judgment in an imaginary case, and thus commit him to a similar judgment in the case of Absalom. But there was a world-wide difference between the purpose of the parable of Nathan and that of the wise woman of Tekoah. Nathan's parable was designed to rouse the king's conscience as against his feelings ; the woman of Tekoah's, as prompted by Joab, to rouse his feelings as against his conscience. Joab found a fitting tool for his purpose in a wise woman of Tekoah, a small town in the south of Judah. She was evidently an accommodating and unscrupulous person ;

but there is no reason to compare her to the woman
of Endor, whose services Saul had resorted to.   She
seems to have been a woman of dramatic faculty,
clever at personating another, and at acting a part.
Her skill in this way becoming known to Joab, he
arranged with her to go to the king with a fictitious
story, and induce him now to bring back Absalom.
Her story bore that she was a widow who had been
left with two sons, one of whom in a quarrel killed his
brother in the field.   All the family were risen against
her to constrain her to give up the murderer to death,
but if she did so her remaining coal would be quenched,
and neither name nor remainder left to her husband
on the face of the earth.   On hearing the case, the
king seems to have been impressed in the woman's
favour, and promised to give an order accordingly.
Further conversation obtained clearer assurances from
him that he would protect her from the avenger of
blood.   Then, dropping so far her disguise, she ven-
tured to remonstrate with the king, inasmuch as he had
not dealt with his own son as he was prepared to deal
with hers.   "Wherefore then hast thou devised such a
thing against the people of God ? for in speaking this
word, the king is as one that is guilty, in that the king
doth not fetch home again his banished one.   For we
must needs die, and are as water spilt upon the ground
which cannot be gathered up again ; neither doth God
take away life, but deviseth means that he that is
banished be not an outcast from Him."   We cannot
but be struck, though not favourably, with the pious
tone which the woman here assumed to David.   She
represents that the continued banishment of Absalom
is against the people of God,—it is not for the nation's
interest that the heir-apparent should be for ever

banished. It is against the example of God, who, in administering His providence, does not launch His arrows at once against the destroyer of life, but rather shows him mercy, and allows him to return to his former condition. Clemency is a divine-like attribute. The king who can disentangle difficulties, and give such prominence to mercy, is like an angel of God. It is a divine-like work he undertakes when he recalls his banished. She can pray, when he is about to undertake such a business, "The Lord thy God be with thee" (R.V.). She knew that any difficulties the king might have in recalling his son would arise from his fears that he would be acting against God's will. The clever woman fills his eye with considerations on one side—the mercy and forbearance of God, the pathos of human life, the duty of not making things worse than they necessarily are. She knew he would be startled when she named Absalom. She knew that though he had given judgment on the general principle as involved in the imaginary case she had put before him, he might demur to the application of that principle to the case of Absalom. Her instructions from Joab were to get the king to sanction Absalom's return. The king has a surmise that the hand of Joab is in the whole transaction, and the woman acknowledges that it is so. After the interview with the woman, David sends for Joab, and gives him leave to fetch back Absalom. Joab goes to Geshur and brings Absalom to Jerusalem.

But David's treatment of Absalom when he returns does not bear out the character for unerring wisdom which the woman had given him. The king refuses to see his son, and for two years Absalom lives in his own house, without enjoying any of the privileges of the king's son.   By this means David took away all the grace of the transaction, and irritated Absalom.   He was afraid to exercise his royal prerogative in pardoning him out-and-out.   His conscience told him it ought not to be done.   To restore at once one who had sinned so flagrantly to all his dignity and power was against the grain.   Though therefore he had given his consent to Absalom returning to Jerusalem, for all practical purposes he might as well have been at Geshur.   And Absalom was not the man to bear this quietly.   How would his proud spirit like to hear of royal festivals at which all were present but he ?   How would he like to hear of distinguished visitors to the king from the surrounding countries, and he alone excluded from their society ?   His spirit would be chafed like that of a wild beast in its cage.   Now it was, we cannot doubt, that he felt a new estrangement from his father, and conceived the project of seizing upon his throne.   Now too it probably was that he began to gather around him the party that ultimately gave him his short-lived triumph.   There would be sympathy for him in some quarters as an ill-used man ; while there would rally to him all who were discontented with David's government, whether on personal or on public grounds.   The enemies of his godliness, emboldened by his conduct towards Uriah, finding there what Daniel's enemies in a future age tried in vain to find in his conduct, would begin to think seriously of the possibility of a change.   Probably Joab began to apprehend the coming danger when he refused once and again to speak to Absalom.   It seemed to be the impression both of David and of Joab that there would be danger to the state in his complete restoration.

Two years of this state of things had passed, and the

patience of Absalom was exhausted. He sent for Joab
to negotiate for a change of arrangements. But Joab
would not see him. A second time he sent, and a
second time Joab declined. Joab was really in a great
difficulty. He seems to have seen that he had made a
mistake in bringing Absalom to Jerusalem, but it was
a mistake out of which he could not extricate himself.
He was unwilling to go back, and he was afraid to go
forward. He had not courage to undo the mistake he
had made in inviting Absalom to return by banishing
him again. If he should meet Absalom he knew he
would be unable to meet the arguments by which he
would press him to complete whāt he had begun when
he invited him back. Therefore he studiously avoided
him. But Absalom was not to be outdone in this way.
He fell on a rude stratagem for bringing Joab to his
presence. Their fields being adjacent to each other,
Absalom sent his servants to set Joab's barley on
fire. The irritation of such an unprovoked injury
overcame Joab's unwillingness to meet Absalom ; he
went to him in a rage and demanded why this had
been done. The matter of the barley would be easy
to arrange ; but now that he had met Joab he showed
him that there were just two modes of treatment open
to David,—either really to pardon, or really to punish
him. This probably was just what Joab felt. There
was no good, but much harm in the half-and-half
policy which the king was pursuing. If Absalom was
pardoned, let him be on friendly terms with the king.
If he was not pardoned, let him be put to death for the
crime he had committed.

Joab was unable to refute Absalom's reasoning.
And when he went to the king he would press that
view on him likewise. And now, after two years of a

half-and-half measure, the king sees no alternative but to yield. " When he had called for Absalom, he came to the king, and bowed himself to his face on the ground before the king ; and the king kissed Absalom." This was the token of reconciliation and friendship. But it would not be with a clear conscience or an easy mind that David saw the murderer of his brother in full possession of the honours of the king's son.

In all this conduct of King David we can trace only the infatuation of one left to the guidance of his own mind. It is blunder after blunder. Like many good but mistaken men, he erred both in inflicting punishments and in bestowing favours. Much that ought to be punished such persons pass over ; what they do select for punishment is probably something trivial ; and when they punish it is in a way so injudicious as to defeat its ends. And some, like David, keep oscillating between punishment and favour so as at once to destroy the effect of the one and the grace of the other. His example may well show all of you who have to do with such things the need of great carefulness in this important matter. Penalties, to be effectual, should be for marked offences, but when incurred should be firmly maintained. Only when the purpose of the punishment is attained ought reconciliation to take place, and when that comes it should be full-hearted and complete, restoring the offender to the full benefit of his place and privilege, both in the home and in the hearts of his parents.

So David lets Absalom loose, as it were, on the people of Jerusalem. He is a young man of fine appearance and fascinating manners. " In all Israel there was none to be so much praised as Absalom for his beauty ; from the sole of the foot even to the crown of the head there was no blemish in him. And when he polled his head (for it was at every year's end that he polled it; because his hair was heavy on him, therefore he polled it) the weight of the hair of his head was two hundred shekels after the king's weight." No doubt this had something to do with David's great liking for him. He could not but look on him with pride, and think with pleasure how much he was admired by others. The affection which owed so much to a cause of this sort was not likely to be of the highest or purest quality. What then are we to say of David's fondness for Absalom? Was it wrong for a father to be attached to his child? Was it wrong for him to love even a wicked child? No one can for a moment think so who remembers that " God *commended His love towards us,* in that *while we were yet sinners* Christ died for us." There is a sense in which loving emotions may warrantably be more powerfully excited in the breast of a godly parent toward an erring child than toward a wise and good one. The very thought that a child is in the thraldom of sin creates a feeling of almost infinite pathos with reference to his condition. The loving desire for his good and his happiness becomes more intense from the very sense of the disorder and misery in which he lies. The sheep that has strayed from the fold is the object of a more profound emotion than the ninety-and-nine that are safe within it. In this sense a parent cannot love his child, even his sinful and erring child, too well. The love that seeks another's highest good can never be too intense, for it is the very counterpart and image of God's love for sinful men.

But, as far as we can gather, David's love for Absalom was not exclusively of this kind. It was a fondness that led him to wink at his faults even when they became flagrant, and that desired to see him occupying a place of honour and responsibility for which he certainly was far from qualified. This was more than the love of benevolence. The love of benevolence has, in the Christian bosom, an unlimited sphere. It may be given to the most unworthy. But the love of complacency, of delight in any one, of desire for his company, desire for close relations with him, confidence in him, as one to whom our own interests and the interests of others may be safely entrusted, is a quite different feeling. This kind of love must ever be regulated by the degree of true excellence, of genuine worth, possessed by the person loved. The fault in David's love to Absalom was not that he was too benevolent, not that he wished his son too well. It was that he had too much complacency or delight in him, delight resting on very superficial ground, and that he was too willing to have him entrusted with the most vital interests of the nation. This fondness for Absalom was a sort of infatuation, to which David never could have yielded if he had remembered the hundred and first Psalm, and if he had thought of the kind of men whom alone when he wrote that psalm he determined to promote to influence in the kingdom.

And on this we found a general lesson of no small importance. Young persons, let us say emphatically young women, and perhaps Christian young women, are apt to be captivated by superficial qualities, qualities like those of Absalom, and in some cases are not only ready but eager to marry those who possess them. In their blindness they are willing to commit not only their own interests but the interests of their children, if they should have any, to men who are not Christians, perhaps barely moral, and who are therefore not worthy of their trust. Here it is that affection should be watched and restrained. Christians should never allow their affections to be engaged by any whom, on Christian grounds, they do not thoroughly esteem. All honour to those who, at great sacrifice, have honoured this rule! All honour to Christian parents who bring up their children to feel that, if they are Christians themselves, they can marry only in the Lord! Alas for those who deem accidental and superficial qualities sufficient grounds for a union which involves the deepest interests of souls for time and for eternity! In David's ill-founded complacency in Absalom, and the woeful disasters which flowed from it, let them see a beacon to warn them against any union which has not mutual esteem for its foundation, and does not recognise those higher interests in reference to which the memorable words were spoken by our Lord, "What is a man profited if he gain the whole world and lose his own soul?"

# CHAPTER XIX.

## *ABSALOM'S REVOLT.*

### 2 SAMUEL xv. 1—12.

WHEN Absalom obtained from his father the position he had so eagerly desired at Jerusalem, he did not allow the grass to grow under his feet. The terms on which he was now with the king evidently gave him a command of money to a very ample degree. By this means he was able to set up an equipage such as had not previously been seen at Jerusalem. "He prepared him a chariot and horses, and fifty men to run before him." To multiply horses to himself was one of the things forbidden by the law of Moses to the king that should be chosen (Deut. xvii. 16), mainly, we suppose, because it was a prominent feature of the royal state of the kings of Egypt, and because it would have indicated a tendency to place the glory of the kingdom in magnificent surroundings rather than in the protection and blessing of the heavenly King. The style of David's living appears to have been quiet and unpretending, notwithstanding the vast treasures he had amassed; for the love of pomp or display was none of his failings. Anything in the shape of elaborate arrangement that he devised seems to have been in connection with the public service of God—for instance, his choir of singers and players (1 Chron. xxiii. 5); his

own personal tastes appear to have been simple and inex-
pensive. And this style undoubtedly befitted a royalty
which rested on a basis so peculiar as that of the
nation of Israel, when the king, though he used that
title, was only the viceroy of the true King of the
nation, and where it was the will of God that a different
spirit should prevail from that prevalent among the
surrounding nations. A modest establishment was
evidently suited to one who recognised his true position
as a subordinate lieutenant, not an absolute ruler.

But Absalom's tastes were widely different, and he
was not the man to be restrained from gratifying them
by any considerations of that sort. The moment he
had the power, though he was not even king, he set
up his imposing equipage, and became the observed of
all observers in Jerusalem. And no doubt there were
many of the people who sympathised with him, and
regarded it as right and proper that, now that Israel
was so renowned and prosperous a kingdom, its court
should shine forth in corresponding splendour. The
plain equipage of David would seem to them paltry
and unimposing, in no way fitted to gratify the pride
or elevate the dignity of the kingdom. Absalom's, on
the other hand, would seem to supply all that David's
wanted. The prancing steeds, with their gay capari-
sons, the troop of outrunners in glittering uniform, the
handsome face and figure of the prince, would create
a sensation wherever he went; There, men would say
emphatically, is the proper state and bearing of a king;
had we such a monarch as that, surrounding nations
would everywhere acknowledge our superiority, and
feel that we were entitled to the first place among the
kingdoms of the East.

But Absalom was far too shrewd a man to base his

popularity merely on outward show. For the daring
game which he was about to play it was necessary to
have much firmer support than that. He understood
the remarkable power of personal interest and sympathy in winning the hearts of men, and drawing them
to one's side. He rose up early, and stood beside the
way of the gate, where in Eastern cities judgment was
usually administered, but where, for some unknown
reason, little seems to have been done by the king or
the king's servants at that time. To all who came to
the gate he addressed himself with winsome affability,
and to those who had "a suit that should come to
the king for judgment" (R.V.) he was especially
encouraging. Well did he know that when a man has
a lawsuit it usually engrosses his whole attention,
and that he is very impatient of delays and hindrances
in the way of his case. Very adroitly did he take
advantage of this feeling,—sympathising with the liti-
gant, agreeing with him of course that he had right
on his side, but much concerned that there was no one
appointed of the king to attend to his business, and
devoutly and fervently wishing that he were made
judge in the land, that every one that had any suit or
cause might come to him, and he would do him justice.
And with regard to others, when they came to do him
homage he seemed unwilling to recognise this token of
superiority, but, as if they were just brothers, he put
forth his hand, took hold of them, and kissed them. If
it were not for what we know now of the hollowness
of it, this would be a pretty picture—an ear so ready
to listen to the tale of wrong, a heart so full of sympathy,
an active temperament that in the early hours of the
morning sent him forth to meet the people and
exchange kindly greetings with them; a form and

figure that graced the finest procession ; a manner that could be alike dignified when dignity was becoming, and humility itself when it was right to be humble. But alas for the hollow-heartedness of the picture ! It is like the fabled apples of Sodom, outside all fair and attractive, but dust within.

But hollow though it was, the policy succeeded—he became exceedingly popular ; he secured the affections of the people. It is a remarkable expression that is used to denote this result—" He stole the hearts of the men of Israel." It was not an honest transaction. It was swindling in high life. He was appropriating valuable property on false pretences. To constitute a man a thief or a swindler it is not necessary that he forge a rich man's name, or that he put his hand into the pocket of his neighbour. To gain a heart by hypocritical means, to secure the confidence of another by lying promises, is equally low and wicked ; nay, in God's sight is a greater crime. It may be that man's law has difficulty in reaching it, and in many cases cannot reach it at all. But it cannot be supposed that those who are guilty of it will in the end escape God's righteous judgment. And if the punishments of the future life are fitted to indicate the due character of the sins for which they are sent, we can think of nothing more appropriate than that those who have stolen hearts in this way, high in this world's rank though they have often been, should be made to rank with the thieves and thimbleriggers and other knaves who are the *habitués* of our prisons, and are scorned universally as the meanest of mankind. With all his fine face and figure and manner, his chariot and horses, his outrunners and other attendants, Absalom after all was but a black-hearted thief.

All this crooked and cunning policy of his Absalom carried on witr unwearied vigour till his plot was ripe. There is reason to apprehend an error of some kind in the text when it is said (ver. 7) that it was " at the end of forty years " that Absalom struck the final blow. The reading of some manuscripts is more likely to be correct,—" at the end of four years," that is, four years after he was allowed to assume the position of prince. During that space of time much might be quietly done by one who had such an advantage of manner, and was so resolutely devoted to his work. For he seems to have laboured at his task without interruption all that time. The dissembling which he had to practise, to impress the people with the idea of his kindly interest in them, must have required a very considerable strain. But he was sustained in it by the belief that in the end he would succeed, and success was worth an infinity of labour. What a power of persistence is often shown by the children of this world, and how much wiser are they in their generation than the children of light as to the means that will achieve their ends ! With what wonderful application and perseverance do many men labour to build up a business, to accumulate a fortune, to gain a distinction ! I have heard of a young man who, being informed that an advertisement had appeared in a newspaper to the effect that if his family would apply to some one they would hear of something to their advantage, set himself to discover that advertisement, went over the advertisements for several years, column by column, first of one paper, then of another and another, till he became so absorbed in the task that he lost first his reason and then his life. Thank God, there are instances not a few of very noble application and perseverance in the spiritual field; but is it not true that the mass even of good men are sadly remiss in the efforts they make for spiritual ends? Does not the energy of the racer who ran for the corruptible crown often put to shame the languor of those who seek for an incorruptible? And does not the manifold secular activity of which we see so much in the world around us sound a loud summons in the ears of all who are at ease in Zion—"Now it is high time to awake out of sleep"?

The copestone which Absalom put on his plot when all was ripe for execution was of a piece with the whole undertaking. It was an act of religious hypocrisy amounting to profanity. It shows how well he must have succeeded in deceiving his father when he could venture on such a finishing stroke. Hypocrite though he was himself, he well knew the depth and sincerity of his father's religion. He knew too that nothing could gratify him more than to find in his son the evidence of a similar state of heart. It is difficult to comprehend the villainy that could frame such a statement as this :—"I pray thee, let me go and pay my vow, which I have vowed unto the Lord, in Hebron. For thy servant vowed a vow, while I abode at Geshur in Syria, saying, If the Lord shall indeed bring me again to Jerusalem, then I will serve" (marg. R.V., worship) "the Lord." We have already remarked that it is not very clear from this whether up to this time Absalom had been a worshipper of the God of Israel. The purport of his pretended vow (that is, what he wished his father to believe) must have been either that, renouncing the idolatry of Geshur, he would now become a worshipper of Israel's God, or (what seems more likely) that in token of his purpose for the future

he would present a special offering to the God of
Israel. This vow he now wished to redeem by making
his offerings to the Lord, and for this purpose he
desired to go to Hebron. But why go to Hebron?
Might he not have redeemed it at Jerusalem? It was
the custom, however, when a vow was taken, to specify
the place where it was to be fulfilled, and in this
instance Hebron was alleged to be the place. But
what are we to think of the effrontery and wickedness of this pretence? To drag sacred things into a
scheme of villainy, to pretend to have a desire to do
honour to God simply for the purpose of carrying out
deception and gaining a worldly end, is a frightful
prostitution of all that ought to be held most sacred.
It seems to indicate one who had no belief in God or
in anything holy, to whom truth and falsehood, right
and wrong, honour and shame, were all essentially
alike, although, when it suited him, he might pretend
to have a profound regard to the honour of God and
a cordial purpose to render that honour. We are reminded of Charles II. taking the Covenant to please
the Scots, and get their help towards obtaining the
crown. But indeed the same great sin is involved in
every act of religious hypocrisy, in every instance
in which pretended reverence is paid to God in order
to secure a selfish end.

The place was cunningly selected. It enjoyed a
sanctity which had been gathering round it for centuries; whereas Jerusalem, as the capital of the nation,
was but of yesterday. Hebron was the place where
David himself had begun his reign, and while it was
far enough from Jerusalem to allow Absalom to work
unobserved by David, it was near enough to allow him
to carry out the schemes which had been set on foot

there.   So little suspicion had the old king of what
was brewing that, when Absalom asked leave to go
to Hebron, he dismissed him with a blessing—"Go in
peace."

What Joab was thinking of all this we have no
means of knowing.   That a man who looked after
his own interests so well as Joab did, should have
stuck to David when his fortunes appeared to be
desperate, is somewhat surprising.   But the truth
seems to be that Absalom never felt very cordial
towards Joab after his refusal to meet him on his
return from Geshur.   It does not appear that Joab
was much impressed by regard to God's will in the
matter of the succession ; his being engaged afterwards
in the insurrection in favour of Adonijah when Solomon
was divinely marked out for the succession shows that
he was not.   His adherence to David on this occasion
was probably the result of necessity rather than choice.
But what are we to say of his want of vigilance in
allowing Absalom's conspiracy to advance as it did
either without suspecting its existence, or at least
without making provision for defending the king's
cause ?   Either he was very blind or he was very
careless.   As for the king himself, we have seen what
cause he had, after his great trespass, for courting
solitude and avoiding contact with the people.   That
he should be ignorant of all that was going on need
not surprise us.   And moreover, from allusions in
some of the Psalms (xxxviii., xxxix., xli.) to a loathsome
and all but fatal illness of David's, and to treachery
practised on him when ill, some have supposed that
this was the time chosen by Absalom for consummating
his plot.   When Absalom said to the men applying
for justice, whom he met at the gate of the city, "There

is no man deputed of the king to hear thee," his words implied that there was something hindering the king from being there in person, and for some reason he had not appointed a deputy. A protracted illness, unfitting David for his personal duties and for super-intending the machinery of government, might have furnished Absalom with the pretext for his lamentation over this want. It gives us a harder impression of his villainy and hardness of heart if he chose a time when his father was enfeebled by disease to inflict a crushing blow on his government and a crowning humiliation on himself.

Three other steps were taken by Absalom before bringing the revolt to a crisis. First, he sent spies or secret emissaries to all the tribes, calling them, on hearing the sound of a trumpet, to acknowledge him as king at Hebron. Evidently he had all the talent for administration that was so conspicuous in his nation and in his house,—if only it had been put to a better use. Secondly, he took with him to Hebron a band of two hundred men, of whom it is said "they went in their simplicity, and they knew not anything' —so admirably was the secret kept. Thirdly, Absalom sent for Ahithophel the Gilonite, David's counsellor, from his city, having reason to believe that Ahithophel was on his side, and knowing that his counsel would be valuable to him in the present emergency. And every arrangement seemed to succeed admirably. The tide ran strongly in his favour—" the conspiracy was strong, for the people increased continually with Absalom." Everything seemed to fall out precisely as he wished ; it looked as if the revolt would not only succeed, but that it would succeed without serious opposition. Absalom must have been full of expecta

tion that in a few days or weeks he would be reigning
unopposed at Jerusalem.

This extraordinary success is difficult to understand.
For what could have made David so unpopular? In
his earliest years he had been singularly popular;
his victories brought him unbounded *éclat;* and when
Ishbosheth died it was the remembrance of these early
services that disposed the people to call him to the
throne. Since that time he had increased his services
in an eminent degree. He had freed his country from
all the surrounding tribes that were constantly attacking it; he had conquered those distant but powerful
enemies the Syrians; and he had brought to the
country a great accumulation of wealth. Add to this
that he was fond of music and a poet, and had written
many of the very finest of their sacred songs. Why
should not such a king be popular? The answer to
this question will embrace a variety of reasons. In the
first place, a generation was growing up who had not
been alive at the time of his early services, and on
whom therefore they would make a very slender
impression. For service done to the public is very
soon forgotten unless it be constantly repeated in
other forms, unless, in fact, there be a perpetual round
of it. So it is found by many a minister of the gospel.
Though he may have built up his congregation from the
very beginning, ministered among them with unceasing
assiduity, and taken the lead in many important and
permanent undertakings, yet in a few years after he
goes away all is forgotten, and his very name comes
to be unknown to many. In the second place, David
was turning old, and old men are prone to adhere
to their old ways; his government had become old-
fashioned, and he showed no longer the life and vigour

of former days.  A new, fresh, lively administration
was eagerly desired by the younger spirits of the nation.
Further, there can be no doubt that David's fervent
piety was disliked by many, and his puritan methods
of governing the kingdom.  The spirit of the world is
sure to be found in every community, and it is always
offended by the government of holy men.  Finally, his
fall in the matter of Uriah had greatly impaired the
respect and affection even of the better part of the
community.  If to all this there was added a period
of feeble health, during which many departments of
government were neglected, we shall have, beyond
doubt, the principal grounds of the king's unpopularity.
The ardent lovers of godliness were no doubt a
minority, and thus even David, who had done so
much for Israel, was ready to be sacrificed in the time
of old age.

But had he not something better to fall back on ?
Was he not promised the protection and the aid of the
Most High ?   Might he not cast himself on Him who
had been his refuge and his strength in every time of
need, and of whom he had sung so serenely that He
is near to them that call on Him in sincerity and in
truth ?  Undoubtedly he might, and undoubtedly he
did.  And the final result of Absalom's rebellion, the
wonderful way in which its back was broken and David
rescued and restored, showed that though cast down
he was not forsaken.  But now, we must remember, the
second element of the chastisement of which Nathan
testified, had come upon him.  " Behold, I will raise
up evil against thee out of thine own house."  That
chastisement was now falling, and while it lasted
the joy and comfort of God's gracious presence must
have been interrupted.  But all the same God was

still with him, even though He was carrying him through the valley of the shadow of death. Like the Apostle Peter, he was brought to the very verge of destruction ; but at the critical moment an unseen hand was stretched out to save him, and in after-years he was able to sing, " He brought me up also out of a fearful pit, and out of the miry clay ; and He set my feet upon a rock and established my goings ; and He hath put a new song in my mouth, even praise unto our God ; many shall see it and shall fear, and shall trust in the Lord."

# CHAPTER XX.

2 SAMUEL xv. 13.

THE trumpet which was to be the signal that
Absalom reigned in Hebron had been sounded,
the flow of people in response to it had begun, when
"a messenger came to David saying, The hearts of
the men of Israel are after Absalom." The narrative
is so concise that we can hardly tell whether or not
this was the first announcement to David of the
real intentions of Absalom. But it is very certain that
the king was utterly unprepared to meet the sudden
revolt. The first news of it all but overwhelmed him.
And little wonder. There came on him three calamities
in one. First, there was the calamity that the great
bulk of the people had revolted against him, and
were now hastening to drive him from the throne, and
very probably to put him to death. Second, there was
the appalling discovery of the villainy, hypocrisy, and
heartless cruelty of his favourite and popular son,—the
most crushing thing that can be thought of to a tender
heart. And third, there was the discovery that the
hearts of the people were with Absalom ; David had
lost what he most prized and desired to possess ; the
intense affection he had for his people now met with
no response ; their love and confidence were given

to a usurper. Fancy an old man, perhaps in infirm health, suddenly confronted with this threefold calamity; who can wonder for the time that he is paralysed, and bends before the storm ?

Flight from Jerusalem seemed the only feasible course. Both policy and humanity seemed to dictate it. He considered himself unable to defend the city with any hope of success against an attack by such a force as Absalom could muster, and he was unwilling to expose the people to be smitten with the sword. Whether he was really as helpless as he thought we can hardly say. We should be disposed to think that his first duty was to stay where he was, and defend his capital. He was there as God's viceroy, and would not God be with him, defending the place where He had set His name, and the tabernacle in which He was pleased to dwell ?  It is not possible for us, ignorant as we are of the circumstances, to decide whether the flight from Jerusalem was the enlightened result of an overwhelming necessity, or the fruit of sudden panic, of a heart so paralysed that it could not gird itself for action. His servants had no other advice to offer. Any course that recommended itself to him they were ready to take. If this did not help to throw light on his difficulties, it must at least have soothed his heart. His friends were not all forsaking him. Amid the faithless a few were found faithful. Friends in such need were friends indeed. And the sight of their honest though perplexed countenances, and the sound of their friendly though trembling voices, would be most soothing to his feelings, and serve to rally the energy that had almost left him. When the world forsakes us, the few friends that remain are of priceless value.

On leaving Jerusalem David at once turned east-

ward, into the wilderness region between Jerusalem and
Jericho, with the view, if possible, of crossing the Jordan,
so as to have that river, with its deep valley, between
him and the rebels. The first halt, or rather the rendez-
vous for his followers, though called in the A.V. "a place
that was far off," is more suitably rendered in the R.V.
Bethmerhak, and the margin "the far house." Probably it was the last house on this side the brook
Kidron. Here, outside the walls of the city, some
hasty arrangements were made before the flight was
begun in earnest.

First, we read that he was accompanied by all his
household, with the exception of ten concubines who
were left to keep the house. Fain would we have
avoided contact at such a moment with that feature of
his house from which so much mischief had come; but
to the end of the day David never deviated in that
respect from the barbarous policy of all Eastern kings.
The mention of his household shows how embarrassed
he must have been with so many helpless appendages,
and how slow his flight. And his household were not the
only women and children of the company; the "little
ones" of the Gittites are mentioned in ver. 22; we
may conceive how the unconcealed terror and excitement
of these helpless beings must have distressed him, as
their feeble powers of walking must have held back the
fighting part of his attendants. When one thinks of
this, one sees more clearly the excellence of the advice
afterwards given by Ahithophel to pursue him without
loss of time with twelve thousand men, to destroy his
person at once; in that case, Absalom must have overtaken him long before he reached the Jordan, and
found him quite unable to withstand his ardent troops.

Next, we find mention of the forces that remained.

faithful to the king in the crisis of his misfortunes.
The Pelethites, the Cherethites, and the Gittites were
the chief of these.  The Pelethites and the Cherethites
are supposed to have been the representatives of the
band of followers that David commanded when hiding
from Saul in the wilderness ; the Gittites appear to have
been a body of refugees from Gath, driven away by the
tyranny of the Philistines, who had thrown themselves
on the protection of David and had been well treated
by him.  The interview between David and Ittai was
most creditable to the feelings of the fugitive king.
Ittai was a stranger who had but lately come to Jerusalem, and as he was not attached to David personally,
it would be safer for him to return to the city and
offer to the reigning king the services which David could
no longer reward.   But the generous proposal of David
was rejected with equal nobility on the part of Ittai.
He had probably been received with kindness by David
when he first came to Jerusalem, the king remembering
well when he himself was in the like predicament, and
thinking, like the African princess to Æneas, "*Haud
ignara mali, miseris succurrere disco*"—"Having had
experience of adversity myself, I know how to succour
the miserable."   Ittai's heart was won to David then ;
and he had made up his mind, like Ruth the Moabitess
with reference to Naomi, that wherever David was, in life
or in death, there also he should be.   How affecting must
it have been to David to receive such an assurance from
a stranger !   His own son, whom he had loaded with
undeserved kindness, was conspiring against him,
while this stranger, who owed him nothing in com-
parison, was risking everything in his cause.   "There
is a friend that sticketh closer than a brother."

Next in David's train presented themselves Zadok

and Abiathar, the priests, carrying the ark of God. The presence of this sacred symbol would have invested the cause of David with a manifestly sacred character in the eyes of all good men ; its absence from Absalom would have equally suggested the absence of Israel's God. But David probably remembered how ill it had fared with Israel in the days of Eli and his sons, when the ark was carried into battle. Moreover, when the ark had been placed on Mount Zion, God had said, " This is My rest ; here will I dwell ;" and even in this extraordinary emergency, David would not disturb that arrangement. He said to Zadok, "Carry back the ark of God into the city : if I shall find favour in the eyes of the Lord, He shall bring me again, and show me both it and His habitation : but if He thus say, I have no delight in thee, behold, here am I ; let Him do to me what seemeth good unto Him." These words show how much God was in David's mind in connection with the events of that humiliating day. They show, too, that he did not regard his case as desperate. But everything turned on the will of God. It might be that, in His great mercy, He would bring him back to Jerusalem. His former promises led him to think of this as a possible, perhaps probable, termination of the insurrec-tion. But it might also be that the Lord had no more delight in him. The chastening with which He was now visiting him for his sin might involve the success of Absalom. In that case, all that David would say was that he was at God's disposal, and would offer no resistance to His holy will. If he was to be restored, he would be restored without the aid of the ark ; if he was to be destroyed, the ark could not save him. Zadok and his Levites must carry it back into the city. The distance was a very short one, and they would be

able to have everything placed in order before Absalom
could be there.

Another thought occurred to David, who was now
evidently recovering his calmness and power of making
arrangements.   Zadok was a seer, and able to use that
method of obtaining light from God which in great
emergencies God was pleased to give when the ruler of
the nation required it.   But the marginal reading of the
R.V., "Seest thou?" instead of "Thou art a seer,"
makes it doubtful whether David referred to this mystic
privilege, which Zadok does not appear to have used ;
the meaning may be simply, that as he was an observ-
ant man, he could be of use to David in the city, by
noticing how things were going and sending him word.
In this way he could be of more use to him in Jerusalem than in the field.   Considering how he was
embarrassed with the women and children, it was
better for David not to be encumbered with another
defenceless body like the Levites.   The sons of the
priests, Ahimaaz and Jonathan, would be of great
service in bringing him information.   Even if he succeeded in reaching the plains (or fords, *marg.* R.V.) of
the wilderness, they could easily overtake him, and tell
him what plan of operations it would be wisest for him
to follow.

These hasty arrangements being made, and the company placed in some sort of order, the march towards
the wilderness now began.   The first thing was to
cross the brook Kidron.   From its bed, the road led up
the slope of Mount Olivet.   To the spectators the sight
was one of overwhelming sadness.   "All the country
wept with a loud voice, and all the people passed over ;
the king also himself passed over the brook Kidron,
and all the people passed over toward the way of the

wilderness." After all, there was a large number who
sympathised with the king, and to whom it was most
affecting to see one who was now "old and grey-headed "
driven from his throne and from his home by an
unprincipled son, aided and abetted by a graceless
generation who had no consideration for the countless
benefits which David had conferred on the nation.    It
is when we find " all the country " expressing their
sympathy that we cannot but doubt whether it was
really necessary for David to fly.    Perhaps "the
country" here may be used in contrast to the city.
Country people are less accessible to secret conspiracies,
and besides are less disposed to change their allegiance.
The event showed that in the more remote country
districts David had still a numerous following.    Time
to gather these friends together was his great need.    If
he had been fallen on that night, weary and desolate
and almost friendless, as was proposed by Ahithophel,
there can be no rational doubt what the issue would
have been.

And the king himself gave way to distress, like the
people, though for different reasons.    "David went up
by the ascent of Mount Olivet, and wept as he went
up, and had his head covered; and he went barefoot;
and all the people that was with him covered every
man his head, and they went up, weeping as they went
up."    The covered head and bare feet were tokens of
humiliation.    They were a humble confession on the
king's part that the affliction which had befallen him
was well deserved by him.    The whole attitude and
bearing of David is that of one " stricken, smitten, and
afflicted."    Lofty looks and a proud bearing had never
been among his weaknesses; but on this occasion, he
is so meek and lowly that the poorest person in his

kingdom could not have assumed a more humble bearing.  It is the feeling that had so wrung his heart in
the fifty-first Psalm come back on him again.  It is the
feeling, Oh, what a sinner I have been! how forgetful
of God I have often proved, and how unworthily I have
acted toward man!  No wonder that God rebukes me
and visits me with these troubles!  And not me only,
but my people too.  These are my children, for whom I
should have provided a peaceful home, driven into the
shelterless wilderness with me!  These kind people
who are compassionating me have been brought by me
into this trouble, which peradventure will cost them
their lives.  "Have mercy upon me, O God, according
to Thy lovingkindness; according unto the multitude
of Thy tender mercies, blot out my transgressions!"

It was at this time that some one brought word to
David that Ahithophel the Gilonite was among the
conspirators.  He seems to have been greatly distressed at the news.  For "the counsel of Ahithophel,
which he counselled in those days, was as if a man
had inquired of the oracle of God" (xvi. 23).  An
ingenious writer has found a reason for this step.
By comparing 2 Sam. xi. 3 with 2 Sam. xxiii. 34, in the
former of which Bathsheba is called the daughter of
Eliam, and in the latter Eliam is called the son of
Ahithophel, it would appear—if it be the same Eliam
in both—that Ahithophel was the grandfather of
Bathsheba.  From this it has been inferred that his
forsaking of David at this time was due to his displeasure at David's treatment of Bathsheba and Uriah.
The idea is ingenious, but after all it is hardly
trustworthy.  For if Ahithophel was a man of such
singular shrewdness, he would not be likely to let his
personal feelings determine his public conduct.  There

can be no reasonable doubt that, judging calmly from
the kind of considerations by which a worldly mind
like his would be influenced, he came to the deliberate
conclusion that Absalom was going to win.  And when
David heard of his defection, it must have given him
a double pang; first, because he would lose so valuable
a counsellor, and Absalom would gain what he would
lose; and second, because Ahithophel's choice showed
the side that, to his shrewd judgment, was going to
triumph.  David could but fall back on that higher
Counsellor on whose aid and countenance he was still
able to rely, and offer a short but expressive prayer, " O
Lord, I pray Thee, turn the counsel of Ahithophel into
foolishness."

It was but a few minutes after this that another
distinguished counsellor, Hushai the Archite, came to
him, with his clothes rent and dust on his head, signify-
ing his sense of the public calamity, and his adherence
to David.  Him too, as well as Ittai and the priests,
David wished to send back.  And the reason assigned
showed that his mind was now calm and clear, and
able to ponder the situation in all its bearings.  Indeed,
he concocts quite a little scheme with Hushai.  First,
he is to go to Absalom and pretend to be on his side.
But his main business will be to oppose the counsel of
Ahithophel, try to secure a little time to David, and
thus give him a chance of escape.  Moreover, he is to
co-operate with the priests Zadok and Abiathar, and
through their sons send word to David of everything
he hears.  Hushai obeys David, and as he returns to
the city from the east, Absalom arrives from the south,
before David is more than three or four miles away.
But for the Mount of Olives intervening, Absalom
might have seen the company that followed his father

creeping slowly along the wilderness, a company that could hardly be called an army, and that, humanly speaking, might have been scattered like a puff of smoke.

Thus Absalom gets possession of Jerusalem without a blow. He goes to his father's house, and takes possession of all that he finds there. He cannot but feel the joy of gratified ambition, the joy of the successful accomplishment of his elaborate and long-prosecuted scheme. Times are changed, he would naturally reflect, since I had to ask my father's leave for everything I did, since I could not even go to Hebron without begging him to allow me. Times are changed since I reared that monument in the vale for want of anything else to keep my name alive. Now that I am king, my name will live without a monument. The success of the revolution was so remarkable, that if Absalom had believed in God, he might have imagined, judging from the way in which everything had fallen out in his favour, that Providence was on his side. But, surely, there must have been a hard constraint and pressure upon his feelings somewhere. Conscience could not be utterly inactive. Fresh efforts to silence it must have been needed from time to time. Amid all the excitement of success, a vague horror must have stolen in on his soul. A vision of outraged justice would haunt him. He might scare away the hideous spectre for a time, but he could not lay it in the grave. " There is no peace, saith my God, to the wicked."

But if Absalom might well be haunted by a spectre because he had driven his father from his house, and God's anointed from his throne, there was a still more fearful reckoning standing against him, in that he had enticed such multitudes from their allegiance, and drawn them into the guilt of rebellion. There was not one of the many thousands that were now shouting "God save the king !" who had not been induced through him to do a great sin, and bring himself under the special displeasure of God. A rough nature like Absalom's would make light of this result of his movement, as rough natures have done since the world began. But a very different judgment was passed by the great Teacher on the effects of leading others into sin. " Whosoever shall break one of these least commandments and teach men so, he shall be called least in the kingdom of God." "Whoso shall cause one of these little ones which believe in Me to stumble, it were better for him that a millstone were hanged about his neck and he were cast in the depth of the sea." Yet how common a thing this has been in all ages of the world, and how common it is still ! To put pressure on others to do wrong ; to urge them to trifle with their consciences, or knowingly to violate them ; to press them to give a vote against their convictions ;—all such methods of disturbing conscience and drawing men into crooked ways, what sin they involve ! And when a man of great influence employs it with hundreds and thousands of people in such ways, twisting consciences, disturbing self-respect, bringing down Divine displeasure, how forcibly we are reminded of the proverb, " One sinner destroyeth much good " !

Most earnestly should every one who has influence over others dread being guilty of debauching conscience, and discouraging obedience to its call. On the other hand, how blessed is it to use one's influence in the opposite direction. Think of the blessedness of a life spent in enlightening others as to truth and duty, and encouraging loyalty to their high but often difficult claims. What a contrast to the other! What a noble aim to try to make men's eye single and their duty easy; to try to raise them above selfish and carnal motives, and inspire them with a sense of the nobility of walking uprightly, and working righteousness, and speaking the truth in their hearts! What a privilege to be able to induce our fellows to walk in some degree even as He walked "who did no sin, neither was guile found in His mouth;" and who, in ways so high above our ways, was ever influencing the children of men " to do justly, and to love mercy, and to walk humbly with their God"!

# CHAPTER XXI.

*FROM JERUSALEM TO MAHANAIM.*

2 SAMUEL xvi. 1—14; xvii. 15—22 and 24—26.

AS David proceeds on his painful journey, there flows from his heart a gentle current of humble contrite, gracious feeling. If recent events have thrown any doubt on the reality of his goodness, this fragrant narrative will restore the balance. Many a man would have been beside himself with rage at the treatment he had undergone. Many another man would have been restless with terror, looking behind him every other moment to see if the usurper's army was not hastening in pursuit of him. It is touching to see David, mild, self-possessed, thoroughly humble, and most considerate of others. Adversity is the element in which he shines; it is in prosperity he falls; in adversity he rises beautifully. After the humbling events in his life to which our attention has been lately called, it is a relief to witness the noble bearing of the venerable saint amid the pelting of this most pitiless storm.

It was when David was a little past the summit of Mount Olivet, and soon after he had sent back Hushai, that Ziba came after him,—that servant of Saul that had told him of Mephibosheth the son of Jonathan, and whom he had appointed to take charge of the property

that had belonged to Saul, now made over to Mephibosheth. The young man himself was to be as one of
the king's sons, and was to eat at the royal table.
Ziba's account of him was, that when he heard of the
insurrection he remained at Jerusalem, in the expectation that on that very day the kingdom of his father
would be restored to him. It can hardly be imagined
that Mephibosheth was so silly as to think or say anything of the kind. Either Ziba must have been slander-
ing him now, or Mephibosheth must have slandered
Ziba when David returned (see 2 Sam. xix. 24-30).
With that remarkable impartiality which distinguishes
the history, the facts and the statements of the parties
are recorded as they occurred, but we are left to form
our own judgment regarding them. All things considered, it is likely that Ziba was the slanderer and
Mephibosheth the injured man. Mephibosheth was
too feeble a man, both in mind and in body, to be
forming bold schemes by which he might benefit from
the insurrection. We prefer to believe that the son
of Jonathan had so much of his father's nobility as to
cling to David in the hour of his trial, and be desirous
of throwing in his lot with him. If, however, Ziba
was a slanderer and a liar, the strange thing about him
is that he should have taken this opportunity to give
effect to his villainy. It is strange that, with a soul full
of treachery, he should have taken the trouble to come
after David at all, and still more that he should have
made a contribution to his scanty stores. We should
have expected such a man to remain with Absalom,
and look to him for the reward of unrighteousness.
He brought with him for David's use a couple of asses
saddled, and two hundred loaves of bread, and an
hundred clusters of raisins, and an hundred of summer

fruits, and a bottle of wine. We get a vivid idea of the extreme haste with which David and his company must have left Jerusalem, and their destitution of the very necessaries of life as they fled, from this catalogue of Ziba's contributions. Not even were there beasts of burden "for the king's household"—even Bathsheba and Solomon may have been going on foot. David was evidently impressed by the gift, and his opinion of Mephibosheth was not so high as to prevent him from believing that he was capable of the course ascribed to him. Yet we cannot but think there was undue haste in his at once transferring to Ziba the whole of Mephibosheth's property. We can only say, in vnidication of David, that his confidence even in those who had been most indebted to him had received so rude a shock in the conduct of Absalom, that he was ready to say in his haste, "All men are liars;" he was ready to suspect every man of deserting him, except those that gave palpable evidence that they were on his side. In this number it seemed at the moment that Ziba was, while Mephibosheth was not; and trusting to his first impression, and acting with the promptitude necessary in war, he made the transfer. It is true that afterwards he discovered his mistake; and some may think that when he did he did not make a sufficient rectification. He directed Ziba and Mephibosheth to divide the property between them; but in explanation it has been suggested that this was equivalent to the old arrangement, by which Ziba was to cultivate the land, and Mephibosheth to receive the fruits; and if half the produce went to the proprietor, and the other half to the cultivator, the arrangement may have been a just and satisfactory one after all.

But if Ziba sinned in the way of smooth treachery,

Shimei, the next person with whom David came in contact, sinned not less in the opposite fashion, by his outrageous insolence and invective. It is said of this man that he was of the family of the house of Saul, and that fact goes far to account for his atrocious behaviour. We get a glimpse of that inveterate jealousy of David which during the long period of his reign slept in the bosom of the family of Saul, and which seemed now. like a volcano, to burst out all the more fiercely for its long suppression. When the throne passed from the family of Saul, Shimei would of course experience a great social fall. To be no longer connected with the royal family would be a great mortification to one who was vain of such distinctions. Outwardly, he was obliged to bear his fall with resignation, but inwardly the spirit of disappointment and jealousy raged in his breast. When the opportunity of revenge against David came, the rage and venom of his spirit poured out in a filthy torrent. There is no mistaking the mean nature of the man to take such an opportunity of venting his malignity on David. To trample on the fallen, to press a man when his back is at the wall, to pierce with fresh wounds the body of a stricken warrior, is the mean resource of ungenerous cowardice. But it is too much the way of the world. "If there be any quarrels, any exceptions," says Bishop Hall, "against a man, let him look to have them laid in his dish when he fares the hardest. This practice have wicked men learned of their master, to take the utmost advantage of their afflictions."

If Shimei had contented himself with denouncing the policy of David, the forbearance of his victim would not have been so remarkable. But Shimei was guilty of every form of offensive and provoking assault. He

threw stones, he called abusive names, he hurled wicked
charges against David; he declared that God was
fighting against him, and fighting justly against such
a man of blood, such a man of Belial. And, as if this
were not enough, he stung him in the most sensitive
part of his nature, reproaching him with the fact that it
was his son that now reigned instead of him, because
the Lord had delivered the kingdom into his hand.
But even all this accumulation of coarse and shameful
abuse failed to ruffle David's equanimity. Abishai,
Joab's brother, was enraged at the presumption of a
fellow who had no right to take such an attitude, and
whose insolence deserved a prompt and sharp castiga-
tion. But David never thirsted for the blood of foes.
Even while the rocks were echoing Shimei's charges,
David gave very remarkable evidence of the spirit of a
chastened child of God. He showed the same forbearance that he had shown twice on former occasions
in sparing the life of Saul. "Why," asked Abishai,
"should this dead dog curse my lord the king? Let
me go, I pray thee, and take off his head." "So let
him curse," was David's answer, "because the Lord hath
said unto him, Curse David." It was but partially true
that the Lord had told him to do so. The Lord had
only permitted him to do it; He had only placed David
in circumstances which allowed Shimei to pour out his
insolence. This use of the expression, "The Lord hath
said unto him," may be a useful guide to its true meaning in some passages of Scripture where it has seemed
at first as if God gave very strange directions. The
pretext that Providence had afforded to Shimei was
this, "Behold, my son, which came out of my bowels,
seeketh my life; how much more then may this
Benjamite do it? Let him alone, and let him curse,

for the Lord hath bidden him.   It may be that the Lord
will requite me good for his cursing this day."   It is
touching to remark how keenly David felt this dreadful
trial as coming from his own son.

> " So the struck eagle stretched upon the plain,
> No more through rolling clouds to soar again,
> Viewed his own feather on the fatal dart
> That winged the shaft that quivered in his heart ;
> Keen were his pangs, but keener far to feel
> He nursed the pinion which impelled the steel ;
> While the same plumage that had warmed his nest
> Drank the last lifedrop of his bleeding breast."

But even the fact that it was his own son that was
the author of all his present calamities would not have
made David so meek under the outrage of Shimei if he
had not felt that God was using such men as instruments to chastise him for his sins.   For though God had
never said to Shimei, " Curse David," He had let him
become an instrument of chastisement and humiliation
against him.   It was the fact of his being such an instrument in God's hands that made the King so unwilling
to interfere with him.   David's reverence for God's
appointment was like that which afterwards led our
Lord to say, " The cup which My Father hath given
Me, shall I not drink of it ? "   Unlike though David and
Jesus were in the cause of their sufferings, yet there is
a remarkable resemblance in their bearing under them.
The meek resignation of David as he went out from the
holy city had a strong resemblance to the meek resignation of Jesus as He was being led from the same city
to Calvary.   The gentle consideration of David for the
welfare of his people as he toiled up Mount Olivet was
parallel to the same feeling of Jesus expressed to the
daughters of Jerusalem as He toiled up to Calvary.
The forbearance of David to Shimei was like the spirit

of the prayer—"Father, forgive them : for they know not what they do." The overawing sense that God had ordained their sufferings was similar in both. David owed his sufferings solely to himself; Jesus owed His solely to the relation in which He had placed Himself to sinners as the Sin-bearer. It is beautiful to see David so meek and lowly under the sense of his sins—breathing the spirit of the prophet's words, "I will stand upon my watch, and set me upon the tower, and will watch to see what he will say unto me, and what I shall answer when I am reproved."

There was another thought in David's mind that helped him to bear his sufferings with meek submission. It is this that is expressed in the words, "It may be that the Lord will requite me good for his cursing this day." He felt that, as coming from the hand of God, all that he had suffered was just and righteous. He had done wickedly, and he deserved to be humbled and chastened by God, and by such instruments as God might appoint. But the particular words and acts of these instruments might be highly unjust to him : though Shimei was God's instrument for humiliating him, yet the curses of Shimei were alike unrighteous and outrageous ; the charge that he had shed the blood of Saul's house, and seized Saul's kingdom by violence, was outrageously false ; but it was better to bear the wrong, and leave the rectifying of it in God's hands ; for God detests unfair dealing, and when His servants receive it He will look to it and redress it in His own time and way. And this is a very important and valuable consideration for those servants of God who are exposed to abusive language and treatment from scurrilous opponents, or, what is too common in our day, scurrilous newspapers. If injustice is done them, let them, like David, trust to God to redress the wrong ; God is a God of justice, and God will not see them treated unjustly.   And hence that remarkable statement which forms a sort of appendix to the seven beatitudes —" Blessed are ye when men shall revile you and persecute you, and speak all manner of evil against you falsely for My name's sake.   Rejoice and be exceeding glad, for great is your reward in heaven ; for so persecuted they the prophets that were before you."

Ere we return to Jerusalem to witness the progress of events in Absalom's camp and cabinet, let us accompany David to his resting-place beyond the Jordan.   Through the counsel of Hushai, afterwards to be considered, he had reachec the plains of Jordan in safety ; had accomplished the passage of the river, and traversed the path on the other side as far as Mahanaim, somewhere to the south of the Lake of Gennesareth, the place where Ishbosheth had held his court.   It was a singular mercy that he was able to accomplish this journey, which in the condition of his followers must have occupied several days, without opposition in front or molestation in his rear.   Tokens of the Lord's loving care were not wanting to encourage him on the way.   It must have been a great relief to him to learn that Ahithophel's proposal of an immediate pursuit had been arrested through the counsel of Hushai.   It was a further token for good, that the lives of the priests' sons, Jonathan and Ahimaaz, which had been endangered as they bore tidings for him, had been mercifully preserved.   After learning the result of Hushai's counsel, they proceeded, incautiously perhaps, to reach David, and were observed and pursued.   But a friendly woman concealed them in a well, as Rahab the harlot had hid the spies in the roof of her house ; and though they ran a great risk, they contrived to reach David's camp in peace.

And when David reached Mahanaim, where he halted to await the course of events, Shobi, the son of Nahash, king of Ammon, and Machir, the son of Ammiel of Lo-debar, and Barzillai the Gileadite of Rogelim, brought beds, and basons, and earthen vessels, and wheat, and barley, and flour, and parched corn, and beans, and lentiles, and parched pulse, and honey, and butter, and sheep, and cheese of kine, for David and for the people that were with him to eat; for they said, The people is hungry, and weary, and thirsty in the wilderness." Some of those who thus befriended him were only requiting former favours. Shobi may be supposed to have been ashamed of his father's insulting conduct when David sent messengers to comfort him on his father's death. Machir, the son of Ammiel of Lo-debar, was the friend who had cared for Mephibosheth, and was doubtless thankful for David's generosity to him. Of Barzillai we know nothing more than is told us here. But David could not have reckoned on the friendship of these men, nor on its taking so useful and practical a turn. The Lord's hand was manifest in the turning of the hearts of these people to him. How hard bestead he and his followers were is but too apparent from the fact that these supplies were most welcome in their condition. And David must have derived no small measure of encouragement even from these trifling matters; they showed that God had not forgotten him, and they raised the expectation that further tokens of His love and care would not be withheld.

The district where David now was, "the other side of Jordan," lay far apart from Jerusalem and the more frequented places in the country, and, in all probability, it was but little affected by the arts of Absalom.   The inhabitants lay under strong obligations to David ; in former times they had suffered most from their neighbours, Moab, Ammon, and especially Syria ; and now they enjoyed a very different lot, owing to the fact that those powerful nations had been brought under David's rule.   It was a fertile district, abounding in all kinds of farm and garden produce, and therefore well adapted to support an army that had no regular means of supply.   The people of this district seem to have been friendly to David's cause.   The little force that had followed him from Jerusalem would now be largely recruited ; and, even to the outward sense, he would be in a far better condition to receive the assault of Absalom than on the day when he left the city.

The third Psalm, according to the superscription— and in this case there seems no cause to dispute it— was composed "when David fled from Absalom his son." It is a psalm of wonderful serenity and perfect trust. It begins with a touching reference to the multitude of the insurgents, and the rapidity with which they increased.   Everything confirms the statement that "the conspiracy was strong, and that the people increased continually with Absalom."   We seem to understand better why David fled from Jerusalem ; even there the great bulk of the people were with the usurper.   We see, too, how godless and unbelieving the conspirators were—"Many there be which say of my soul, There is no help for him in God."   God was cast out of their reckoning as of no consideration in the case ; it was all moonshine, his pretended trust in Him. Material forces were the only real power ; the idea of God's favour was only cant, or at best but "a devout imagination." But the foundation of his trust was too firm to be shaken either by the multitude of the insurgents or the bitterness of their sneers. "Thou, Lord, art a shield unto me"—ever protecting me, "my glory,"—ever honouring me, "and the lifter up of mine head,"—ever setting me on high because I have known Thy name. No doubt he had felt some tumult of soul when the insurrection began. But prayer brought him tranquillity. "I cried unto God with my voice, and He heard me out of His holy hill." How real the communion must have been that brought tranquillity to him amid such a sea of trouble! Even in the midst of his agitation he can lie down and sleep, and awake refreshed in mind and body. "I will not be afraid of ten thousands of the people that have set themselves against me round about." Faith already sees his enemies defeated and receiving the doom of ungodly men. "Arise, O Lord; save me, O my God; for Thou hast smitten all mine enemies upon the cheek bone; Thou hast broken the teeth of the ungodly." And he closes as confidently and serenely as if victory had already come—"Salvation belongeth unto the Lord; Thy blessing is upon Thy people."

If, in this solemn crisis of his history, David is a pattern to us of meek submission, not less is he a pattern of perfect trust. He is strong in faith, giving glory to God, and feeling assured that what He has promised He is able also to perform. Deeply conscious of his own sin, he at the same time most cordially believes in the word and promise of God. He knows that, though chastened, he is not forsaken. He bows his head in meek acknowledgment of the righteousness of the chastisement; but he lays hold with unwavering trust on the mercy of God. This union of submission and trust, is one of priceless value, and much to be sought by every good man. Under the deepest sense of sin and unworthiness, you may rejoice and you ought to rejoice, in the provision of grace. And while rejoicing most cordially in the provision of grace, you ought to be contrite and humble for your sin. You are grievously defcetive if you want either of these elements. If the sense of ain weighs on you with unbroken pressure, if it keeps you from believing in forgiving mercy, if it hinders you from looking to the cross, to Him who taketh away the sin of the world, there is a grievous defect. If your joy in forgiving mercy has no element of contrition, no chastened sense of unworthiness, there is no less grievous a defect in the opposite direction. Let us try at once to feel our unworthiness, and to rejoice in the mercy that freely pardons and accepts. Let us look to the rock whence we are hewn, and to the hole of the pit whence we are digged ; feeling that we are great sinners, but that the Lord Jesus Christ is a great Saviour ; and finding our joy in that faithful saying, ever worthy of all acceptation, that " Jesus Christ came into the world to save sinners," even the chief.

# CHAPTER XXII.

## *ABSALOM IN COUNCIL.*

**2 SAMUEL xvi. 15—23 ; xvii. 1—14, and ver. 23.**

WE must now return to Jerusalem, and trace the course of events there on that memorable day when David left it, to flee toward the wilderness, just a few hours before Absalom entered it from Hebron.

When Absalom came to the city, there was no trace of an enemy to oppose him. His supporters in Jerusalem would no doubt go out to meet him, and conduct him to the palace with great demonstrations of delight. Eastern nations are so easily roused to enthusiasm that we can easily believe that, even for Absalom, there would be an overpowering demonstration of loyalty. Once within the palace, he would receive the adherence and congratulations of his friends.

Among these, Hushai the Archite presents himself, having returned to Jerusalem at David's request, and it is to Hushai's honour that Absalom was surprised to see him. He knew him to be too good a man, too congenial with David " his friend," to be likely to follow such a standard as his. There is much to be read between the lines here. Hushai was not only a counsellor, but a friend, of David's. They were probably of kindred feeling in religious matters, earnest in serving God. A man of this sort did not seem to be in his own place among the supporters of Absalom. It was a silent confession by Absalom that his supporters were a godless crew, among whom a man of godliness must be out of his element. The sight of Hushai impressed Absalom as the sight of an earnest Christian in a gambling saloon or on a racecourse would impress the greater part of worldly men. For even the world has a certain faith in godliness,—to this extent, at least, that it ought to be consistent. You may stretch a point here and there in order to gain favour with worldly men ; you may accommodate yourselves to their ways, go to this and to that place of amusement, adopt their tone of conversation, join with them in ridiculing the excesses of this or that godly man or woman ; but you are not to expect that by such approaches you will rise in their esteem. On the contrary, you may expect that in their secret hearts they will despise you. A man that acts according to his convictions and in the spirit of what he professes they may very cordially hate, but they are constrained to respect. A man that does violence to the spirit of his religion, in his desire to be on friendly terms with the world and further his interests, and that does many things to please them, they may not hate so strongly, but they will not respect. There is a fitness of things to which the world is sometimes more alive than Christians themselves. Jehoshaphat is not in his own place making a league with Ahab, and going up with him against Ramoth-gilead ; he lays himself open to the rebuke of the seer—" Shouldest thou help the ungodly, and love them that hate the Lord ? therefore is wrath upon thee from before the Lord." There is no New Testament precept needing to be more pondered than this—" Be ye not unequally yoked with unbelievers ; for what communion hath light with darkness? or what fellowship hath Christ with Belial? or what communion hath he that believeth with an infidel?"

But Hushai was not content with putting in a silent appearance for Absalom. When his consistency is challenged, he must repudiate the idea that he has any preference for David; he is a loyal man in this sense, that he attaches himself to the reigning monarch, and as Absalom has received overwhelming tokens in his favour from every quarter, Hushai is resolved to stand by him. But can we justify these professions of Hushai? It is plain enough he went on the principle of fighting Absalom with his own weapons, of paying him with his own coin; Absalom had dissembled so profoundly, he had made treachery, so to speak, so much the current coin of the kingdom, that Hushai determined to use it for his own purposes. Yet, even in these circumstances, the deliberate dissembling of Hushai grates against every tender conscience, and more especially his introduction of the name of Jehovah —" Nay, but whom the Lord, and this people, and all the men of Israel choose, his will I be, and with him will I abide." Was not this taking the name of the Lord his God in vain? The stratagem had been suggested by David; it was not condemned by the voice of the age; and we are not prepared to say that stratagem is always to be condemned; but surely, in our time, the claims of truth and fair dealing would stamp it as a disreputable device, not sanctified by the end for which it was resorted to, and not worthy the followers of Him "who did no sin, neither was guile found in His mouth."

Having established himself in the confidence of Absalom, Hushai gained a right to be consulted in

the deliberations of the day. He enters the room
where the new king's counsellors are met, but he finds
it a godless assemblage. In planning the most awful
wickedness, a cool deliberation prevails that shows
how familiar the counsellors are with the ways of
sin. "Give counsel among you," says the royal presi-
dent, "what we shall do." How different from David's
way of opening the business—" Bring hither the ephod,
and enquire of the Lord." In Absalom's council help
of that kind is neither asked nor desired.

The first to propose a course is Ahithophel, and
there is something so revolting in the first scheme
which he proposed that we wonder much that such
a man should ever have been a counsellor of David.
His first piece of advice, that Absalom should publicly
take possession of his father's concubines, was designed
to put an end to any wavering among the people; it
was, according to Eastern ideas, the grossest insult
that could be offered to a king, and that king a father,
and it would prove that the breach between David and
Absalom was irreparable, that it was vain to hope for
any reconciliation. They must all make up their minds
to take a side, and as Absalom's cause was so popular,
it was far the most likely they would side with him.
Without hesitation Absalom complied with the advice.
It is a proof how hard his heart had become, that he
did not hesitate to mock his father by an act which
was as disgusting as it was insulting. And what a
picture we get of the position of women even in the
court of King David! They were slaves in the worst
sense of the term, with no right even to guard their
virtue, or to protect their persons from the very worst
of men; for the custom of the country, when it gave
him the throne, gave him likewise the bodies and

souls of the women of the harem to do with as he pleased!

The next piece of Ahithophel's counsel was a master-piece alike of sagacity and of wickedness. He proposed to take a select body of twelve thousand out of the troops that had already flocked to Absalom's standard, and follow the fugitive king. That very night he would set out; and in a few hours they would over-take the king and his handful of defenders; they would destroy no life but the king's only; and thus, by an almost bloodless revolution, they would place Absalom peacefully on the throne. The advantages of the plan were obvious. It was prompt, it seemed certain of success, and it would avoid an unpopular slaughter. So strongly was Ahithophel impressed with the advan-tages that it seemed impossible that it could be opposed, far less rejected. One element only he left out of his reckoning—that " as the mountains are round about Jerusalem, so the Lord God is round about His people from henceforth even for ever." He forgot how many methods of protecting David God had already employed From the lion and the bear He had delivered him in his youth, by giving strength to his arm and courage to his heart; from the uncircumcised Philistine He had delivered him by guiding the stone projected from his sling to the forehead of the giant; from Saul, at one time through Michal letting him down from a window; at another, through Jonathan taking his side; at a third, by an invasion of the Philistines calling Saul away; and now He was preparing to deliver him from Absalom by a still different method: by causing the shallow proposal of Hushai to find more favour than the sagacious counsel of Ahithophel.

It must have been a moment of great anxiety to

Hushai when the man whose counsel was as the oracle
of God sat down amid universal approval, after having
propounded the very advice of which he was most afraid.
But he shows great coolness and skill in recommending
his own course, and in trying to make the worse
appear the better reason. He opens with an implied
compliment to Ahithophel—his counsel is not good *at
this time.* It may have been excellent on all other
occasions, but the present is an exception. Then he
dwells on the warlike character of David and his men,
and on the exasperated state of mind in which they
might be supposed to be; probably they were at that
moment in some cave, where no idea of their numbers
could be got, and from which they might make a
sudden sally on Absalom's troops; and if, on occasion
of an encounter between the two armies, some of
Absalom's were to fall, people would take it as a defeat;
a panic might seize the army, and his followers might
disperse as quickly as they had assembled.

But the concluding stroke was the masterpiece. He
knew that vanity was Absalom's besetting sin. The
young man that had prepared chariots and horses, and
fifty men to run before him, that had been accustomed
to poll his head from year to year and weigh it with
so much care, and whose praise was throughout all
Israel for beauty, must be flattered by a picture of the
whole host of Israel marshalled around him, and going
forth in proud array, with him at its head. " Therefore
I counsel that all Israel be generally gathered unto thee,
from Dan even to Beersheba, as the sand that is by
the sea for multitude, and that thou go to battle in
thine own person. So shall we come upon him in
some place where he may be found, and we will light
upon him as the dew falleth on the ground; and of

him and of all the men that are with him there shall not be left so much as one.  Moreover, if he be gotten into a city, then shall all Israel bring ropes to that city, and we will draw it into the river until there shall not be one small stone left there."

It is with counsel as with many other things : what pleases best is thought best; solid merit gives way to superficial plausibility.  The counsel of Hushai pleased better than that of Ahithophel, and so it was preferred.  Satan had outwitted himself.  He had nursed in Absalom an overweening vanity, intending by its means to overturn the throne of David ; and now that very vanity becomes the means of defeating the scheme, and laying the foundation of Absalom's ruin.  The turning-point in Absalom's mind seems to have been the magnificent spectacle of the whole of Israel mustered for battle, and Absalom at their head.  He was fascinated by the brilliant imagination.  How easily may God, when He pleases, defeat the most able schemes of His enemies !  He does not need to create weapons to oppose them ; He has only to turn their own weapons against themselves.  What an encouragement to faith even when the fortunes of the Church are at their lowest ebb !  " The kings of the earth set themselves, and the rulers take counsel together against the Lord, and against His anointed, saying, Let us break their bonds asunder, and cast away their cords from us.  He that sitteth in the heavens shall laugh; the Lord shall have them in derision.  Then shall He speak to them in wrath, and vex them in His sore displeasure.  Yet have I set my king upon my holy hill of Zion."

The council is over ; Hushai, unspeakably relieved, hastens to communicate with the priests, and through them send messengers to David ; Absalom withdraws to

delight himself with the thought of the great military
muster that is to flock to his standard ; while Ahithophel, in high dudgeon, retires to his house.   The
character of Ahithophel was a singular combination.
To deep natural sagacity he united great spiritual
blindness and lack of true manliness.   He saw at once
the danger to the cause of Absalom in the plan that
had been preferred to his own ; but it was not that
consideration, it was the gross affront to himself that
preyed on him, and drove him to commit suicide.
"When Ahithophel saw that his counsel was not
followed, he saddled his ass and arose and gat him
home to his house, to his city, and put his household
in order, and hanged himself and died, and was buried
in the sepulchre of his father."   In his own way he
was as much the victim of vanity as Absalom.   The
one was vain of his person, the other of his wisdom.
In each case it was the man's vanity that was the
cause of his death.   What a contrast Ahithophel was
to David in his power of bearing disgrace !—David,
though with bowed head, bearing up so bravely, and
even restraining his followers from chastising some
of those who were so vehemently affronting him ;
Ahithophel unable to endure life because for once
another man's counsel had been preferred to his.   Men
of the richest gifts have often shown themselves babes
in self-control.   Ahithophel is the Judas of the New
Testament, lays plans for the destruction of his master,
and, like Judas, falls almost immediately, by his own
hand.   "What a mixture," says Bishop Hall, "do we
find here of wisdom and madness !   Ahithophel will
needs hang himself, *there* is madness ; he will yet set
his house in order, *there* is wisdom.   And could it be
possible that he that was so wise as to set his house

in order was so mad as to hang himself ? that he should be so careful to order his house who had no care to order his unruly passions ? that he should care for his house who cared not for his body or his soul ? How vain is it for man to be wise if he is not wise in God. How preposterous are the cares of idle world-lings, that prefer all other things to themselves, and while they look at what they have in their coffers forget what they have in their breasts."

This council-chamber of Absalom is full of material for profitable reflection. The manner in which he was turned aside from the way of wisdom and safety is a re-markable illustration of our Lord's principle— " If thine eye be single, thy whole body shall be full of light." We are accustomed to view this principle chiefly in its relation to moral and spiritual life ; but it is applicable likewise even to worldly affairs. Absalom's eye was not single. Success, no doubt, was the chief object at which he aimed, but another object was the gratification of his vanity. This inferior object was allowed to come in and disturb his judgment. If Absalom had had a single eye, even in a worldly sense, he would have felt profoundly that the one thing to be considered was, how to get rid of David and establish himself firmly on the throne. But instead of studying this one thing with firm and immovable purpose, he allowed the vision of a great muster of troops commanded by himself to come in, and so to distract his judgment that he gave his decision for the latter course. No doubt he thought that his position was so secure that he could afford the few days' delay which this scheme involved. All the same, it was this disturbing element of personal vanity that gave a twist to his vision, and led him to the con-clusion which lost him everything.

For even in worldly things, singleness of eye is a great
help towards a sound conclusion. " To the upright there
ariseth light in the darkness." And if this rule hold true
in the worldly sphere, much more in the moral and
spiritual. It is when you have the profoundest desire
to do what is right that you are in the best way to
know what is wise. In the service of God you are
grievously liable to be distracted by private feelings and
interests of your own. It is when these private interests
assert themselves that you are most liable to lose the
clear line of duty and of wisdom. You wish to do
God's will, but at the same time you are very unwilling
to sacrifice this interest, or expose yourself to that
trouble. Thus your own feeling becomes a screen that
dims your vision, and prevents you from seeing the path
of duty and wisdom alike. You have not a clear sight
of the right path. You live in an atmosphere of per-
plexity ; whereas men of more single purpose, and
more regardless of their own interests, see clearly and
act wisely. Was there anything more remarkable in
the Apostle Paul than the clearness of his vision, the
decisive yet admirable way in which he solved perplexing
questions, and the high practical wisdom that guided
him throughout ? And is not this to be connected with
his singleness of eye, his utter disregard of personal
interests in his public life—his entire devotion to the
will and to the service of his Master? From that
memorable hour on the way to Damascus, when he put
the question, " Lord, what wilt Thou have me to
do ? " onward to the day when he laid his head on the
block in imperial Rome, the one interest of his heart,
the one thought of his mind, was to do the will of Christ.
Never was an eye more single, and never was a body
more full of light.

But again, from that council-chamber of Absalom and its results we learn how all projects founded on godlessness and selfishness carry in their bosom the elements of dissolution. They have no true principle of coherence, no firm, binding element, to secure them against disturbing influences arising from further manifestations of selfishness on the part of those engaged in them. Men may be united by selfish interest in some undertaking up to a certain point, but, like a rocket in the air, selfishness is liable to burst up in a thousand different directions, and then the bond of union is destroyed. The only bond of union that can resist distracting tendencies is an immovable regard to the will of God, and, in subordination thereto, to the welfare of men. In our fallen world it is seldom—rather, it is never —that any great enterprise is undertaken and carried forward on grounds where selfishness has no place whatever. But we may say this very confidently, that the more an undertaking is based on regard to God's will and the good of men, the more stability and true prosperity will it enjoy; whereas every element of selfishness or self-seeking that may be introduced into it is an element of weakness, and tends to its dissolution. The remark is true of Churches and religious societies, of religious movements and political movements too.

Men that are not overawed, as it were, by a supreme regard to the will of God; men to whom the consideration of that will is not strong enough at once to smite down every selfish feeling that may arise in their minds, will always be liable to desire some object of their own rather than the good of the whole. They will begin to complain if they are not sufficiently considered and honoured. They will allow jealousies and suspicions towards those who have most influence to arise in their hearts. They will get into caves to air their discontent with those like-minded. All this tends to weakness and dissolution. Selfishness is the serpent that comes crawling into many a hopeful garden, and brings with it division and desolation. In private life, it should be watched and thwarted as the grievous foe of all that is good and right. The same course should be taken with regard to it in all the associations of Christians. And it is Christian men only that are capable of uniting on grounds so high and pure as to give some hope that this evil spirit will not succeed in disuniting them—that is to say, men who feel and act on the obligations under which the Lord Jesus Christ has placed them ; men that feel that their own redemption, and every blessing they have or hope to have, come through the wonderful self-denial of the Son of God, and that if they have the faintest right to His holy name they must not shrink from the like self-denial. It is a happy thing to be able to adopt as our rule—" None of us liveth to himself ; for whether we live, we live unto the Lord, or whether we die, we die unto the Lord ; whether we live therefore or die, we are the Lord's." The more this rule prevails in Churches and Christian societies, the more will there be of union and stability too; but with its neglect, all kinds of evil and trouble will come in, and very probably, disruption and dissolution in the end.

# CHAPTER XXIII.

2 SAMUEL xviii. 1—18.

## *ABSALOM'S DEFEAT AND DEATH.*

WHATEVER fears of defeat and destruction might occasionally flit across David's soul between his flight from Jerusalem and the battle in the wood of Ephraim, it is plain both from his actions and from his songs that his habitual frame was one of serenity and trust. The number of psalms ascribed to this period of his life may be in excess of the truth; but that his heart was in near communion with God all the time we cannot doubt. Situated as his present refuge was not far from Peniel, where Jacob had wrestled with the angel, we may believe that there were wrestlings again in the neighbourhood not unworthy to be classed with that from which Peniel derived its memorable name.

In the present emergency the answer to prayer consisted, first, in the breathing-time secured by the success of Hushai's counsel; second, in the countenance and support of the friends raised up to David near Mahanaim; and last, not least, in the spirit of wisdom and harmony with which all the arrangements were made for the inevitable encounter. Every step was taken with prudence, while every movement of his opponents seems to have been a blunder. It was wise in David, as we have already seen, to cross the Jordan

and retire into Gilead ; it was wise in him to make
Mahanaim his headquarters ; it was wise to divide his
army into three parts, for a reason that will presently
be seen ; and it was wise to have a wood in the neighbourhood of the battlefield, though it could not have
been foreseen how this was to bear on the individual
on whose behalf the insurrection had taken place.

By this time the followers of David had grown to
the dimensions of an army. We are furnished with no
means of knowing its actual number. Josephus puts it
at four thousand, but, judging from some casual expressions ("David set captains of hundreds and *captains
of thousands* over them," ver. 1 ; " Now thou art worth
*ten thousand* of us," ver. 3 ; "The people came by
thousands," ver. 4), we should infer that David's force
amounted to a good many thousands. The division of
the army into three parts, however, reminding us, as
it does, of Gideon's division of his little force into
three, would seem to imply that David's force was far
inferior in number to Absalom's. The insurrectionary
army must have been very large, and stretching over a
great breadth of country, would have presented far too
wide a line to be effectually dealt with by a single body
of troops, comparatively small. Gideon had divided his
handful into three that he might make a simultaneous
impression on three different parts of the Midianite
host, and thus contribute the better to the defeat of the
whole. So David divided his army into three, that,
meeting Absalom's at three different points, he might
prevent a concentration of the enemy that would have
swallowed up his whole force. David had the advantage of choosing his ground, and his military instinct
and long experience would doubtless enable him to do
this with great effect. His three generals were able

and valuable leaders. The aged king was prepared to take part in the battle, believing that his presence would be helpful to his men; but the people would not allow him to run the risk. Aged and somewhat infirm as he seems to have been, wearied with his flight, and weakened with the anxieties of so distressing an occasion, the excitement of the battle might have proved too much for him, even if he had escaped the enemy's sword. Besides, everything depended on him; if his place were discovered by the enemy, their hottest assault would be directed to it; and if he should fall, there would be left no cause to fight for. " It is better," they said to him, " that thou succour us out of the city." What kind of succour could he render there? Only the succour that Moses and his two attendants rendered to Israel in the fight with Amalek in the wilderness, when Moses held up his hands, and Aaron and Hur propped them up. He might pray for them; he could do no more.

By this time Absalom had probably obtained the great object of his ambition; he had mustered Israel from Dan to Beersheba, and found himself at the head of an array very magnificent in appearance, but, like most Oriental gatherings of the kind, somewhat unwieldy and unworkable. This great conglomeration was now in the immediate neighbourhood of Mahanaim, and must have seemed as if by sheer weight of material it would crush any force that could be brought against it. We read that the battle took place " in the wood of Ephraim." This could not be a wood in the tribe of Ephraim, for that was on the other side of Jordan, but a wood in Gilead, that for some reason unknown to us had been called by that name. The whole region is still richly wooded, and among its prominent trees is one called the prickly oak. A *dense* wood would obviously be unsuitable for battle, but a wooded district, with clumps here and there, especially on the hill-sides, and occasional trees and brushwood scattered over the plains, would present many advantages to a smaller force opposing the onset of a larger. In the American war of 1755 some of the best troops of England were nearly annihilated in a wood near Pittsburg in Pennsylvania, the Indians levelling their rifles unseen from behind the trees, and discharging them with yells that were even more terrible than their weapons. We may fancy the three battalions of David making a vigorous onslaught on Absalom's troops as they advanced into the wooded country, and when they began to retreat through the woods, and got entangled in brushwood, or jammed together by thickset trees, discharging arrows at them, or falling on them with the sword, with most disastrous effect. " There was a great slaughter that day of twenty thousand men. For the battle there was scattered over the face of all the country, and the wood devoured more people that day than the sword devoured." Many of David's men were probably natives of the country, and in their many encounters with the neighbouring nations had become familiar with the warfare of "the bush." Here was one benefit of the choice of Mahanaim by David as his rallying-ground. The people that joined him from that quarter knew the ground, and knew how to adapt it to fighting purposes; the most of Absalom's forces had been accustomed to the bare wadies and limestone rocks of Western Palestine, and, when caught in the thickets, could neither use their weapons nor save themselves by flight.

Very touching, if not very business-like, had been

David's instructions to his generals about Absalom :
" The king commanded Joab and Abishai and Ittai
saying, Deal gently for my sake with the young man,
even with Absalom.    And all the people heard when
the king gave all the captains charge concerning
Absalom."   It is interesting to observe that David fully
expects to win.    There is no hint of any alternative,
as if Absalom would not fall into their hands.    David
knows that he is going to conquer, as well as he knew
it when he went against the giant.    The confidence
which is breathed in the third Psalm is apparent here.
Faith saw his enemies already defeated.    " Thou hast
smitten all mine enemies upon the cheekbone ; Thou
hast broken the teeth of the ungodly.    Salvation belongeth unto the Lord ; Thy blessing is upon Thy
people."    In a pitched battle, God could not give
success to a godless crew, whose whole enterprise was
undertaken to drive God's anointed one from his
throne.    Temporary and partial successes they might
have, but final success it was morally impossible for
God to accord.    It was not the spirit of his own troops,
nor the undisciplined condition of the opposing host,
that inspired this confidence, but the knowledge that
there was a God in Israel, who would not suffer His
anointed to perish, nor the impious usurper to triumph
over him.

We cannot tell whether Absalom was visited with
any misgivings as to the result before the battle began.
Very probably he was not.    Having no faith in God,
he would make no account whatever of what David
regarded as the Divine palladium of his cause.    But
if he entered on the battle confident of success, his
anguish is not to be conceived when he saw his troops
yield to panic, and, in wild disorder, try to dash through

the wood.  Dreadful miseries must have overwhelmed
him.  He does not appear to have made any attempt
to rally his troops.  Riding on a mule, in his haste to
escape, he probably plunged into some thick part of the
wood, where his head came in contact with a mass of
prickly oak ; struggling to make a way through it, he
only entangled his hair more hopelessly in the thicket ;
then, raising himself in the saddle to attack it with
his hands, his mule went from under him, and left him
hanging between heaven and earth, maddened by pain,
enraged at the absurdity of his plight, and storming
against his attendants, none of whom was near him
in his time of need.  Nor was this the worst of it.
Absalom was probably among the foremost of the
fugitives, and we can hardly suppose but that many of
his own people fled that way after him.  Could it be
that all of them were so eager to escape that not one
of them would stop to help their king ?  What a contrast the condition of Absalom when fortune turned
against him to that of his father !  Dark though
David's trials had been, and seemingly desperate his
position, he had not been left alone in its sudden
horrors ; the devotion of strangers, as well as the
fidelity of a few attached friends, had cheered him, and
had the worst disaster befallen him, had his troops
been routed and his cause ruined, there were warm
and bold hearts that would not have deserted him in
his extremity, that would have formed a wall around
him, and with their lives defended his grey hairs.  But
when the hour of calamity came to Absalom it found
him alone.  Even Saul had his armour-bearer at his
side when he fled over Gilboa ; but neither armour-
bearer nor friend attended Absalom as he fled from
the battle of the wood of Ephraim.  It would have

been well for him if he had really gained a few of the many hearts he stole. Much though moralists tell us of the heartlessness of the world in the hour of adversity, we should not have expected to light on so extreme a case of it. We can hardly withhold a tear at the sight of the unhappy youth, an hour ago with thousands eager to obey him, and a throne before him, apparently secure from danger; now hanging helpless between earth and heaven, with no companion but an evil conscience, and no prospect but the judgment of an offended God.

A recent writer, in his "History of the English People" (Green), when narrating the fall of Cardinal Wolsey, powerfully describes the way of Providence in suffering a career of unexampled wickedness and ambition to go on from one degree of prosperity to another, till the moment of doom arrives, when all is shattered by a single blow. There was long delay, but "the hour of reckoning at length arrived. Slowly the hand had crawled along the dial-plate, slowly as if the event would never come; and wrong was heaped on wrong, and oppression cried, and it seemed as if no ear had heard its voice, till the measure of the wickedness was at length fulfilled. The finger touched the hour; and as the strokes of the great hammer rang out above the nation, in an instant the whole fabric of iniquity was shivered to ruins."

This hour had now come to Absalom. He had often been reproved, but had hardened his heart, and was now to be destroyed, and that without remedy. In the person of Joab, God found a fitting instrument for carrying His purpose into effect. The character of Joab is something of a riddle. We cannot say that he was altogether a bad man, or altogether without the

fear of God. Though David bitterly complained of him
in some things, he must have valued him on the whole,
for during the whole of his reign Joab had been his
principal general. That he wanted all tenderness of
heart seems very plain. That he was subject to
vehement and uncontrollable impulses, in the heat of
which fearful deeds of blood were done by him, but
done in what seemed to him the interest of the public,
is also clear. There is no evidence that he was habitually savage or grossly selfish. When David charged
him and the other generals to deal tenderly with the
young man Absalom, it is quite possible that he was
minded to do so. But in the excitement of the battle,
that uncontrollable impulse seized him which urged
him to the slaughter of Amasa and Abner. The chance
of executing judgment on the arch-rebel who had caused
all this misery, and been guilty of crimes never before
heard of in Israel, and thus ending for ever an insurrection that might have dragged its slow length along
for harassing years to come, was too much for him.
"How could you see Absalom hanging in an oak and
not put an end to his mischievous life?" he asks the
man that tells him he had seen him in that plight. And
he has no patience with the man's elaborate apology.
Seizing three darts, he rushes to the place, and thrusts
them through Absalom's heart. And his ten armour-
bearers finish the business with their swords. We need
not suppose that he was altogether indifferent to the
feelings of David; but he may have been seized by an
overwhelming conviction that Absalom's death was the
only effectual way of ending this most guilty and pernicious insurrection, and so preserving the country from
ruin. Absalom living, whether banished or imprisoned,
would be a constant and fearful danger. Absalom dead,

great though the king's distress for the time might be, would be the very salvation of the country. Under the influence of this conviction he thrust the three darts through his heart, and he allowed his attendants to hew that comely body to pieces, till the fair form that all had admired so much became a mere mass of hacked and bleeding flesh. But whatever may have been the process by which Joab found himself constrained to disregard the king's order respecting Absalom, it is plain that to his dying day David never forgave him.

The mode of Absalom's death, and also the mode of his burial, were very significant. It had probably never happened to any warrior, or to any prince, to die from a similar cause. And but for the vanity that made him think so much of his bodily appearance, and especially of his hair, death would never have come to him in such a form. Vanity of one's personal appearance is indeed a weakness rather than a crime. It would be somewhat hard to punish it directly, but it is just the right way of treating it, to make it punish itself. And so it was in the case of Absalom. His bitterest enemy could have desired nothing more ludicrously tragical than to see those beautiful locks fastening him as with a chain of gold to the arm of the scaffold, and leaving him dangling there like the most abject malefactor. And what of the beautiful face and handsome figure that often, doubtless, led his admirers to pronounce him every inch a king? So slashed and mutilated under the swords of Joab's ten men, that no one could have told that it was Absalom that lay there. This was God's judgment on the young man's vanity.

The mode of his burial is particularly specified. "They took Absalom and cast him into a great pit in the wood, and laid a very great heap of stones upon him ; and all Israel fled every one to his tent." The purpose of this seems to have been to show that Absalom was deemed worthy of the punishment of the rebellious son, as appointed by Moses; and a more significant expression of opinion could not have been given. The punishment for the son who remained incorrigibly rebellious was to be taken beyond the walls of the city, and stoned to death. It is said by Jewish writers that this punishment was never actually inflicted, but the mode of Absalom's burial was fitted to show that he at least was counted as deserving of it. The ignominious treatment of that graceful body, which he adorned and set off with such care, did not cease even after it was gashed by the weapons of the young men ; no place was found for it in the venerable cave of Machpelah ; it was not even laid in the family sepul-chre at Jerusalem, but cast ignominiously into a pit in the wood ; it was bruised and pounded by stones, and left to rot there, like the memory of its possessor, and entail eternal infamy on the place. What a lesson to all who disown the authority of parents ! What a warning to all who cast away the cords of self-restraint! It is said by Jewish writers that every by-passer was accustomed to throw a stone on the heap that covered the remains of Absalom, and as he threw it to say, "Cursed be the memory of rebellious Absalom ; and cursed for ever be all wicked children that rise up in rebellion against their parents !"

And here it may be well to say a word to children. You all see the lesson that is taught by the doom of Absalom, and you all feel that in that doom, terrible though it was, he just reaped what he had sowed. You see the seed of his offence, disobedience to parents, bringing forth the most hideous fruit, and receiving in God's providence a most frightful punishment. You see it without excuse and without palliation ; for David had been a kind father, and had treated Absalom better than he deserved. Mark, then, that this is the final fruit of that spirit of disobedience to parents which often begins with very little offences. These little offences are big enough to show that you prefer your own will to the will of your parents. If you had a just and true respect for their authority, you would guard against little transgressions—you would make con-science of obeying in all things great and small. Then remember that every evil habit must have a beginning, and very often it is a small beginning. By imperceptible stages it may grow and grow, till it becomes a hideous vice, like this rebellion of Absalom. Nip it in the bud; if you don't, who can tell whether it may not grow to something terrible, and at last brand you with the brand of Absalom ?

If this be the lesson to children from the doom of Absalom, the lesson to parents is not less manifest from the case of David. The early battle between the child's will and the parent's is often very difficult and trying ; but God is on the parent's side, and will give him the victory if he seeks it aright. It certainly needs great vigilance, wisdom, patience, firmness, and affection. If you are careless and unwatchful, the child's will will speedily assert itself. If you are foolish, and carry discipline too far, if you thwart the child at every point, instead of insisting on one thing, or perhaps a few things, at a time, you will weary him and weary yourself without success. If you are fitful, insisting at one time and taking no heed at another, you will convey the impression of a very elastic law, not entitled to much respect. If you lose your tempei, and speak unadvisedly, instead of mildly and lovingly, you will most effectually set the child's temper up against the very thing you wish him to do. If you forget that you are not independent agents, but have got the care of your beloved child from God, and ought to bring him up as in God's stead, and in the most humble and careful dependence on God's grace, you may look for blunder upon blunder in sad succession, with results in the end that will greatly disappoint you. How close every Christian needs to lie to God in the exercise of this sacred trust! And how much, when conscious of weakness and fearing the consequences, ought he to prize the promise— "My grace is sufficient for thee!"

# CHAPTER XXIV.

## *DAVID'S GRIEF FOR ABSALOM.*

### 2 SAMUEL xviii. 19-33; xix. 1-4.

"NEXT to the calamity of losing a battle," a great general used to say, "is that of gaining a victory." The battle in the wood of Ephraim left twenty thousand of King David's subjects dead or dying on the field. It is remarkable how little is made of this dismal fact. Men's lives count for little in time of war, and death, even with its worst horrors, is just the common fate of warriors. Yet surely David and his friends could not think lightly of a calamity that cut down more of the sons of Israel than any battle since the fatal day of Mount Gilboa. Nor could they form a light estimate of the guilt of the man whose inordinate vanity and ambition had cost the nation such a fearful loss.

But all thoughts of this kind were for the moment brushed aside by the crowning fact that Absalom himself was dead. And this fact, as well as the tidings of the victory, must at once be carried to David. Mahanaim, where David was, was probably but a little distance from the field of battle. A friend offered to Joab to carry the news—Ahimaaz, the son of Zadok the priest. He had formerly been engaged in the same way, for he was one of those that had brought word to David of the result of Absalom's council, and of other things that were going on in Jerusalem. But Joab did not wish that Ahimaaz should be the bearer of the news. He would not deprive him of the character of kirg's messenger, but he would employ him as such another time. Meanwhile the matter was entrusted to another man, called in the Authorized Version Cushi, but in the Revised Version the Cushite. Whoever this may have been, he was a simple official, not like Ahimaaz, a personal friend of David. And this seems to have been Joab's reason for employing him. It is evident that physically he was not better adapted to the task than Ahimaaz, for when the latter at last got leave to go he overran the Cushite. But Joab appears to have felt that it would be better that David should receive his first news from a mere official than from a personal friend. The personal friend would be likely to enter into details that the other would not give. It is clear that Joab was ill at ease in reference to his own share in the death of Absalom. He would fain keep that back from David, at least for a time; it would be enough for him at the first to know that the battle had been gained, and that Absalom was dead.

But Ahimaaz was persistent, and after the Cushite had been despatched he carried his point, and was allowed to go. Very graphic is the description of the running of the two men and of their arrival at Mahanaim. The king had taken his place at the gate of the city, and stationed a watchman on the wall above to look out eagerly lest any one should come bringing news of the battle. In those primitive times there was no more rapid way of despatching important news than by a swift well-trained runner on foot. In the clear atmosphere of the East first one man, then another, was seen running alone. By-and-bye, the watchman surmised that the foremost of the two was Ahimaaz; and when the king heard it, remembering his former message, he concluded that such a man must be the bearer of good tidings. As soon as he came within hearing of the king, he shouted out, " All is well." Coming close, he fell on his face and blessed God for delivering the rebels into David's hands. Before thanking him or thanking God, the king showed what was uppermost in his heart by asking, " Is the young man Absalom safe ? " And here the moral courage of Ahimaaz failed him, and he gave an evasive answer: " When Joab sent the king's servant, and me thy servant, I saw a great tumult, but I knew not what it was." When he heard this the king bade him stand aside, till he should hear what the other messenger had to say. And the official messenger was more frank than the personal friend. For when the king repeated the question about Absalom, the answer was, " The enemies of my lord the king, and all that rise against thee to do thee hurt, be as that young man is." The answer was couched in skilful words. It suggested the enormity of Absalom's guilt, and of the danger to the king and the state which he had plotted, and the magnitude of the deliverance, seeing that he was now beyond the power of doing further evil.

But such soothing expressions were lost upon the king. The worst fears of his heart were realized—Absalom was dead. Gone from earth for ever, beyond reach of the yearnings of his heart ; gone to answer for crimes that were revolting in the sight of God and man. " The king was much moved ; and he went up to the chamber over the gate and wept ; and as he went, thus he said, ○ my son Absalom ! my son, my son Absalom !

Would God I had died for thee, O Absalom, my son, my son!"

He had been a man of war, a man of the sword; he had been familiar with death, and had seen it once and again in his own family; but the tidings of Absalom's death fell upon him with all the force of a first bereavement. Not more piercing is the wail of the young widow when suddenly the corpse of her beloved is borne into the house, not more overwhelming is her sensation, as if the solid earth were giving way beneath her, than the emotion that now prostrated King David.

Grief for the dead is always sacred; and however unworthy we may regard the object of it, we cannot but respect it in King David. Viewed simply as an expression of his unquenched affection for his son, and separated from its bearing on the interests of the kingdom, and from the air of repining it seemed to carry against the dispensation of God, it showed a marvellously tender and forgiving heart. In the midst of an odious and disgusting rebellion, and with the one object of seeking out his father and putting him to death, the heartless youth had been arrested and had met his deserved fate. Yet so far from showing satisfaction that the arm that had been raised to crush him was laid low in death, David could express no feelings but those of love and longing. Was it not a very wonderful love, coming very near to the feeling of Him who prayed, " Father, forgive them, for they know not what they do," like that "love Divine, all love excelling," that follows the sinner through all his wanderings, and clings to him amid all his rebellions; the love of Him that not merely wished in a moment of excitement that He could die for His guilty children, but did die for them, and in dying bore their guilt and took it away, and of which the brief but matchless record is that "having once loved His own that were with Him in the world, He loved them even unto the end?"

The elements of David's intense agony, when he heard of Absalom's death, were mainly three. In the first place, there was the loss of his son, of whom he could say that, with all his faults, he loved him still. A dear object had been plucked from his heart, and left it sick, vacant, desolate. A face he had often gazed on with delight lay cold in death. He had not been a good son, he had been very wicked; but affection has always its visions of a better future, and is ready to forgive unto seventy times seven. And then death is so dreadful when it fastens on the young. It seems so cruel to fell to the ground a bright young form; to extinguish by one blow his every joy, every hope, every dream; to reduce him to nothingness, so far as this life is concerned. An infinite pathos, in a father's experience, surrounds a young man's death. The regret, the longing, the conflict with the inevitable, seem to drain him of all energy, and leave him helpless in his sorrow.

Secondly, there was the terrible fact that Absalom had died in rebellion, without expressing one word of regret, without one request for forgiveness, without one act or word that it would be pleasant to recall in time to come, as a foil to the bitterness caused by his unnatural rebellion. Oh, if he had had but an hour to think of his position, to realise the lesson of his defeat, to ask his father's forgiveness, to curse the infatuation of the last few years! How would one such word have softened the sting of his rebellion in his father's breast! What a change it would have given to the aspect of his evil life! But not even the faint vestige

of such a thing was ever shown ; the unmitigated glare
of that evil life must haunt his father evermore !

Thirdly, there was the fact that in this rebellious
condition he had passed to the judgment of God.
What hope could there be for such a man, living and
dying as he had done ?   Where could he be now ?
Was not "the great pit in the wood," into which his
unhonoured carcase had been flung, a type of another
pit, the receptacle of his soul ?   What agony to the
Christian heart is like that of thinking of the misery
of dear ones who have died impenitent and un-
pardoned ?

To these and similar elements of grief David appears
to have abandoned himself without a struggle.    But
was this right ?   Ought he not to have made some
acknowledgment of the Divine hand in his trial, as he
did when Bathsheba's child died ?   Ought he not to have
acted as he did on another occasion, when he said, " I
was dumb with silence, I opened not my mouth, because Thou didst it " ?   We have seen that in domestic
matters he was not accustomed to place himself so
thoroughly under the control of the Divine will as in
the more public business of his life ; and now we see
that, when his parental feelings are crushed, he is left
without the steadying influence of submission to the
will of God.   And in the agony of his private grief he
forgets the public welfare of the nation.   Noble and
generous though the wish be, "Would God I had died
for thee," it was on public grounds out of the question.
Let us imagine for one moment the wish realized.
David has fallen and Absalom survives.   What sort
of kingdom would it have been ?   What would have
been the fate of the gallant men who had defended
David ?   What would have been the condition of God's

servants throughout the kingdom? What would have
been the influence of so godless a monarch upon the
interests of truth and the cause of God? It was a
rash and unadvised utterance of affection. But for the
rough faithfulness of Joab, the consequences would have
been disastrous. " The victory that day was turned
into mourning, for the people heard say that day how
the king was grieved for his son." Every one was
discouraged. The man for whom they had risked
their lives had not a word of thanks to any of them,
and could think of no one but that vile son of his, who
was now dead. In the evening Joab came to him, and
in his blunt way swore to him that if he was not more
affable to the people they would not remain a night
longer in his service. Roused by the reproaches and
threatenings of his general, the king did now present
himself among them. The people responded and came
before him, and the effort he made to show himself
agreeable kept them to their allegiance, and led on to
the steps for his restoration that soon took place.

But it must have been an effort to abstract his
attention from Absalom, and fix it on the brighter
results of the battle. And not only that night, in the
silence of his chamber, but for many a night, and
perhaps many a day, during the rest of his life, the
thought of that battle and its crowning catastrophe
must have haunted David like an ugly dream. We
seem to see him in some still hour of reverie recalling
early days;—happy scenes rise around him; lovely
children gambol at his side; he hears again the merry
laugh of little Tamar, and smiles as he recalls some
childish saying of Absalom; he is beginning, as of old,
to forecast the future and shape out for them careers
of honour and happiness; when, horror of horrors!

the spell breaks; the bright vision gives way to dismal realities—Tamar's dishonour, Amnon's murder, Absalom's insurrection, and, last not least, Absalom's death, glare in the field of memory ! Who will venture to say that David did not smart for his sins ? Who that reflects would be willing to take the cup of sinful indulgence from his hands, sweet though it was in his mouth, when he sees it so bitter in the belly ?

Two remarks may appropriately conclude this chapter, one with reference to grief from bereavements in general, the other with reference to the grief that may arise to Christians in connection with the spiritual condition of departed children.

1. With reference to grief from bereavements in general, it is to be observed that they will prove either a blessing or an evil according to the use to which they are turned. All grief in itself is a weakening thing— weakening both to the body and the mind, and it were a great error to suppose that it *must* do good in the end. There are some who seem to think that to resign themselves to overwhelming grief is a token of regard to the memory of the departed, and they take no pains to counteract the depressing influence. It is a painful thing to say, yet it is true, that a long-continued manifestation of overwhelming grief, instead of exciting sympathy, is more apt to cause annoyance. Not only does it depress the mourner himself, and unfit him for his duties to the living, but it depresses those that come in contact with him, and makes them think of him with a measure of impatience. And this suggests another remark. It is not right to obtrude our grief overmuch on others, especially if we are in a public position. Let us take example in this respect from our blessed Lord. Was any sorrow like unto His sorrow ? Yet how little did

He obtrude it even on the notice of His disciples! It
was towards the end of His ministry before He even
began to tell them of the dark scenes through which He
was to pass; and even when He did tell them how He
was to be betrayed and crucified, it was not to court
their sympathy, but to prepare them for their part
of the trial. And when the overwhelming agony of
Gethsemane drew on, it was only three of the twelve
that were permitted to be with Him. All such considerations show that it is a more Christian thing to
conceal our griefs than to make others uncomfortable
by obtruding them upon their notice. David was on
the very eve of losing the affections of those who had
risked everything for him, by abandoning himself to
anguish for his private loss, and letting his distress for
the dead interfere with his duty to the living.

And how many things are there to a Christian mind
fitted to abate the first sharpness even of a great
bereavement. Is it not the doing of a Father, infinitely
kind? Is it not the doing of Him "who spared not
His own Son, but delivered Him up for us all"? You
say you can see no light through it,—it is dark, all dark,
fearfully dark. Then you ought to fall back on the
inscrutability of God. Hear Him saying, "What I do,
thou knowest not now, but thou shalt know hereafter.'
Resign yourself patiently to His hands, till He make
the needed revelation, and rest assured that when it is
made it will be worthy of God. "Ye have heard of
the patience of Job, and have seen the end of the Lord,
that the Lord is very pitiful and of tender mercy."
Meanwhile, be impressed with the vanity of this life,
and the infinite need of a higher portion. "Set your
affection on things above, and not on the things on the
earth. For ye are dead, and your life is hid with Christ

in God.   When Christ, who is your Life, shall appear,
then shall ye also appear with Him in glory."

2.  The other remark that falls to be made here con-
cerns the grief that may arise to Christians in connection with the spiritual condition of departed children.

When the parent is either in doubt as to the happiness of a beloved one, or has cause to apprehend that
the portion of that child is with the unbelievers, the
pang which he experiences is one of the most acute
which the human heart can know.   Now here is a
species of suffering which, if not peculiar to believers,
falls on them far the most heavily, and is, in many
cases, a haunting spectre of misery.   The question
naturally arises, Is it not strange that their very
beliefs, as Christians, subject them to such acute sufferings ?   If one were a careless, unbelieving man, and
one's child died without evidence of grace, one would
probably think nothing of it, because the things that
are unseen and eternal are never in one's thoughts.
But just because one believes the testimony of God
on this great subject, one becomes liable to a peculiar
agony.   Is this not strange indeed ?

Yes, there is a mystery in it which we cannot wholly
solve.   But we must remember that it is in thorough
accordance with a great law of Providence, the operation of which, in other matters, we cannot overlook.
That law is, that the cultivation and refinement of any
organ or faculty, while it greatly increases your capacity
of enjoyment, increases at the same time your capacity,
and it may be your occasions, of suffering.   Let us
take, for example, the habit of cleanliness.   Where
this habit prevails, there is much more enjoyment in
life ; but let a person of great cleanliness be surrounded by filth, his suffering is infinitely greater.   Or

take the cultivation of taste, and let us say of musical
taste.   It adds to life an immense capacity of enjoyment, but also a great capacity and often much
occasion of suffering, because bad music or tasteless
music, such as one may often have to endure, creates
a misery unknown to the man of no musical culture.
To a man of classical taste, bad writing or bad speaking,
such as is met with every day, is likewise a source of
irritation and suffering.   If we advance to a moral and
spiritual region, we may see that the cultivation of one's
ordinary affections, apart from religion, while on the
whole it increases enjoyment, does also increase sorrow.
If I lived and felt as a Stoic, I should enjoy family life
much less than if I were tender-hearted and affectionate; but when I suffered a family bereavement I should
suffer much less.   These are simply illustrations of the
great law of Providence that culture, while it increases
happiness, increases suffering too.   It is a higher
application of the same law, that gracious culture, the
culture of our spiritual affections under the power of the
Spirit of God, in increasing our enjoyment does also
increase our capacity of suffering.   In reference to that
great problem of natural religion, Why should a God
of infinite benevolence have created creatures capable
of suffering? one answer that has often been given is,
that if they had not been capable of suffering they
might not have been capable of enjoyment.   But in
pursuing these inquiries we get into an obscure region,
in reference to which it is surely our duty patiently to
wait for that increase of light which is promised to us
in the second stage of our existence.

   Yet still it remains to be asked, What comfort can
there possibly be for Christian parents in such a case
as David's?   What possible consideration can ever

reconcile them to the thought that their beloved ones
have gone to the world of woe? Are not their
children parts of themselves, and how is it possible
for them to be completely saved if those who are so
identified with them are lost? How can they ever be
happy in a future life if eternally separated from
those who were their nearest and dearest on earth?
On such matters it has pleased God to allow a great
cloud to rest which our eyes cannot pierce. We cannot
solve this problem. We cannot reconcile perfect
personal happiness, even in heaven, with the knowledge
that beloved ones are lost. But God must have some
way, worthy of Himself, of solving the problem. And
we must just wait for His time of revelation. "God is
His own interpreter, and He will make it plain." The
Judge of all the earth must act justly. And the song
which will express the deepest feelings of the redeemed,
when from the sea of glass, mingled with fire, they
look back on the ways of Providence toward them, will
be this: "Great and marvellous are Thy works, Lord
God Almighty; *just and true are all Thy ways*, Thou
King of saints. Who would not fear Thee and glorify
Thy name, for Thou only art holy?"

# CHAPTER XXV.

## *THE RESTORATION.*

### 2 SAMUEL xix. 5—30.

TO rouse one's self from the prostration of grief, and grapple anew with the cares of life, is hard indeed. Among the poorer classes of society, it is hardly possible to let grief have its swing; amid suppressed and struggling emotions the poor man must return to his daily toil. The warrior, too, in the heat of conflict has hardly time to drop a tear over the tomb of his comrade or his brother. But where leisure is possible, the bereaved heart does crave a time of silence and solitude; and it seems reasonable, in order that its fever may subside a little, before the burden of daily work is resumed. It was somewhat hard upon David, then, that his grief could not get a single evening to flow undisturbed. A rough voice called him to rouse himself, and speak comfortably to his people, otherwise they would disband before morning, and all that he had gained would be lost to him again. In the main, Joab was no doubt right; but in his manner there was a sad lack of consideration for the feelings of the king. He might have remembered that, though he had gained a battle, David had lost a son, and that, too, under circumstances peculiarly heart-breaking. Faithful in the main and shrewd as Joab was, he was no doubt a useful officer;

but his harshness and want of feeling went far to neutralise the benefit of his services. It ought surely to be one of the benefits of civilisation and culture that, where painful duties have to be done, they should be done with much consideration and tenderness. For the real business of life is not so much to get right things done in any way, as to diffuse a right spirit among men, and get them to do things well. Men of enlightened goodness will always aim at purifying the springs of conduct, at increasing virtue, and deepening faith and holiness. The call to the royal bridegroom in the forty-fifth Psalm is to "gird his sword on his thigh, and ride forth prosperously, *because of truth, and meekness, and righteousness.*" To increase these three things is to increase the true wealth of nations and advance the true prosperity of kingdoms. In his eagerness to get a certain thing done, Joab showed little or no regard for those higher interests to which outward acts should ever be subordinate.

But David felt the call of duty—"He arose and sat in the gate. And they told unto all the people saying, Behold, the king doth sit in the gate. And all the people came before the king: for Israel had fled every man to his tent." And very touching it must have been to look on the sad, pale, wasted face of the king, and mark his humble, chastened bearing, and yet to receive from him words of winning kindness that showed him still caring for them and loving them, as a shepherd among his sheep; in no wise exasperated by the insurrection, not breathing forth threatenings and slaughter on those who had taken part against him; but concerned as ever for the welfare of the whole kingdom, and praying for Jerusalem, for his brethren and companions' sakes, "Peace be within thee."

It was now open to him to follow either of two courses: either to march to Jerusalem at the head of his victorious army, take military possession of the capital, and deal with the remains of the insurrection in the stern fashion common among kings ; or to wait till he should be invited back to the throne from which he had been driven, and then magnanimously proclaim an amnesty to all the rebels. We are not surprised that he preferred the latter alternative. It is more agreeable to any man to be offered what is justly due to him by those who have deprived him of it than to have to claim it as his right. It was far more like him to return in peace than in that vengeful spirit that must have hecatombs of rebels slain to satisfy it. The people knew that David was in no bloodthirsty mood. And it was natural for him to expect that an advance would be made to him, after the frightful wrong which he had suffered from the people. He was therefore in no haste to leave his quarters at Mahanaim.

The movement that he looked for did take place, but it did not originate with those who might have been expected to take the lead. It was among the ten tribes of Israel that the proposal to bring him back was first discussed, and his own tribe, the tribe of Judah, held back after the rest were astir. He was much chagrined at this backwardness on the part of Judah. It was hard that his own tribe should be the last to stir, that those who might have been expected to head the movement should lag behind. But in this David was only experiencing the same thing as the Son of David a thousand years after, when the people of Nazareth, His own city, not only refused to listen to Him, but were about to hurl Him over the edge of a precipice.

So important, however, did he see it to be for the general welfare that Judah should share the movement, that he sent Zadok and Abiathar the priests to stir them up to their duty. He would not have taken this step but for his jealousy for the honour of Judah; it was the fact that the movement was now going on in some places and not in all that induced him to interfere. He dreaded disunion in any case, especially a disunion between Judah and Israel. For the jealousy between these two sections of the people that afterwards broke the kingdom into two under Jeroboam was now beginning to show itself, and, indeed, led soon after to the revolt of Sheba.

Another step was taken by David, of very doubtful expediency, in order to secure the more cordial support of the rebels. He superseded Joab, and gave the command of his army to Amasa, who had been general of the rebels. In more ways than one this was a strong measure. To supersede Joab was to make for himself a very powerful enemy, to rouse a man whose passions, when thoroughly excited, were capable of any crime. But on the other hand, David could not but be highly offended with Joab for his conduct to Absalom, and he must have looked on him as a very unsuitable coadjutor to himself in that policy of clemency that he had determined to pursue. This was significantly brought out by the appointment of Amasa in room of Joab. Both were David's nephews, and both were of the tribe of Judah; but Amasa had been at the head of the insurgents, and therefore in close alliance with the insurgents of Judah. Most probably the reason why the men of Judah hung back was that they were afraid lest, if David were restored to Jerusalem, he would make an example of them; for it was at Hebron, in the tribe of Judah, that Absalom had been first proclaimed, and the people of Jerusalem

who had favoured him were mostly of that tribe.
But when it became known that the leader of the rebel
forces was not only not to be punished, but actually
promoted to the highest office in the king's service, all
fears of that sort were completely scattered. It was an
act of wonderful clemency. It was such a contrast to
the usual treatment of rebels! But this king was not
like other kings; he gave gifts even to the rebellious.
There was no limit to his generosity. Where sin
abounded grace did much more abound. Accordingly
a new sense of the goodness and generosity of their
ill-treated but noble king took possession of the people.
" He bowed the heart of the men of Judah, even as the
heart of one man, so that they sent this word unto the
king, Return thou, and all thy servants." From the
extreme of backwardness they started to the extreme
of forwardness ; the last to speak for David, they were
the first to act for him ; and such was their vehemence
in his cause that the evil of national disunion which
David dreaded from their indifference actually sprang
from their over-impetuous zeal.

Thus at length David bade farewell to Mahanaim,
and began his journey to Jerusalem. His route in
returning was the reverse of that followed in his flight.
First he descends the eastern bank of the Jordan as
far as opposite Gilgal ; then he strikes up through the
wilderness the steep ascent to Jerusalem. At Gilgal
several events of interest took place.

The first of these was the meeting with the representatives of Judah, who came to conduct the king over
Jordan, and to offer him their congratulations and loyal
assurances. This step was taken by the men of Judah
alone, and without consultation or co-operation with
the other tribes. A ferry-boat to convey the king's

household over the river, and whatever else might be required to make the passage comfortable, these men of Judah provided. Some have blamed the king for accepting these attentions from Judah, instead of inviting the attendance of all the tribes. But surely, as the king had to pass the Jordan, and found the means of transit provided for him, he was right to accept what was offered. Nevertheless, this act of Judah and its acceptance by David gave serious offence, as we shall presently see, to the other tribes.

Neither Judah nor Israel comes out well in this little incident. We get an instructive glimpse of the hotheadedness of the tribes, and the childishness of their quarrels. It is members of the same nation a thousand years afterwards that on the very eve of the Crucifixion we see disputing among themselves which of them should be the greatest. Men never appear in a dignified attitude when they are contending that on some occasion or other they have been treated with too little consideration. And yet how many of the quarrels of the world, both public and private, have arisen from this, that some one did not receive the attention which he deserved ! Pride lies at the bottom of it all. And quarrels of this kind will sometimes, nay often, be found even among men calling themselves the followers of Christ. If the blessed Lord Himself had acted on this principle, what a different life He would have led ! If He had taken offence at every want of etiquette, at every want of the honour due to the Son of God, when would our redemption ever have been accomplished ? Was His mother treated with due consideration when forced into the stable, because there was no room for her in the inn ? Was Jesus Himself treated with due honour when the people of

Nazareth took Him to the brow of the hill, or when the
foxes had holes, and the birds of the air had nests, but
the Son of Man had not where to lay His head ?   What
if He had resented the denial of Peter, the treachery
of Judas, and the forsaking of Him by all the apostles?
How admirable was the humility that made Himself of
no reputation, so that when He was reviled He reviled
not again, when He suffered He threatened not, but
committed Himself to Him that judgeth righteously !
Yet how utterly opposite is the bearing of many, who
are ever ready to take offence if anything is omitted to
which they have a claim—standing upon their rights,
claiming precedence over this one and the other, maintaining that it would never do to allow themselves to
be trampled on, thinking it spirited to contend for their
honours !   It is because this tendency is so deeply
seated in human nature that you need to be so watch-
ful against it.   It breaks out at the most unseasonable
times.   Could any time have been more unsuitable
for it on the part of the men of Israel and Judah than
when the king was giving them such a memorable
example of humility, pardoning every one, great and
small, that had offended him, even though their offence
was as deadly as could be conceived ?   Or could any
time have been more unsuitable for it on the part of
the disciples of our Lord than when He was about to
surrender His very life, and submit to the most shameful form of death that could be devised ?   Why do
men not see that the servant is not above his lord,
nor the disciple above his master ?   " Is not the heart
deceitful above all things and desperately wicked " ?
Let him that thinketh he standeth take heed lest he
fall.

The next incident at Gilgal was the cringing entreaty

of Shimei, the Benjamite, to be pardoned the insult which he had offered the king when he left Jerusalem. The conduct of Shimei had been such an outrage on all decency that we wonder how he could have dared to present himself at all before David, even though, as a sort of screen, he was accompanied by a thousand Benjamites. His prostration of himself on the ground before David, his confession of his sin and abject depreciation of the king's anger, are not fitted to raise him in our estimation ; they were the fruits of a base nature that can insult the fallen, but lick the dust off the feet of men in power. It was not till David had made it known that his policy was to be one of clemency that Shimei took this course ; and even then he must have a thousand Benjamites at his back before he could trust himself to his mercy. Abishai, Joab's brother, would have had him slain ; but his proposal was rejected by David with warmth and even indignation. He knew that his restoration was an accomplished fact, and he would not spoil a policy of forgiveness by shedding the blood of this wicked man. Not content with passing his word to Shimei, " he sware unto him." But he afterwards found that he had carried clemency too far, and in his dying charge to Solomon he had to warn him against this dangerous enemy, and instruct him to bring down his hoar head with blood. But this needs not to make us undervalue the singular quality of heart which led David to show such forbearance to one utterly unworthy. It was a strange thing in the annals of Eastern kingdoms, where all rebellion was usually punished with the most fearful severity. It brings to mind the gentle clemency of the great Son of David in His dealings, a thousand years after, with another Benjamite as he was travelling, on that very route, on the way to Damascus, breathing out threatenings and slaughter against His disciples. Was there ever such clemency as that which met the persecutor with the words, Saul, Saul, why persecutest thou Me? Only in this case the clemency accomplished its object; in Shimei's case it did not. In the one case the persecutor became the chief of Apostles; in the other he acted more like the evil spirit in the parable, whose last end was worse than the first.

The next incident in the king's return was his meeting with Mephibosheth. He came down to meet the king, "and had neither dressed his feet, nor trimmed his beard, nor washed his clothes from the day the king departed unto the day when he came again in peace." Naturally, the king's first question was an inquiry why he had not left Jerusalem with him. And Mephibosheth's reply was simply, that he had wished to do so, but, owing to his lameness, had not been able. And, moreover, Ziba had slandered him to the king when he said that Mephibosheth hoped to receive back the kingdom of his grandfather. The words of this poor man had all the appearance of an honest narrative. The ass which he intended to saddle for his own use was probably one of those which Ziba took away to present to David, so that Mephibosheth was left helpless in Jerusalem. If the narrative commends itself by its transparent truthfulness, it shows also how utterly improbable was the story of Ziba, that he had expectations of being made king. For he seems to have been as feeble in mind as he was frail in body, and he undoubtedly carried his compliments to David to a ridiculous pitch when he said, "All my father's house were but dead men before my lord the king." Was that a fit way to speak of his father Jonathan?

We cannot greatly admire one who would depreciate his family to such a degree because he desired to obtain David's favour. And for some reason David was somewhat sharp to him. No man is perfect, and we cannot but wonder that the king who was so gentle to Shimei should have been so sharp to Mephibosheth. "Why speakest thou any more of thy matters? I have said, Thou and Ziba divide the land." David appears to have been irritated at discovering his mistake in believing Ziba, and hastily transferring Mephibosheth's property to him. Nothing is more common than such irritation, when men discover that through false information they have made a blunder, and gone into some arrangement that must be undone. But why did not the king restore all his property to Mephibosheth? Why say that he and Ziba were to divide it? Some have supposed (as we remarked before) that this meant simply that the old arrangement was to be continued—Ziba to till the ground, and Mephibosheth to receive as his share half the produce. But in that case Mephibosheth would not have added, "Yea, let him take all, forasmuch as my lord the king is come again in peace unto his own house." Our verdict would have been the very opposite,—Let Mephibosheth take all. But David was in a difficulty. The temper of the Benjamites was very irritable; they had never been very cordial to David, and Ziba was an important man among them. There he was, with his fifteen sons and twenty servants, a man not to be hastily set aside. For once the king appeared to prefer the rule of expediency to that of justice. To make some amends for his wrong to Mephibosheth, and at the same time not to turn Ziba into a foe, he resorted to this rough-and-ready method of dividing the land between them.   But surely it was an unworthy arrangement.  Mephibosheth had been loyal, and should never have lost his land.   He had been slandered by Ziba, and therefore deserved some solace for his wrong.   David restores but half his land, and has no soothing word for the wrong he has done him.   Strange that when so keenly sensible of the wrong done to himself when he lost his kingdom unrighteously, he should not have seen the wrong he had done to Mephibosheth.   And strange that when his whole kingdom had been restored to himself, he should have given back but half to Jonathan's son.

The incident connected with the meeting with Barzillai we reserve for separate consideration.

Amid the greatest possible diversity of circumstance, we are constantly finding parallels in the life of David to that of Him who was his Son according to the flesh. Our Lord can hardly be said to have ever been driven from His kingdom.   The hosannahs of to-day were indeed very speedily exchanged into the "Away with Him! away with Him!  Crucify Him! crucify Him!" of to-morrow.   But what we may remark of our Lord is rather that He has been kept out of His kingdom than driven from it.   He who came to redeem the world, and of whom the Father said, "Yet have I set My King upon My holy hill of Zion," has never been suffered to exercise His sovereignty, at least in a conspicuous manner and on a universal scale.   Here is a truth that ought to be a constant source of humiliation and sorrow to every Christian.   Are you to be content that the rightful Sovereign should be kept in the background, and the great ruling forces of the world should be selfishness, and mammon, and pleasure, the lust of the flesh, and the lust of the eye, and the pride of life ?   Why speak ye not of bringing the King back to His house ? You say you can do so little. But every subject of King David might have said the same. The question is, not whether you are doing much or little, but whether you are doing what you can. Is the exaltation of Jesus Christ to the supreme rule of the world an object dear to you ? Is it matter of humiliation and concern to you that He does not occupy that place ? Do you humbly try to give it to Him in your own heart and life ? Do you try to give it to Him in the Church, in the State, in the world ? The supremacy of Jesus Christ must be the great rallying cry of the members of the Christian Church, whatever their denomination. It is a point on which surely all ought to be agreed, and agreement there might bring about agreement in other things. Let us give our minds and hearts to realise in our spheres that glorious plan of which we read in the first chapter of Ephesians : " That, in the dispensation of the fulness of time, God might gather together in one all things in Christ, both which are in heaven, and which are on earth, even in Him, in whom also we have obtained an inheritance, being predestinated according to the purpose of Him who worketh all things according to the counsel of His own will, that we should be to the praise of His glory, who first trusted in Christ."

# CHAPTER XXVI.

## DAVID AND BARZILLAI.

2 SAMUEL xix. 31—40.

IT is very refreshing to fall in with a man like Barzillai in a record which is so full of wickedness,
and without many features of a redeeming character.
He is a sample of humanity at its best—one of those
men who diffuse radiance and happiness wherever
their influence extends. Long before St. Peter wrote
his epistle, he had been taught by the one Master
to "put away all wickedness, and all guile, and
hypocrisies, and envies, and evil-speakings;" and he
had adopted St. Paul's rule for rich men, "that they
do good, that they be rich in good works, that
they be ready to distribute, willing to communicate."
We cannot well conceive a greater contrast than
that between Barzillai and another rich farmer with
whom David came in contact at an earlier period
of his life—Nabal of Carmel: the one niggardly,
beggarly, and bitter, not able even to acknowledge
an obligation, far less to devise anything liberal,
adding insult to injury when David modestly stated his
claim, humiliating him before his messengers, and
meeting his request with a flat refusal of everything
great or small; the other hastening from his home
when he heard of David's distress, carrying with him

whatever he could give for the use of the king and his
followers, continuing to send supplies while he was at
Mahanaim, and now returning to meet him on his way
to Jerusalem, conduct him over Jordan, and show his
loyalty and goodwill in every available way. While
we grieve that there are still so many Nabals let us
bless God that there are Barzillais too.

Of Barzillai's previous history we know nothing.
We do not even know where Rogelim, his place of
abode, was, except that it was among the mountains of
Gilead. The facts stated regarding him are few, but
suggestive.

1. He was "a very great man." The expression
seems to imply that he was both rich and influential.
Dwelling among the hills of Gilead, his only occupation,
and main way of becoming rich, must have been as
a farmer. The two and a half tribes that settled on
the east of the Jordan, while they had a smaller share
of national and spiritual privileges, were probably
better provided in a temporal sense. That part of the
country was richer in pasturage, and therefore better
adapted for cattle. It is probable, too, that the allot-
ments were much larger. The kingdoms of Sihon and
Og, especially the latter, were of wide extent. If the
two and a half tribes had been able thoroughly to
subdue the original inhabitants, they would have had
possessions of great extent and value. Barzillai's
ancestors had probably received a valuable and extensive allotment, and had been strong enough and coura-
geous enough to keep it for themselves. Consequently,
when their flocks and herds multiplied, they were not
restrained within narrow dimensions, but could spread
over the mountains round about. But however his
riches may have been acquired, Barzillai was evidently

a man of very large means.  He was rich apparently
both in flocks and servants, a kind of chief or sheikh,
not only with a large establishment of his own, but
enjoying the respect, and in some degree able to command the services, of many of the humble people
around him.

2. His generosity was equal to his wealth.  The
catalogue of the articles which he and another friend
of David's brought him in his extremity (2 Sam. xvii.
28, 29) is instructive from its minuteness and its length.
Like all men liberal in heart, he devised liberal things.
He did not ask to see a subscription list, or inquire
what other people were giving.  He did not consider
what was the smallest amount that he could give without appearing to be shabby.  His only thought seems
to have been, what there was he had to give that could
be of use to the king.  It is this large inborn generosity manifested to David that gives one the assurance
that he was a kind, generous helper wherever there
was a case deserving and needing his aid.  We class
him with the patriarch of Uz, with whom no doubt he
could have said, "When the eye saw me, then it
blessed me, and when the ear heard me, it bare witness
unto me ; the blessing of him that was ready to perish
came upon me, and I made the widow's heart to leap
for joy."

3. His loyalty was not less thorough than his
generosity.  When he heard of the king's troubles, he
seems never to have hesitated one instant as to throwing in his lot with him.  It mattered not that the king
was in great trouble, and apparently in a desperate
case.  Neighbours, or even members of his own family,
might have whispered to him that it would be better
not to commit himself, seeing the rebellion was so

strong. He was living in a sequestered part of the country; there was no call on him to declare himself at that particular moment; and if Absalom got the upper hand, he would be sure to punish severely those who had been active on his father's side. But none of these things moved him. Barzillai was no sunshine courtier, willing to enjoy the good things of the court in days of prosperity, but ready in darker days to run off and leave his friends in the midst of danger. He was one of those true men that are ready to risk their all in the cause of loyalty when persuaded that it is the cause of truth and right. We cannot but ask, What could have given him a feeling so strong? We are not expressly told that he was a man deeply moved by the fear of God, but we have every reason to believe it. If so, the consideration that would move him most forcibly in favour of David must have been that he was God's anointed. God had called him to the throne, and had never declared, as in the case of Saul, that he had forfeited it; the attempt to drive him from it was of the devil, and therefore to be resisted to the last farthing of his property, and if he had been a younger man, to the last drop of his blood. Risk? Can you frighten a man like this by telling him of the risk he runs by supporting David in the hour of adversity? Why, he is ready not only to risk all, but to lose all, if necessary, in a cause which appears so obviously to be Divine, all the more because he sees so well what a blessing David has been to the country. Why, he has actually made the kingdom. Not only has he expelled all its internal foes, but he has cowed those troublesome neighbours that were constantly pouncing upon the tribes, and especially the tribes situated in Gilead and Bashan. Moreover, he has given unity and stability to all the internal arrangements of the kingdom. See what a grand capital he has made for it at Jerusalem. Look how he has planted the ark on the strongest citadel of the country, safe from every invading foe. Consider how he has perfected the arrangements for the service of the Levites, what a delightful service of song he has instituted, and what beautiful songs he has composed for the use of the sanctuary. Doubtless it was considerations of this kind that roused Barzillai to such a pitch of loyalty. And is not a country happy that has such citizens, men who place their personal interest far below the public weal, and are ready to make any sacrifice, of person or of property, when the highest interests of their country are concerned ? We do not plead for the kind of loyalty that clings to a monarch simply because he is king, apart from all considerations, personal and public, bearing on his worthiness or unworthiness of the office. We plead rather for the spirit that makes duty to country stand first, and personal or family interest a long way below. We deprecate the spirit that sneers at the very idea of putting one's self to loss or trouble of any kind for the sake of public interests. We long for a generation of men and women that, like many in this country in former days, are willing to give " all for the Church and a little less for the State." And surely in these days, when no deadly risk is incurred, the demand is not so very severe. Let Christian men lay it on their consciences to pay regard to the claims under which they lie to serve their country. Whether it be in the way of serving on some public board, or fighting against some national vice, or advancing some great public interest, let it be considered even by busy men that their country, and    must add, their Church, have true

claims upon them. Even heathens and unbelievers
have said, " It is sweet and glorious to die for one's
country." It is a poor state of things when in a
Christian community men are so sunk in indolence
and selfishness that they will not stir a finger on its
behalf.

4. Barzillai was evidently a man of attractive personal qualities. The king was so attracted by him,
that he wished him to come with him to Jerusalem,
and promised to sustain him at court. The heart of
King David was not too old to form new attachments.
And towards Barzillai he was evidently drawn. We
can hardly suppose but that there were deeper qualities
to attract the king than even his loyalty and generosity.
It looks as if David perceived a spiritual congeniality
that would make Barzillai, not only a pleasant inmate,
but a profitable friend. For indeed in many ways
Barzillai and David seem to have been like one another.
God had given them both a warm, sunny nature. He
had prospered them in the world. He had given them
a deep regard for Himself and delight in His fellowship. David must have found in Barzillai a friend
whose views on the deepest subjects were similar to
his own. At Jerusalem the men who were of his mind
were by no means too many. To have Barzillai beside
him, refreshing him with his experiences of God's
ways and joining with him in songs of praise and
thanksgiving, would be delightful. " Behold, how
good and how pleasant it is for brethren to dwell
together in unity!" But however pleasant the prospect
may have been to David, it was not one destined to be
realized.

5. For Barzillai was not dazzled even by the highest
offers of the king, because he felt that the proposal was

unsuitable for his years. He was already eighty, and every day was adding to his burden, and bringing him sensibly nearer the grave. Even though he might be enjoying a hale old age, he could not be sure that he would not break down suddenly, and thus become an utter burden to the king. David had made the offer as a compliment to Barzillai, although it might also be a favour to himself, and as a compliment the aged Gileadite was entitled to view it. And viewing it in that light, he respectfully declined it. He was a home-loving man, his habits had been formed for a quiet domestic sphere, and it was too late to change them. His faculties were losing their sharpness; his taste had become dulled, his ear blunted, so that both savoury dishes and elaborate music would be comparatively thrown away on him. The substance of his answer was, I am an old man, and it would be unsuitable in me to begin a courtier's life. In a word, he understood what was suitable for old age. Many a man and woman too, perhaps, even of Barzillai's years, would have jumped at King David's offer, and rejoiced to share the dazzling honours of a court, and would have affected youthful feelings and habits in order to enjoy the exhilaration and the excitement of a courtier's life. In Barzillai's choice, we see the predominance of a sanctified common sense, alive to the proprieties of things, and able to see how the enjoyment most suitable to an advanced period of life might best be had. It was not by aping youth or grasping pleasures for which the relish had gone. Some may think this a painful view of old age. Is it so that as years multiply the taste for youthful enjoyments passes away, and one must resign one's self to the thought that life itself is near its end ? Undoubtedly it is. But even a

heathen could show that this is by no means an evil.
The purpose of Cicero's beautiful treatise on old age,
written when he was sixty-two, but regarded as spoken
by Cato at the age of eighty-four, was to show that the
objections commonly brought against old age were not
really valid. These objections were—that old age
unfits men for active business, that it renders the
body feeble, that it deprives them of the enjoyment of
almost all pleasures, and that it heralds the approach
of death. Let it be granted, is the substance of Cicero's
argument; nevertheless, old age brings enjoyments of
a new order that compensate for those which it withdraws. If we have wisdom to adapt ourselves to our
position, and to lay ourselves out for those compensa-
tory pleasures, we shall find old age not a burden, but
a joy. Now, if even a heathen could argue in that
way, how much more a Christian! If he cannot
personally be so lively as before, he may enjoy the
young life of his children and grandchildren or other
young friends, and delight to see them enjoying what
he cannot now engage in. If active pleasures are not to
be had, there are passive enjoyments—the conversation
of friends, reading, meditation, and the like—of which
all the more should be made. If one world is gliding
from him, another is moving towards him. As the
outward man perisheth, let the inward man be renewed
day by day.

There are few more jarring scenes in English history
than the last days of Queen Elizabeth. As life was
passing away, a historian of England says, " she clung
to it with a fierce tenacity. She hunted, she danced,
she jested with her young favourites, she coquetted, and
frolicked, and scolded at sixty-seven as she had done at
thirty." "The Queen," wrote a courtier, "a few months

before her death was never so gallant these many years, nor so set upon jollity." She persisted, in spite of opposition, in her gorgeous progresses from country house to country house. She clung to business as of old, and rated in her usual fashion one " who minded not to giving up some matter of account." And then a strange melancholy settled on her. Her mind gave way, and food and rest became alike distasteful. Clever woman, yet very foolish in not discerning how vain it was to attempt to carry the brisk habits of youth into old age, and most profoundly foolish in not having taken pains to provide for old age the enjoyments appropriate to itself! How differently it has fared with those who have been wise in time and made the best provision for old age! "I have waited for Thy salvation, O my God," says the dying Jacob, relieved and happy to think that the object for which he had waited had come at last. "I am now ready to be offered," says St. Paul, " and the time of my departure is at hand. I have fought the good fight ; I have finished my course ; I have kept the faith : henceforth there is laid up for me a crown of righteousness, which the Lord, the righteous Judge, will give me at that day, and not to me only, but unto all them also that love His appearing." Which is the better portion—he whose old age is spent in bitter lamentation over the departed joys and brightness of his youth ? or he whose sun goes down with the sweetness and serenity of an autumn sunset, but only to rise in a brighter world, and shine forth in the glory of immortal youth ?

6. Holding such views of old age, it was quite natural and suitable for Barzillai to ask for his son Chimham what he respectfully declined for himself. For his declinature was not a rude rejection of an honour

deemed essentially false and vain. Barzillai did not
tell the king that he had lived to see the folly and the
sin of those pleasures which in the days of youth and
inexperience men are so greedy to enjoy. That
would have been an affront to David, especially as he
was now getting to be an old man himself. He recognised that a livelier mode of life than befitted the old
was suitable for the young. The advantages of residence at the court of David were not to be thought
little of by one beginning life, especially where the
head of the court was such a man as David, himself
so affectionate and attractive, and so deeply imbued
with the fear and love of God. The narrative is so
short that not a word is added as to how it fared with
Chimham when he came to Jerusalem. Only one thing
is known of him : it is said that, after the destruction of
Jerusalem by Nebuchadnezzar, when Johanan conducted
to Egypt a remnant of Jews that he had saved from the
murderous hand of Ishmael, "they departed and dwelt
in the habitation of Chimham, which is by Bethlehem,
to go into Egypt." We infer that David bestowed on
Chimham some part of his paternal inheritance at
Bethlehem. The vast riches which he had amassed
would enable him to make ample provision for his
sons ; but we might naturally have expected that the
whole of the paternal inheritance would have remained
in the family. For some reason unknown to us,
Chimham seems to have got a part of it. We cannot
but believe that David would desire to have a good
man there, and it is much in favour of Chimham that he
should have got a settlement at Bethlehem. And there
is another circumstance that tells in his favour: during
the five centuries that elapsed between David's time
and the Captivity, the name of Chimham remained

in connection with that property, and even so late as the time of Jeremiah it was called "Chimham's habitation." Men do not thus keep alive dishonoured names, and the fact that Chimham's was thus preserved would seem to indicate that he was one of those of whom it is said, "The memory of the just is blessed."

Plans for life were speedily formed in those countries; and as Rebekah wished no delay in accompanying Abraham's servant to be the wife of Isaac, nor Ruth in going forth with Naomi to the land of Judah, so Chimham at once went with the king. The interview between David and Barzillai was ended in the way that in those countries was the most expressive sign of regard and affection : " David kissed Barzillai," but " Chimham went on with him."

The meeting with Barzillai and the finding of a new son in Chimham must have been looked back on by David with highly pleasant feelings. In every sense of the term, he had lost a son in Absalom; he seems now to find one in Chimham. We dare not say that the one was compensation for the other. Such a blank as the death of Absalom left in the heart of David could never be filled up from any earthly source whatever. Blanks of that nature can be filled only when God gives a larger measure of His own presence and His own love. But besides feeling very keenly the blank of Absalom's death, David must have felt distressed at the loss as it seemed, of power, to secure the affections of the younger generation of his people, many of whom, there is every reason to believe, had followed Absalom. The ready way in which Chimham accepted of the proposal in regard to him would therefore be a pleasant incident in his experience ; and the remembrance of his father's fast attachment and most useful friendship would ever be in David's memory like an oasis in the desert.

We return for a moment to the great lesson of this passage. Aged men, it is a lesson for you. Titus was instructed to exhort the aged men of Crete to be "sober, grave, temperate, sound in faith, in charity, in patience." It is a grievous thing to see grey hairs dishonoured. It is a humiliating sight when Noah excites either the shame or the derision of his sons. But "the hoary head is a crown of glory if it is found in the way of uprightness." And the crown is described in the six particulars of the exhortation to Titus. It is a crown of six jewels. Jewel the first is "sobriety," meaning here self-command, self-control, ability to stand erect before temptation, and calmness under provocation and trial. Jewel the second is "gravity," not sternness, nor sullenness, nor censoriousness, but the bearing of one who knows that "life is real, life is earnest," in opposition to the frivolous tone of those who act as if there were no life to come. Jewel the third is "temperance," especially in respect of bodily indulgence, keeping under the body, never letting it be master, but in all respects a servant. Jewel the fourth, "soundness in faith," holding the true doctrine of eternal life, and looking forward with hope and expectation to the inheritance of the future. Jewel the fifth, "soundness in charity," the charity of the thirteenth chapter of 1 Corinthians, itself a coruscation of the brightest gem in the Christian cabinet. Jewel the sixth, "soundness in patience," that grace so needful, but so often neglected, that grace that gives an air of serenity to one's character, that allies it to heaven, that gives it sublimity, that bears the unbearable, and hopes and rejoices on the very edge of despair.

Onward, then, ye aged men, in this glorious path! By God's grace, gather round your head these incorruptible jewels, which shine with the lustre of God's holiness, and which are the priceless gems of heaven. Happy are ye, if indeed you have these jewels for your crown; and happy is your Church where the aged men are crowned with glory like the four-and-twenty elders before the throne!

But what of those who dishonour God, and their own grey hairs, and the Church of Christ by stormy tempers, profane tongues, drunken orgies, and disorderly lives? "O my soul, come not thou into their secret! To their assembly, mine honour, be not thou united!"

# CHAPTER XXVII.

## THE INSURRECTION OF SHEBA.

2 SAMUEL xix. 41—43 ; xx.

DAVID was now virtually restored to his kingdom ;
but he had not even left Gilgal when fresh troubles
began. The jealousy between Judah and Israel broke
out in spite of him. The cause of complaint was on
the part of the ten tribes ; they were offended at not
having been waited for to take part in escorting the
king to Jerusalem. First, the men of Israel, in harsh
language, accused the men of Judah of having stolen
the king away, because they had transported him over
the Jordan. To this the men of Judah replied that the
king was of their kin ; therefore they had taken
the lead, but they had received no special reward or
honour in consequence. The men of Israel, however,
had an argument in reply to this : they were ten
tribes, and therefore had so much more right to the
king ; and Judah had treated them with contempt in not
consulting or co-operating with them in bringing him
back. It is added that the words of the men of Judah
were fiercer than the words of the men of Israel.

It is in a poor and paltry light that both sides
appear in this inglorious dispute. There was no solid
grievance whatever, nothing that might not have been
easily settled if the soft answer that turneth away

wrath had been resorted to instead of fierce and exasperating words. Alas ! that miserable tendency of our nature to take offence when we think we have been overlooked,—what mischief and misery has it bred in the world ! The men of Israel were foolish to take offence ; but the men of Judah were neither magnanimous nor forbearing in dealing with their unreasonable humour. The noble spirit of clemency that David had shown awakened but little permanent response. The men of Judah, who were foremost in Absalom's rebellion, were like the man in the parable that had been forgiven ten thousand talents, but had not the generosity to forgive the trifling offence committed against them, as they thought, by their brethren of Israel. So they seized their fellow-servant by the throat and demanded that he should pay them the uttermost farthing. Judah played false to his national character; for he was not " he whom his brethren should praise."

What was the result ? Any one acquainted with human nature might have foretold it with tolerable certainty. Given on one side a proneness to take offence, a readiness to think that one has been overlooked, and on the other a want of forbearance, a readiness to retaliate,—it is easy to see that the result will be a serious breach. It is just what we witness so often in children. One is apt to be dissatisfied, and complains of ill-treatment ; another has no forbearance, and retorts angrily : the result is a quarrel, with this difference, that while the quarrels of children pass quickly away, the quarrels of nations or of factions last miserably long.

Much inflammable material being thus provided, a casual spark speedily set it on fire. Sheba, an artful

Benjamite, raised the standard of revolt against David, and the excited ten tribes, smarting with the fierce words of the men of Judah, flocked to his standard. Most miserable proceeding! The quarrel had begun about a mere point of etiquette, and now they cast off God's anointed king, and that, too, after the most signal token of God's anger had fallen on Absalom and his rebellious crew. There are many wretched enough slaveries in this world, but the slavery of pride is perhaps the most mischievous and humiliating of all.

And here it cannot be amiss to call attention to the very great neglect of the rules and spirit of Christianity that is apt, even at the present day, to show itself among professing Christians in connection with their disputes. This is so very apparent that one is apt to think that the settlement of quarrels is the very last matter to which Christ's followers learn to apply the example and instructions of their Master. When men begin in earnest to follow Christ, they usually pay considerable attention to certain of His precepts; they turn away from scandalous sins, they observe prayer, they show some interest in Christian objects, and they abandon some of the more frivolous ways of the world. But alas! when they fall into differences, they are prone in dealing with them to leave all Christ's precepts behind them. See in what an unlovely and unloving spirit the controversies of Christians have usually been conducted; how much of bitterness and personal animosity they show, how little forbearance and gene-rosity; how readily they seem to abandon themselves to the impulses of their own hearts. Controversy rouses temper, and temper creates a tempest through which you cannot see clearly. And how many are the

quarrels in Churches or congregations that are carried
on with all the heat and bitterness of unsanctified men!
How much offence is taken at trifling neglects or
mistakes! Who remembers, even in its spirit, the
precept in the Sermon on the Mount, "If any man
smite thee on the right cheek, turn to him the other
also"? Who remembers the beatitude, "Blessed are
the peacemakers, for they shall be called the children of
God"? Who bears in mind the Apostle's horror at
the unseemly spectacle of saints carrying their quarrels
to heathen tribunals, instead of settling them as Christians quietly among themselves? Who weighs the
earnest counsel, "Endeavour to keep the unity of the
Spirit in the bond of peace"? Who prizes our gracious
Lord's most blessed legacy, "Peace I leave with you,
My peace I give unto you; not as the world giveth give
I unto you"? Do not all such texts show that it is
incumbent on Christians to be most careful and watch-
ful, when any difference arises, to guard against carnal
feeling of every kind, and strive to the very utmost to
manifest the spirit of Christ? Yet is it not at such
times that they are most apt to leave all their Christianity behind them, and engage in unseemly wrangles
with one another? Does not the devil very often get
it all his own way, whoever may be in the right, and
whoever in the wrong? And is not frequent occasion
given thereby to the enemy to blaspheme, and, in the
very circumstances that should bring out in clear and
strong light the true spirit of Christianity, is there not
often, in place of that, an exhibition of rudeness and
bitterness that makes the world ask, What better are
Christians than other men?

But let us return to King David and his people.
The author of the insurrection was "a man of Belial,

whose name was Sheba." He is called "the son of
Bichri, a Benjamite." Benjamin had a son whose
name was Becher, and the adjective formed from that
would be Bichrite ; some have thought that Bichri
denotes not his father, but his family. Saul appears
to have been of the same family (see *Speaker's
Commentary in loco*). It is thus quite possible that Sheba
was a relation of Saul, and that he had always
cherished a grudge against David for taking the throne
which he had filled. Here, we may remark in passing,
would have been a real temptation to Mephibosheth
to join an insurrection, for if this had succeeded he was
the man who would naturally have become king. But
there is no reason to believe that Mephibosheth
favoured Sheba, and therefore no reason to doubt the
truth of the account he gave of himself to David. The
war-cry of Sheba was an artful one—"We have no
part in David, neither have we inheritance in the son
of Jesse." It was a scornful and exaggerated mockery
of the claim that Judah had asserted as being of the
same tribe with the king, whereas the other tribes
stood in no such relation to him. "Very well," was
virtually the cry of Sheba—"if we have no part in
David, neither any inheritance in the son of Jesse, let
us get home as fast as possible, and leave his friends,
the tribe of Judah, to make of him what they can."
It was not so much a setting up of a new rebellion
as a scornful repudiation of all interest in the existing
king. Instead of going with David from Gilgal to
Jerusalem, they went up every man to his tent or
to his home. It is not said that they intended actively
to oppose David, and from this part of the narrative
we should suppose that all that they intended was
to make a public protest against the unworthy treat-

ment which they held that they had received.  It must
have greatly disturbed the pleasure of David's return
to Jerusalem that this unseemly secession occurred
by the way.  A chill must have fallen upon his heart
just as it was beginning to recover its elasticity.  And
much anxiety must have haunted him as to the issue
— whether or not the movement would go on to another
insurrection like Absalom's ;  or whether, having discharged their dissatisfied feeling, the people of Israel
would return sullenly to their allegiance.

Nor could the feelings of King David be much
soothed when he re-entered his home.  The greater
part of his family had been with him in his exile, and
when he returned his house was occupied by the ten
women whom he had left to keep it, and with whom
Absalom had behaved dishonourably.  And here was
another trouble resulting from the rebellion that could
not be adjusted in a satisfactory way.  The only way
of disposing of them was to put them in ward, to
shut them up in confinement, to wear out the rest of
their lives in a dreary, joyless widowhood.  All joy
and brightness was thus taken out of their lives, and
personal freedom was denied them.  They were doomed,
for no fault of theirs, to the weary lot of captives, cursing the day, probably, when their beauty had brought
them to the palace, and wishing that they could
exchange lots with the humblest of their sisters that
breathed the air of freedom.  Strange that, with all his
spiritual instincts, David could not see that a system
which led to such miserable results must lie under
the curse of God !

As events proceeded, it appeared that active mischief
was likely to arise from Sheba's movement.  He was
accompanied by a body of followers, and the king was

afraid lest he should get into some fenced city, and escape the correction which his wickedness deserved. He accordingly sent Amasa to assemble the men of Judah, and return within three days. This was Amasa's first commission after his being appointed general of the troops. Whether he found the people unwilling to go out again immediately to war, or whether they were unwilling to accept him as their general, we are not told, but certainly he tarried longer than the time appointed. Thereupon the king, who was evidently alarmed at the serious dimensions which the insurrection of Sheba was assuming, sent for Abishai, Joab's brother, and ordered him to take what troops were ready and start immediately to punish Sheba. Abishai took " Joab's men, and the Cherethites and the Pelethites, and all the mighty men." With these he went out from Jerusalem to pursue after Sheba. How Joab conducted himself on this occasion is a strange but characteristic chapter of his history. It does not appear that he had any dealings with David, or that David had any dealings with him. He simply went out with his brother, and, being a man of the strongest will and greatest daring, he seems to have resolved on some fit occasion to resume his command in spite of all the king's arrangements.

They had not gone farther from Jerusalem than the Pool of Gibeon when they were overtaken by Amasa, followed doubtless by his troops. When Joab and Amasa met, Joab, actuated by jealousy towards him as having superseded him in the command of the army, treacherously slew him, leaving his dead body on the ground, and, along with Abishai, prepared to give pursuit after Sheba. An officer of Joab's was stationed beside Amasa's dead body, to call on the soldiers, when they saw that their chief was dead, to follow Joab as the friend of David. But the sight of the dead body of Amasa only made them stand still—horrified, most probably, at the crime of Joab, and unwilling to place themselves under one who had been guilty of such a crime. The body of Amasa was accordingly removed from the highway into the field, and his soldiers were then ready enough to follow Joab. Joab was now in undisturbed command of the whole force, having set aside all David's arrangements as completely as if they had never been made. Little did David thus gain by superseding Joab and appointing Amasa in his room. The son of Zeruiah proved himself again too strong for him. The hideous crime by which he got rid of his rival was nothing to him. How he could reconcile all this with his duty to his king we are unable to see. No doubt he trusted to the principle that "success succeeds," and believed firmly that if he were able entirely to suppress Sheba's insurrection and return to Jerusalem with the news that every trace of the movement was obliterated, David would say nothing of the past, and silently restore the general who, with all his faults, did so well in the field.

Sheba was quite unable to offer opposition to the force that was thus led against him. He retreated northwards from station to station, passing in succession through the different tribes, until he came to the extreme northern border of the land. There, in a town called Abel-beth-Maachah, he took refuge, till Joab and his forces, accompanied by the Berites, a people of whom we know nothing, having overtaken him at Abel, besieged the town. Works were raised for the purpose of capturing Abel, and an assault was made on the wall for the purpose of throwing it down. Then a

woman, gifted with the wisdom for which the place
was proverbial, came to Joab to remonstrate against the
siege.   The ground of her remonstrance was that the
people of Abel had done nothing on account of which
their city should be destroyed.   Joab, she said, was
trying to destroy " a city and a mother in Israel," and
thereby to swallow up the inheritance of the Lord.   In
what sense was Joab seeking to destroy a *mother* in
Israel ?   The word seems to be used to denote a
mother-city or district capital, on which other places
were depending.   What you are trying to destroy is
not a mere city of Israel, but a city which has its family
of dependent villages, all of which must share in the
ruin if we are destroyed.   But Joab assured the woman
that he had no such desire.   All that he wished was to
get at Sheba, who had taken refuge within the city.
If that be all, said the woman, I will engage to throw
his head to thee over the wall.   It was the interest of
the people of the city to get rid of the man who was
bringing them into so serious a danger.   It was not
difficult for them to get Sheba decapitated, and to throw
his head over the wall to Joab.   By this means the
conspiracy was ended.   As in Absalom's case, the
death of the leader was the ruin of the cause.   No
further stand was made by any one.   Indeed, it is
probable that the great body of Sheba's followers had
fallen away from him in the course of his northern
flight, and that only a handful were with him in Abel.
So " Joab blew a trumpet, and they retired from the
city, every man to his tent.   And Joab returned unto
Jerusalem, to the king."

Thus, once again, the land had rest from war.   At
the close of the chapter we have a list of the chief
officers of the kingdom, similar to that given in

ch. viii. at the close of David's foreign wars. It would appear that, peace being again restored, pains were taken by the king to improve and perfect the arrangements for the administration of the kingdom. The changes on the former list are not very numerous. Joab was again at the head of the army; Benaiah, as before, commanded the Cherethites and the Pelethites; Jehoshaphat was still recorder; Sheva (same as Seraiah) was scribe; and Zadok and Abiathar were priests. In two cases there was a change. A new office had been instituted—"Adoram was over the tribute;" the subjugation of so many foreign states which had to pay a yearly tribute to David called for this change. In the earlier list it is said that the king's sons were chief rulers. No mention is made of king's sons now; the chief ruler is Ira the Jairite. On the whole, there was little change; at the close of this war the kingdom was administered in the same manner and almost by the same men as before.

There is nothing to indicate that the kingdom was weakened in its external relations by the two insurrections that had taken place against David. It is to be observed that both of them were of very short duration. Between Absalom's proclamation of himself at Hebron and his death in the wood of Ephraim there must have been a very short interval, not more than a fortnight. The insurrection of Sheba was probably all over in a week. Foreign powers could scarcely have heard of the beginning of the revolts before they heard of the close of them. There would be nothing therefore to give them any encouragement to rebel against David, and they do not appear to have made any such attempt. But in another and higher sense these revolts left painful consequences behind them. The chastening to which David was exposed in connection with them was very humbling. His glory as king was seriously impaired. It was humiliating that he should have had to fly from before his own son. It was hardly less humiliating that he was seen to lie so much at the mercy of Joab. He is unable to depose Joab, and when he tries to do so, Joab not only kills his successor, but takes possession by his own authority of the vacant place. And David can say nothing. In this relation of David to Joab we have a sample of the trials of kings. Nominally supreme, they are often the servants of their ministers and officers. Certainly David was not always his own master. Joab was really above him; frustrated, doubtless, some excellent plans; did great service by his rough patriotism and ready valour, but injured the good name of David and the reputation of his government by his daring crimes. The retrospect of this period of his reign could have given little satisfaction to the king, since he had to trace it, with all its calamities and sorrows, to his own evil conduct. And yet what David suffered, and what the nation suffered, was not, strictly speaking, the punishment of his sin. God had forgiven him his sin. David had sung, "Blessed is the man whose iniquity is forgiven, whose sin is covered." What he now suffered was not the visitation of God's wrath, but a fatherly chastening, designed to deepen his contrition and quicken his vigilance. And surely we may say, If the fatherly chastening was so severe, what would the Divine retribution have been? If these things were done in the green tree, what would have been done in the dry? If David, even though forgiven, could not but shudder at all the terrible results of that course of sin which began with his allowing himself to lust after

Bathsheba, what must be the feeling of many a lost soul, in the world of woe, recalling its first step in open rebellion against God, and thinking of all the woes, innumerable and unutterable, that have sprung therefrom? Oh, sin, how terrible a curse thou bringest! What serpents spring up from the dragon's teeth! And how awful the fate of those who awake all too late to a sense of what thou art! Grant, O God, of Thine infinite mercy, that we all may be wise in time; that we may ponder the solemn truth, that "the wages of sin is death"; and that, without a day's delay, we may flee for refuge to lay hold of the hope set before us, and find peace in believing on Him who came to take sin away by the sacrifice of Himself!

# CHAPTER XXVIII.

## THE FAMINE.

2 SAMUEL xxi. 1—14.

WE now enter on the concluding part of the reign of David. Some of the matters in which he was most occupied during this period are recorded only in Chronicles. Among these, the chief was his preparations for the building of the temple, which great work was to be undertaken by his son. In the concluding part of Samuel the principal things recorded are two national judgments, a famine and a pestilence, that occurred in David's reign, the one springing from a transaction in the days of Saul, the other from one in the days of David. Then we have two very remarkable lyrical pieces, one a general song of thanksgiving, forming a retrospect of his whole career ; the other a prophetic vision of the great Ruler that was to spring from him, and the effects of His reign. In addition to these, there is also a notice of certain wars of David's, not previously recorded, and a fuller statement respecting his great men than we have elsewhere. The whole of this section has more the appearance of a collection of pieces than a chronological narrative. It is by no means certain that they are all recorded in the order of their occurrence. The most characteristic of the pieces are the two songs or psalms—the

one looking back, the other looking forward; the one
commemorating the goodness and mercy that had
followed him all the days of his life, the other picturing
goodness still greater and mercy more abundant, yet
to be vouchsafed under David's Son.

The conjunction "then" at the beginning of the
chapter is replaced in the Revised Version by "and."
It does not denote that what is recorded here took
place immediately after what goes before. On the
contrary, the note of time is found in the general
expression, "in the days of David," that is, some time
in David's reign. On obvious grounds, most recent
commentators are disposed to place this occurrence
comparatively early. It is likely to have happened
while the crime of Saul was yet fresh in the public
recollection. By the close of David's reign a new
generation had come to maturity, and the transactions
of Saul's reign must have been comparatively forgotten.
It is clear from David's excepting Mephibosheth, that
the transaction occurred after he had been discovered
and cared for. Possibly the narrative of the discovery
of Mephibosheth may also be out of chronological
order, and that event may have occurred earlier than
is commonly thought. It will remove some of the
difficulties of this difficult chapter if we are entitled
to place the occurrence at a time not very far remote
from the death of Saul.

It was altogether a singular occurrence, this famine
in the land of Israel. The calamity was remarkable,
the cause was remarkable, the cure most remarkable
of all. The whole narrative is painful and perplexing;
it places David in a strange light,—it seems to place
even God Himself in a strange light; and the only
way in which we can explain it, in consistency with

a righteous government, is by laying great stress on a principle accepted without hesitation in those Eastern countries, which made the father and his children " one concern," and held the children liable for the misdeeds of the father.

1. As to the calamity. It was a famine that continued three successive years, causing necessarily an increase of misery year after year. There is a presumption that it occurred in the earlier part of David's reign, because, if it had been after the great enlargement of the kingdom which followed his foreign wars, the resources of some parts of it would probably have availed to supply the deficiency. At first it does not appear that the king held that there was any special significance in the famine,—that it came as a reproof for any particular sin. But when the famine extended to a third year, he was persuaded that it must have a special cause. Did he not in this just act as we all are disposed to do? A little trial we deem to be nothing; it does not seem to have any significance or to be connected with any lesson. It is only when the little trial swells into a large one, or the brief trouble into a long-continued affliction, that we begin to inquire why it was sent. If small trials were more regarded, heavy trials would be less needed. The horse that springs forward at the slightest touch of the whip or prick of the spur needs no heavy lash; it is only when the lighter stimulus fails that the heavier has to be applied. Man's tendency, even under God's chastenings, has ever been to ignore the source of them,—when God "poured upon him the fury of His anger and the strength of battle, and it set him on fire round about, yet he knew not; and it burned him, yet he laid it not to heart" (Isa. xlii. 25). Trials

would neither be so long nor so severe if more regard
were had to them in an earlier stage; if they were
accepted more as God's message—" Thus saith the
Lord of hosts, Consider your ways."

2. The cause of the calamity was made known when
David inquired of the Lord—" It is for Saul and his
bloody house, because he slew the Gibeonites."

The history of the crime for which this famine was
sent can be gathered only from incidental notices.
It appears from the narrative before us that Saul
" consumed the Gibeonites, and devised against them
that they should be destroyed from remaining in any of
the coasts of Israel."   The Gibeonites, as is well known,
were a Canaanite people, who, through a cunning
stratagem, obtained leave from Joshua to dwell in their
old settlements, and being protected by a solemn
national oath, were not disturbed even when it was
found out that they had been practising a fraud.   They
possessed cities, situated principally in the tribe of
Benjamin; the chief of them, Gibeon, " was a great city,
one of the royal cities, greater than Ai."   In the time
of Saul they were a quiet, inoffensive people; yet he
seems to have fallen on them with a determination to
sweep them from all the coasts of Israel.   Death or
banishment was the only alternative he offered.   His
desire to exterminate them evidently failed, otherwise
David would have found none of them to consult; but
the savage attack which he made on them affords an
incidental proof that it was no feeling of humanity that
led him to spare the Amalekites when he was ordered
to destroy them.

We are not told of any offence that the Gibeonites
had committed; and perhaps covetousness lay at the
root of Saul's policy.   There is reason to believe that

when he saw his popularity declining and David's advancing, he had recourse to unscrupulous methods of increasing his own. Addressing his servants, before the slaughter of Abimelech and the priests, he asked, " Hear now, ye Benjamites ; will the son of Jesse give you fields and vineyards, that all of you have conspired against me ? " Evidently he had rewarded his favourites, especially those of his own tribe, with fields and vineyards. But how had he got these to bestow ? Very probably by dispossessing the Gibeonites. Their cities, as we have seen, were in the tribe of Benjamin. But to prevent jealousy, others, both of Judah and of Israel, would get a share of the spoil. For he is said to have sought to slay the Gibeonites " in his zeal for the children of Israel and Judah." If this was the way in which the slaughter of the Gibeonites was compassed, it was fair that the nation should suffer for it. If the nation profited by the unholy transaction, and was thus induced to wink at the violation of the national faith and the massacre of an inoffensive people, it shared in Saul's guilt, and became liable to chastisement. Even David himself was not free from blame. When he came to the throne he should have seen justice done to this injured people. But probably he was afraid. He felt his own authority not very secure, and probably he shrank from raising up enemies in those whom justice would have required him to dispossess. Prince and people therefore were both at fault, and both were suffering for the wrongdoing of the nation. Perhaps Solomon had this case in view when he wrote : " Rob not the poor because he is poor, neither oppress the afflicted in the gate ; for the Lord will plead their cause, and spoil the soul of those that spoiled them."

But whatever may have been Saul's motive, it is certain that by his attempt to massacre and banish the Gibeonites a great national sin was committed, and that for this sin the nation had never humbled itself, and never made reparation.

3. What, then, was now to be done? The king left it to the Gibeonites themselves to prescribe the satisfaction which they claimed for this wrong. This was in accordance with the spirit of the law that gave a murdered man's nearest of kin a right to exact justice of the murderer. In their answer the Gibeonites disclaimed all desire for compensation in money; and very probably this was a surprise to the people. To surrender lands might have been much harder than to give up lives. What the Gibeonites asked had a grim look of justice; it showed a burning desire to bring home the punishment as near as possible to the offender: "The man that consumed us, and that devised against us that we should be destroyed from remaining in any of the coasts of Israel, let seven men of his sons be delivered unto us, and we will hang them up unto the Lord in Gibeah of Saul, whom the Lord did choose." Seven was a perfect number, and therefore the victims should be seven. Their punishment was, to be hanged or crucified, but in inflicting this punishment the Jews were more merciful than the Romans; the criminals were first put to death, then their dead bodies were exposed to open shame. They were to be hanged "unto the Lord," as a satisfaction to expiate His just displeasure. They were to be hanged "in Gibeah of Saul," to bring home the offence visibly to him, so that the expiation should be at the same place as the crime. And when mention is made of Saul, the

Gibeonites add, " Whom the Lord did choose." For Jehovah was intimately connected with Saul's call to the throne ; He was in some sense publicly identified with him ; and unless something were done to dis-connect Him with this crime, the reproach of it would, in measure, rest upon Him.

Such was the demand of the Gibeonites ; and David deemed it right to comply with it, stipulating only that the descendants of Jonathan should not be surrendered. The sons or descendants of Saul that were given up for this execution were the two sons of Rizpah, Saul's concubine, and along with them five sons of Michal, or, as it is in the margin, of Merab, the elder daughter of Saul, whom she bare (R. V.—not "brought up," A. V.) to Adriel the Meholathite. These seven men were put to death accordingly, and their bodies exposed in the hill near Gibeah.

The transaction has a very hard look to us, though it had nothing of the kind to the people of those days. Why should these unfortunate men be punished so terribly for the sin of their father ? How was it pos-sible for David, in cold blood, to give them up to an ignominious death ? How could he steel his heart against the supplications of their friends ? With regard to this latter aspect of the case, it is ridiculous to cast reproach on David. As we have remarked again and again, if he had acted like other Eastern kings, he would have consigned every son of Saul to destruction when he came to the throne, and left not one remaining, for no other offence than being the children of their father. On the score of clemency to Saul's family the character of David is abundantly vindicated.

The question of justice remains. Is it not a law of

nature, it may be asked, and a law of the Bible too, that the son shall not bear the iniquity of the father, but that the soul that sinneth it shall die? It is undoubtedly the rule both of nature and the Bible that the son is not to be substituted *for* the father when the father is there to bear the penalty. But it is neither the rule of the one nor of the other that the son is never to suffer *with* the father for the sins which the father has committed. On the contrary, it is what we see taking place, in many forms, every day. It is an arrangement of Providence that almost baffles the philanthropist, who sees that children often inherit from their parents a physical frame disposing them to their parents' vices, and who sees, moreover, that, when brought up by vicious parents, children are deprived of their natural rights, and are initiated into a life of vice. But the law that identified children and parents in Old Testament times was carried out to consequences which would not be tolerated now. Not only were children often punished because of their physical connection with their fathers, but they were regarded as judicially one with them, and so liable to share in their punishment. The Old Testament (as Canon Mozley has so powerfully shown *) was in some respects an imperfect economy ; the rights of the individual were not so clearly acknowledged as they are under the New ; the family was a sort of moral unit, and the father was the responsible agent for the whole. When Achan sinned, his whole household shared his punishment. The solidarity of the family was such that all were involved in the sin of the father. However strange it may seem to us, it did not appear at all strange in David's time

* Lectures on the Old Testament. Lecture V. : " Visitation of Sins of Fathers on Children."

that this rule should be applied in the case of Saul. On the contrary, it would probably be thought that it showed considerable moderation of feeling not to demand the death of the whole living posterity of Saul, but to limit the demand to the number of seven. Doubtless the Gibeonites had suffered to an enormous extent. Thousands upon thousands of them had probably been slain. People might be sorry for the seven young men that had to die, but that there was anything essentially unjust or even harsh in the transaction is a view of the case that would occur to no one. Justice is often hard; executions are always grim; but here was a nation that had already experienced three years of famine for the sin of Saul, and that would experience yet far more if no public expiation should take place; and seven men were not very many to die for a nation.

The grimness of the mode of punishment was softened by an incident of great moral beauty, which cannot but touch the heart of every man of sensibility. Rizpah, the concubine of Saul, and mother of two of the victims, combining the tenderness of a mother and the courage of a hero, took her position beside the gibbet; and, undeterred by the sight of the rotting bodies and the stench of the air, she suffered neither the birds of the air to rest on them by day nor the beasts of the field by night. The poor woman must have looked for a very different destiny when she became the concubine of Saul. No doubt she expected to share in the glory of his royal state. But her lord perished in battle, and the splendour of royalty passed for ever from him and his house. Then came the famine; its cause was declared from heaven, its cure was announced by the Gibeonites. Her two sons were

among the slain. Probably they were but lads, not
yet beyond the age which rouses a mother's sensi-
bilities to the full. (This consideration likewise points
to an early date.) We cannot attempt to picture her
feelings. The last consolation that remained for her
was to guard their remains from the vulture and the
tiger. Unburied corpses were counted to be disgraced,
and this, in some degree, because they were liable to
be devoured by birds and beasts of prey. Rizpah
could not prevent the exposure, but she could try to
prevent the wild animals from devouriug them. The
courage and self-denial needed for this work were
great, for the risk of violence from wild beasts was
very serious. All honour to this woman and her noble
heart! David appears to have been deeply impressed
by her heroism. When he heard of it he went and
collected the bones of Jonathan and his sons, which
had been buried under a tree at Jabesh-gilead, and
likewise the bones of the men that had been hanged;
and he buried the bones of Saul and Jonathan in
Zelah, in the sepulchre of Kish, Saul's father. And
after that God was entreated for the land.

We offer a concluding remark, founded on the tone
of this narrative. It is marked, as every one must
perceive, by a subdued, solemn tone. Whatever may
be the opinion of our time as to the need of apologizing
for it, it is evident that no apology was deemed necessary for the transaction at the time this record was
written. The feeling of all parties evidently was, that
it was indispensable that things should take the course
they did. No one expressed wonder when the famine
was accounted for by the crime of Saul. No one
objected when the question of expiation was referred
to the Gibeonites. The house of Saul made no protest

when seven of his sons were demanded for death. The men themselves, when they knew what was coming, seem to have been restrained from attempting to save themselves by flight. It seemed as if God were speaking, and the part of man was simply to obey. When unbelievers object to passages in the Bible like this, or like the sacrifice of Isaac, or the death of Achan, they are accustomed to say that they exemplify the worst passions of the human heart consecrated under the name of religion. We affirm that in this chapter there is no sign of any outburst of passion whatever; everything is done with gravity, with composure and solemnity. And, what is more, the graceful piety of Rizpah is recorded, with simplicity, indeed, but in a tone that indicates appreciation of her tender motherly soul. Savages thirsting for blood are not in the habit of appreciating such touching marks of affection. And further, we are made to feel that it was a pleasure to David to pay that mark of respect for Rizpah's feelings in having the men buried. He did not desire to lacerate the feelings of the unhappy mother; he was glad to soothe them as far as he could. To him, as to his Lord, judgment was a strange work, but he delighted in mercy. And he was glad to be able to mingle a slight streak of mercy with the dark colours of a picture of God's judgment on sin.

To all right minds it is painful to punish, and when punishment has to be inflicted it is felt that it ought to be done with great solemnity and gravity, and with an entire absence of passion and excitement. In a sinful world God too must inflict punishment. And the future punishment of the wicked is the darkest thing in all the scheme of God's government. But it must

take place. And when it does take place it will be
done deliberately, solemnly, sadly. There will be no
exasperation, no excitement. There will be no disregard
of the feelings of the unhappy victims of the Divine
retribution. What they are able to bear will be well
considered. What condition they shall be placed in
when the punishment comes, will be calmly weighed.
But may we not see what a distressing thing it will be
(if we may use such an expression with reference to
God) to consign His creatures to punishment? How
different His feelings when He welcomes them to eternal
glory! How different the feelings of His angels when
that change takes place by which punishment ceases to
hang over men, and glory takes its place! "There is
joy in the presence of the angels of God over one sinner
that repenteth." Is it not blessed to think that this is
the feeling of God, and of all Godlike spirits? Will
you not all believe this,—believe in the mercy of God,
and accept the provision of His grace? "For God so
loved the world that He gave His only-begotten Son,
that whosoever believeth on Him should not perish,
but should have eternal life."

# CHAPTER XXIX.

## *LAST BATTLES AND THE MIGHTY MEN.*

### 2 SAMUEL xxi. 15—22 ; xxiii. 8—39.

IN entering on the consideration of these two portions of the history of David, we must first observe that the events recorded do not appear to belong to the concluding portion of his reign. It is impossible for us to assign a precise date to them, or at least to most of them, but the displays of physical activity and courage which they record would lead us to ascribe them to a much earlier period. Originally, they seem to have formed parts of a record of David's wars, and to have been transferred to the Books of Samuel and Chronicles in order to give a measure of completeness to the narrative. The narrative in Chronicles is substantially the same as that in Samuel, but the text is purer. From notes of time in Chronicles it is seen that some at least of the encounters took place after the war with the children of Ammon.

Why have these passages been inserted in the history of the reign of David? Apparently for two chief purposes. In the first place, to give us some idea of the dangers to which he was exposed in his military life, dangers manifold and sometimes overwhelming, and all but fatal ; and thus enable us to see how wonderful were the deliverances he experienced,

and prepare us for entering into the song of thanksgiving which forms the twenty-second chapter, and of
which these deliverances form the burden.    In the
second place, to enable us to understand the human
instrumentality by which he achieved so brilliant a
success, the kind of men by whom he was helped,
the kind of spirit by which they were animated, and
their intense personal devotion to David himself.   The
former purpose is that which is chiefly in view in the
end of the twenty-first chapter, the latter in the
twenty-third.   The exploits themselves occur in encounters with the Philistines, and may therefore be
referred partly to the time after the slaughter of
Goliath, when he first distinguished himself in warfare, and the daughters of Israel began to sing, "Saul
hath slain his thousands, but David his tens of thousands;" partly to the time in his early reign when
he was engaged driving them out of Israel, and putting a bridle on them to restrain their inroads ; and
partly to a still later period.   It is to be observed
that nothing more is sought than to give a sample
of David's military adventures, and for this purpose
his wars with the Philistines alone are examined.   If
the like method had been taken with all his other campaigns,—against Edom, Moab, and Ammon ; against
the Syrians of Rehob, and Maacah, and Damascus,
and the Syrians beyond the river,—we might borrow
the language of the Evangelist, and say that the world
itself would not have been able to contain the books
that should be written.

Four exploits are recorded in the closing verses of
the twenty-first chapter, all with "sons of the giant,"
or, as it is in the margin, of Rapha.   The first was with
a man who is called Ishbi-benob, but there is reason to

suspect that the text is corrupt here, and in Chronicles this incident is not mentioned. The language applied to David, " David and his servants went down," would lead us to believe that the incident happened at an early period, when the Philistines were very powerful in Israel, and it was a mark of great courage to " go down " to their plains, and attack them in their own country. To do this implied a long journey, over steep and rough roads, and it is no wonder if between the journey and the fighting David "waxed faint." Then it was that the son of the giant, whose spear or spear-head weighed three hundred shekels of brass, or about eight pounds, fell upon him " with a new sword, and thought to have slain him." There is no noun in the original for sword ; all that is said is, that the giant fell on David with something new, and our translators have made it a sword. The Revised Version in the margin gives " new armour." The point is evidently this, that the newness of the thing made it more formidable. This could hardly be said of a common sword, which would be really more formidable after it had ceased to be quite new, since, by having used it, the owner would know it better and wield it more perfectly. It seems better to take the marginal reading " new armour," that is, new defensive armour, against which the weary David would direct his blows in vain. Evidently he was in the utmost peril of his life, but was rescued by his nephew Abishai, who killed the giant. The risk to which he was exposed was such that his people vowed they would not let him go out with them to battle any more, lest the light of Israel should be quenched.

During the rest of that campaign the vow seems to have been respected, for the other three giants were not slain by David personally, but by others. As to other campaigns, David usually took his old place as leader of the army, until the battle against Absalom, when his people prevailed on him to remain in the city.

Three of the four duels recorded here took place at Gob,—a place not now known, but most probably in the neighbourhood of Gath. In fact, all the encounters probably took place near that city. One of the giants slain is said in Samuel, by a manifest error, to have been Goliath the Gittite; but the error is corrected in Chronicles, where he is called the brother of Goliath. The very same expression is used of his spear as in the case of Goliath : " the staff of whose spear was like a weaver's beam." Of the fourth giant it is said that he defied Israel, as Goliath had done. Of the whole four it is said that " they were born to the giant in Gath." This does not necessarily imply that they were all sons of the same father, " the giant " being used generically to denote the race rather than the individual.

But the tenor of the narrative and many of its expressions carry us back to the early days of David. There seems to have been a nest at Gath of men of gigantic stature, brothers or near relations of Goliath. Against these he was sent, perhaps in one of the expeditions when Saul secretly desired that he should fall by the hand of the Philistines. If it was in this way that he came to encounter the first of the four, Saul had calculated well, and was very nearly carrying his point. But though man proposes, God disposes. The example of David in his encounter with Goliath, even at this early period, had inspired several young men of the Hebrews, and even when David was interdicted from going himself into battle, others were raised up to take his place. Every one of the giants found a match either in David or among his men. It was indeed highly perilous work; but David was encompassed by a Divine Protector, and being destined for high service in the kingdom of God, he was " immortal till his work was done."

We have said that these were but samples of David's trials, and that they were probably repeated again and again in the course of the many wars in which he was enggaed. One can see that the danger was often very imminent, making him feel that his only possible deliverance must come from God. Such dangers, therefore, were wonderfully fitted to exercise and discipline the spirit of trust. Not once or twice, but hundreds of times, in his early experience he would find himself constrained to cry to the Lord. And protected as he was, delivered as he was, the conviction would become stronger and stronger that God cared for him and would deliver him to the end. We see from all this how unnecessary it is to ascribe all the psalms where David is pressed by enemies either to the time of Saul or to the time of Absalom. There were hundreds of other times in his life when he had the same experience, when he was reduced to similar straits, and his appeal lay to the God of his life.

And this was in truth the healthiest period of his spiritual life. It was amid these perilous but bracing experiences that his soul prospered most. The north wind of danger and difficulty braced him to spiritual self-denial and endurance; the south wind of prosperity and luxurious enjoyment was what nearly destroyed him. Let us not become impatient when anxieties multiply around us, and we are beset by troubles, and labours, and difficulties. Do not be tempted to contrast your miserable lot with that of others, who have health while you are sick, riches while you are poor, honour while you are despised, ease and enjoyment while you have care and sorrow.  By all these things God desires to draw you to Himself, to discipline your soul, to lead you away from the broken cisterns that can hold no water to the fountain of living waters.  Guard earnestly against the unbelief that at such times would make your hands hang down and your heart despond ; rally your sinking spirit.  "Why art thou cast down, O my soul, and why art thou disquieted within me ? "  Remember the promise, " I will never leave you nor forsake you ; " and one day you shall have cause to look back on this as the most useful, the most profitable, the most healthful, period of your spiritual life.

We pass to the twenty-third chapter, which tells us of David's mighty men.  The narrative, at some points, is not very clear; but we gather from it that David had an order of thirty men distinguished for their valour; that besides these there were three of supereminent merit, and another three, who were also eminent, but who did not attain to the distinction of the first three.  Of the first three, the first was Jashobeam the Hachmonite (see 1 Chron. xi. 11), the second Eleazar, and the third Shammah.  Of the second three, who were not quite equal to the first, only two are mentioned, Abishai and Benaiah ; thereafter we have the names of the thirty.  It is remarkable that Joab's name does not occur in the list, but as he was captain of the host, he probably held a higher position than any.  Certainly Joab was not wanting in valour, and must have held the highest rank in a legion of honour.

Of the three mighties of the first rank, and the two

of the second, characteristic exploits of remarkable
courage and success are recorded. The first of the
first rank, whom the Chronicles call Jashobeam, lifted
up his spear against three hundred slain at one time.
(In Samuel the number is eight hundred.) The exploit
was worthy to be ranked with the famous achievement
of Jonathan and his armour-bearer at the pass of
Michmash. The second, Eleazar, defied the Philistines
when they were gathered to battle, and when the men
of Israel had gone away he smote the Philistines till
his hand was weary. The third, Shammah, kept the
Philistines at bay on a piece of ground covered with
lentils, after the people had fled, and slew the Philistines, gaining a great victory.

Next we have a description of the exploit of three of
the mighty men when the Philistines were in possession
of Bethlehem, and David in a hold near the cave of
Adullam (see 2 Sam. v. 15-21). The occasion of their
exploit was an interesting one. Contemplating the
situation, and grieved to think that his native town
should be in the enemy's hands, David gave expression
to a wish—"Oh that some one would give me water to
drink of the well of Bethlehem which is before the
gate!" It was probably meant for little more than the
expression of an earnest wish that the enemy were
dislodged from their position—that there were no
obstruction between him and the well, that access to it
were as free as in the days of his youth. But the three
mighty men took him at his word, and breaking
through the host of the Philistines, brought the water
to David. It was a singular proof of his great personal
influence; he was so loved and honoured that to
gratify his wish these three men took their lives in
their hands to obtain the water. Water got at such a

cost was sacred in his eyes ; it was a thing too holy
for man to turn to his use, so he poured it out before
the Lord.

Next we have a statement bearing on two of the
second three. Abishai, David's nephew, who was one
of them, lifted up his spear against three hundred and
slew them.   Benaiah, son of Jehoiada, slew two lion-like
men of Moab (the two sons of Ariel of Moab, R.V.);
also, in time of snow, he slew a lion in a pit; and finally
he slew an Egyptian, a powerful man, attacking him
when he had only a staff in his hand, wrenching his
spear from him, and killing him with his own spear.
The third of this trio has not been mentioned ; some
conjecture that he was Amasa ("chief of the captains "
—"the thirty," R.V., I Chron. xii. 18), and that his
name was not recorded because he deserted David to
side with Absalom.   Among the other thirty, we cannot
but be struck with two names—Eliam the son of
Ahithophel the Gilonite, and apparently the father of
Bathsheba ; and Uriah the Hittite.   The sin of David
was all the greater if it involved the dishonour of
men who had served him so bravely as to be enrolled
in his legion of honour.

With regard to the kind of exploits ascribed to some
of these men, a remark is necessary.   There is an
appearance of exaggeration in statements that ascribe
to a single warrior the routing and killing of hundreds
through his single sword or spear.   In the eyes of some
such statements give the narrative an unreliable look,
as if the object of the writer had been more to give *éclat*
to the warriors than to record the simple truth.   But
this impression arises from our tendency to ascribe the
conditions of modern warfare to the warfare of these
times.   In Eastern history, cases of a single warrior

putting a large number to flight, and even killing them, are not uncommon. For though the strength of the whole number was far more than a match for his, the strength of each individual was far inferior; and if the mass of them were scarcely armed, and the few who had arms were far inferior to him, the result would be that after some had fallen the rest would take to flight; and the destruction of life in a retreat was always enormous. The incident recorded of Eleazar is very graphic and truth-like. "He smote the Philistines until his hand was weary, and his hand clave unto his sword." A Highland sergeant at Waterloo had done such execution with his basket-handled sword, and so much blood had coagulated round his hand, that it had to be released by a blacksmith, so firmly were they glued together. The style of Eastern warfare was highly favourable to deeds of great courage being done by individuals, and in the terrific panic which followed their first successes prodigious slaughter often ensued. Under present conditions of fighting such things cannot be done.

The glimpse which these little notices give us of King David and his knights is extremely interesting. The story of Arthur and his Knights of the Round Table bears a resemblance to it. We see the remarkable personal influence of David, drawing to himself so many men of spirit and energy, firing them by his own example, securing their warm personal attachment, and engaging them in enterprises equal to his own. How far they shared his devotional spirit we have no means of judging. If the historian reflects the general sentiment in recording their victories when he says, once and again, "The Lord wrought a great victory that day" (xxiii. 10, 12), we should say that trust in God must have been the general sentiment. "If it had not been the Lord that was on our side, . . . they had swallowed us up quick, when their wrath was kindled against us." It is no wonder that David soon gained a great military renown. Such a king, surrounded by such a class of lieutenants, might well spread alarm among all his enemies. One who, besides having such a body of helpers, could claim the assistance of the Lord of hosts, and could enter battle with the shout, "Let God arise; and let His enemies be scattered; and let them also that hate Him flee before Him," might well look for universal victory. Trustworthy generals, we are told, double the value of the troops; and the soldiers that were led by such leaders, trusting in the Lord of hosts, could hardly fail of triumph.

And thus, too, we may see how David came to be thoroughly under the influence of the military spirit, and of some of the less favourable features of that spirit. Accustomed to such scenes of bloodshed, he would come to think lightly of the lives of his enemies. A hostile army he would be prone to regard as a kind of infernal machine, an instrument of evil only, and therefore to be destroyed. Hence the complacency he expresses in the destruction of his enemies. Hence the judgment he calls down on those who thwarted and opposed him. If, in the songs of David, this feeling sometimes disappears, and the expressed desire of his heart is that the nations may be glad and sing for joy, that the people may praise God, that all the people may praise Him, this seems to be in the later period of his life, when all his enemies had been subdued, and he had rest on every side. Even in earnest and spiritually-minded men, religion is often coloured by their worldly calling; and in no case more so, sometimes for better

and sometimes for worse, than in those who follow the
profession of arms.

But in all this military career and influence of David,
may we not trace a type of character which was
realised in a far higher sphere, and to far grander purpose, in the career of Jesus, David's Son ?   David on an
earthly level is Jesus on a higher.   Every noble quality
of David, his courage, his activity, his affection, his
obedience and trust toward God, his devotion to the
welfare of others, reappears purer and higher in Jesus.
If David is surrounded by his thirty mighties and his
two threes, so is Jesus by His twelve apostles, His
seventy disciples, and pre-eminently the three apostles
who went with Him into the innermost scenes.   If
David's men are roused by his example to deeds of
daring like his own, so the apostles and disciples go
into the world to teach, to fight, to heal, and to bless,
as Christ had done before them.   Looking back from
the present moment to David's time, what young man
of spirit but feels that it would have been a great joy to
belong to his company, much better than to be among
those who were always carping and criticising, and
laughing at the men who shared his danger and sacrifices ?   And does any one think that, when another
cycle of ages has gone past, he will have occasion to
congratulate himself that while he lived on earth he
had nothing to do with Christ and earnest Christians,
that he bore no part in any Christian battle, that he
kept well away from Christ and His staff, that he preferred the service and pleasure of the world ?   Surely
no.   Shall any of us, then, deliberately do to-day what
we know we shall repent to-morrow ?   Is it not certain
that Jesus Christ is an unrivalled Commander, pure and
noble above all His fellows, that His life was the most

glorious ever led on earth, and that His service is by far the most honourable ?   We do not dwell at this moment on the great fact that only in His faith and fellowship can any of us escape the wrath to come, or gain the favour of God.   We ask you to say in what company you can spend your lives to most profit, under whose influence you may receive the highest impulses, and be made to do the best service for God and man ? It must have been interesting in David's time to see his people "willing in the day of his power," to see young men flocking to his standard in the beauties of holiness, like dewdrops from the womb of the morning.   And still more glorious is the sight when young men, even the highest born and the highest gifted, having had grace to see who and what Jesus Christ is, find no manner of life worthy to be compared in essential dignity and usefulness with His service, and, in spite of the world, give themselves to Him.   Oh that we could see many such rallying to His standard, contrasting, as St. Paul did, the two services, and counting all things but loss for the excellency of the knowledge of Christ Jesus their Lord !

# CHAPTER XXX.

## *THE SONG OF THANKSGIVING.*

### 2 SAMUEL xxii.

SOME of David's actions are very characteristic of himself; there are other actions quite out of harmony with his character. This psalm of thanksgiving belongs to the former order. It is quite like David, at the conclusion of his military enterprises, to cast his eye gratefully over the whole, and acknowledge the goodness and mercy that had followed him all along. Unlike many, he was as careful to thank God for mercies past and present as to entreat Him for mercies to come. The whole Book of Psalms resounds with halleluiahs, especially the closing part. In the song before us we have something like a grand halleluiah, in which thanks are given for all the deliverances and mercies of the past, and unbounded confidence expressed in God's mercy and goodness for the time to come.

The date of this song is not to be determined by the place which it occupies in the history. We have already seen that the last few chapters of Samuel consist of supplementary narratives, not introduced at their regular places, but needful to give completeness to the history. It is likely that this psalm was written considerably before the end of David's reign. Two considerations make it all but certain that its date is earlier than Absalom's rebellion. In the first place, the mention of the name of Saul in the first verse—" in the day when God delivered him out of the hand of all his enemies and out of the hand of Saul "—would seem to imply that the deliverance from Saul was somewhat recent, certainly not so remote as it would have been at the end of David's reign. And secondly, while the affirmation of David's sincerity and honesty in serving God might doubtless have been made at any period of his life, yet some of his expressions would not have been likely to be used after his deplorable fall. It is not likely that after that, he would have spoken, for example, of the cleanness of his hands, stained as they had been by wickedness that could hardly have been surpassed. On the whole, it seems most likely that the psalm was written about the time referred to in 2 Sam. vii. 1—" when the Lord had given him rest from all his enemies round about." This was the time when it was in his heart to build the temple, and we know from that and other circumstances that he was then in a state of overflowing thankfulness.

Besides the introduction, the song consists of three leading parts not very definitely separated from each other, but sufficiently marked to form a convenient division, as follows :—

I. Introduction : the leading thought of the song, an adoring acknowledgment of what God had been and was to David (vv. 2-4).

II. A narrative of the Divine interpositions on his behalf, embracing his dangers, his prayers, and the Divine deliverances in reply (vv. 5-19).

III. The grounds of his protection and success (vv. 20-30).

IV. References to particular acts of God's goodness in various parts of his life, interspersed with reflections on the Divine character, from all which the assurance is drawn that that goodness would be continued to him and his successors, and would secure through coming ages the welfare and extension of the kingdom. And here we observe what is so common in the Psalms : a gradual rising above the idea of a mere earthly kingdom ; the type passes into the antitype ; the kingdom of David melts, as in a dissolving view, into the kingdom of the Messiah ; thus a more elevated tone is given to the song, and the assurance is conveyed to every believer that as God protected David and his kingdom, so shall He protect and glorify the kingdom of His Son for ever.

I. In the burst of adoring gratitude with which the psalm opens as its leading thought, we mark David's recognition of Jehovah as the source of all the protection, deliverance, and success he had ever enjoyed, along with a special assertion of closest relationship to Him, in the frequent use of the word "my," and a very ardent acknowledgment of the claim to his gratitude thus arising—" God, who is worthy to be praised."

The feeling that recognised God as the Author of all his deliverances was intensely strong, for every expression that can denote it is heaped together : " My rock, my portion, my deliverer ; the God of my rock, my shield ; the horn of my salvation, my high tower, my refuge, my Saviour." He takes no credit to himself ; he gives no glory to his captains ; the glory is all the Lord's. He sees God so supremely the Author of his deliverance that the human instruments that helped him are for the moment quite out of view.

He who, in the depths of his penitence, sees but one supremely injured Being, and says, " Against Thee, Thee only, have I sinned," at the height of his prosperity sees but one gracious Being, and adores Him, who only is his rock and his salvation. In an age when all the stress is apt to be laid on the human instruments, and God left out of view, this habit of mind is instructive and refreshing. It was a touching incident in English history when, after the battle of Agincourt, Henry V. of England directed the hundred and fifteenth Psalm to be sung ; prostrating himself on the ground, and causing his whole army to do the same, when the words were sounded out, " Not unto us, O Lord, not unto us, but to Thy name give glory."

The emphatic use of the pronoun "my" by the Psalmist is very instructive. It is so easy to speak in general terms of what God is, and what God does ; but it is quite another thing to be able to appropriate Him as ours, and rejoice in that relation. Luther said of the twenty-third Psalm that the word " my " in the first verse was the very hinge of the whole. There is a whole world of difference between the two expressions, " The Lord is a Shepherd " and " The Lord is my Shepherd." The use of the " my " indicates a personal transaction, a covenant relation into which the parties have solemnly entered. No man is entitled to use this expression who has merely a reverential feeling towards God, and respect for His will. You must have come to God as a sinner, owning and feeling your unworthiness, and casting yourself on His grace. You must have transacted with God in the spirit of His exhortation, " Come out from among them, and he ye separate, and touch not the unclean thing ; and

I will be a Father unto you ; and ye shall be My sons and daughters, saith the Lord Almighty."

One other point has to be noticed in this introduction —when David comes to express his dependence on God, he very specially sets Him before his mind as "worthy to be praised." He calls to mind the gracious character of God,—not an austere God, reaping where He has not sown, and gathering where He has not strawed, but "the Lord, the Lord God merciful and gracious, long-suffering and abundant in goodness and truth." "This doctrine," says Luther, "is in tribulation the most ennobling and truly golden. One cannot imagine what assistance such praise of God is in pressing danger. For as soon as you begin to praise God the sense of the evil will also begin to abate, the comfort of your heart will grow ; and then God will be called on with confidence. There are some who cry to the Lord and are not heard. Why is this ? Because they do not praise the Lord when they cry to Him, but go to Him with reluctance ; they have not represented to themselves how sweet the Lord is, but have looked only to their own bitterness. But no one gets deliverance from evil by looking simply upon his evil and becoming alarmed at it ; he can get deliverance only by rising above his evil, hanging it on God, and having respect to His goodness. Oh, hard counsel, doubtless, and a rare thing truly, in the midst of trouble to conceive of God as sweet, and worthy to be praised ; and when He has removed Himself from us and is incomprehensible, even then to regard Him more intensely than we regard our misfortune that keeps us from Him ! Only let one try it, and make the endeavour to praise God, though in little heart for it he will soon experience an enlightenment."

II. We pass on to the part of the song where the Psalmist describes his trials and God's deliverances in his times of danger (vv. 5-20).

The description is eminently poetical. First, there is a vivid picture of his troubles. "The waves of death compassed me, and the floods of ungodly men made me afraid; the sorrows of hell compassed me; the snares of death prevented me" ("The cords of death compassed me, and the floods of ungodliness made me afraid; the cords of sheol were round about me; the snares of death came upon me," R.V.). It is no overcharged picture. With Saul's javelins flying at his head in the palace, or his best troops scouring the wilderness in search of him; with Syrian hosts bearing down on him like the waves of the sea, and a confederacy of nations conspiring to swallow him up, he might well speak of the waves of death and the cords of Hades. He evidently desires to describe the extremest peril and distress that can be conceived, a situation where the help of man is vain indeed. Then, after a brief account of his calling upon God, comes a most animated description of God coming to his help. The description is ideal, but it gives a vivid view how the Divine energy is roused when any of God's children are in distress. It is in heaven as in an earthly home when an alarm is given that one of the little children is in danger, has wandered away into a thicket where he has lost his way: every servant is summoned, every passer-by is called to the rescue, the whole neighbourhood is roused to the most strenuous efforts; so when the cry reached heaven that David was in trouble, the earthquake and the lightning and all the other messengers of heaven were sent out to his aid; nay, these were not enough; God Himself flew, riding on a cherub, yea, He did fly upon

the wings of the wind.    Faith saw God bestirring Him
self for his deliverance, as if every agency of nature
had been set in motion on his behalf.

And this being done, his deliverance was conspicuous
and complete.    He saw God's hand stretched out with
remarkable distinctness.    There could be no more doubt
that it was God that rescued him from Saul than that
it was He that snatched Israel from Pharaoh when
literally " the channels of the sea appeared, the foundations of the world were discovered, at the rebuking of
the Lord, at the blast of the breath of His nostrils."
There could be no more doubt that it was God who protected David when men rose to swallow him up than that
it was He who drew Moses from the Nile—"He sent from
above, He took me, He drew me out of many waters."
No miracles had been wrought on David's behalf;
unlike Moses and Joshua before him, and unlike Elijah
and Elisha after him, he had not had the laws of nature
suspended for his protection ; yet he could see the hand
of God stretched out for him as clearly as if a miracle
had been wrought at every turn.    Does this not show
that ordinary Christians, if they are but careful to watch,
and humble enough to watch in a chastened spirit, may
find in their history, however quietly it may have
glided by, many a token of the interest and care of
their Father in heaven ?    And what a blessed thing to
have accumulated through life a store of such provi-
dences—to have Ebenezers reared along the whole
line of one's history !    What courage after looking over
such a past might one feel in looking forward to the
future !

III. The next section of the song sets forth the
grounds on which the Divine protection was thus enjoyed by David.    Substantially these grounds were the

uprightness and faithfulness with which he had served
God. The expressions are strong, and at first sight
they have a flavour of self-righteousness. " The Lord
rewarded me according to my righteousness ; according
to the cleanness of my hands hath He recompensed
me. For I have kept the ways of the Lord, and have
not wickedly departed from my God. For all His
judgments were before me, and I put not away His
statutes from me. I was also perfect with Him, and
I kept myself from mine iniquity." But it is impossible
to read this Psalm without feeling that it is not pervaded by the spirit of the self-righteous man. It is
pervaded by a profound sense of dependence on God,
and of obligation to His mercy and love. Now that is
the very opposite of the self-righteous spirit. We may
surely find another way of accounting for such expressions used by David here. We may surely believe that
all that was meant by him was to express the unswerving sincerity and earnestness with which he had
endeavoured to serve God, with which he had resisted
every temptation to conscious unfaithfulness, with which
he had resisted every allurement to idolatry on the one
hand or to the neglect of the welfare of God's nation on
the other. What he here celebrates is, not any personal
righteousness that might enable him as an individual
to claim the favour and reward of God, but the ground
on which he, as the public champion of God's cause
before the world, enjoyed God's countenance and
obtained His protection. There would be no self-
righteousness in an inferior officer of the navy or the
army who had been sent on some expedition saying, " I
obeyed your instructions in every particular ; I never
deviated from the course you prescribed." There would
have been no self-righteousness in such a man as Luther

saying, " I constantly maintained the principles of the Bible ; I never once abandoned Protestant ground." Such affirmations would never be held to imply a claim of personal sinlessness during the whole course of their lives. Substantially all that is asserted is, that in their public capacity they proved faithful to the cause entrusted to them ; they never consciously betrayed their public charge. Now it is this precisely that David affirms of himself. Unlike Saul, who abandoned the law of the kingdom, David uniformly endeavoured to carry it into effect. The success which followed he does not claim as any credit to himself, but as due to his having followed the instructions of his heavenly Lord. It is the very opposite of a self-righteous spirit. He would have us understand that if ever he had abandoned the guidance of God, if ever he had relied on his own wisdom and followed the counsels of his own heart, everything would have gone wrong with him ; the fact that he had been successful was due altogether to the Divine wisdom that guided and the Divine strength that upheld him.

Even with this explanation, some of the expressions may seem too strong. How could he speak of the cleanness of his hands, and of his not having wickedly departed from his God? Granting that the song was written before his sin in the case of Uriah, yet remembering how he had lied at Nob and equivocated at Gath, might he not have used less sweeping words? But it is not the way of burning, enthusiastic minds to be for ever weighing their words, and guarding against misunderstandings. Enthusiasm sweeps along in a rapid current. And David correctly describes the prevailing features of his public endeavours. His public life was unquestionably marked by a sincere and commonly successful endeavour to follow the will of God. In contrast with Saul and Ishbosheth, side by side with Absalom or Sheba, his career was purity itself, and bore out the rule of the Divine government, " With the merciful Thou wilt show Thyself merciful, and with the upright man Thou wilt show Thyself upright. With the pure Thou wilt show Thyself pure, and with the froward Thou wilt show Thyself unsavoury." If God is to prosper us, there must be an inner harmony between us and Him. If the habit of our life be opposed to God, the result can only be collision and rebuke. David was conscious of the inner harmony, and therefore he was able to rely on being supported and blessed.

IV. In the wide survey of his life and of his providential mercies, the eye of the Psalmist is particularly fixed on some of his deliverances, in the remembrance of which he specially praises God. One of the earliest appears to be recalled in the words, " By my God have I leaped over a wall,"—the wall, it may be supposed, of Gibeah, down which Michal let him when Saul sent to take him in his house. Still further back, perhaps, in his life is the allusion in another expression —" Thy gentleness hath made me great." He seems to go back to his shepherd life, and in the gentleness with which he dealt with the feeble lamb that might have perished in rougher hands to find an emblem of God's method with himself. If God had not dealt gently with him, he never would have become what he was. The Divine gentleness had made paths easy that rougher treatment would have made intolerable. And who of us that looks back but must own our obligations to the gentleness of God, the tender, forbearing, nay loving, treatment He has bestowed on us, even in the

midst of provocations that would have justified far
harsher treatment ?

But what ?  Can David praise God's gentleness and
in the next words utter such terrible words against his
foes ?   How can he extol God's gentleness to him
and immediately dwell on his tremendous severity to
them ?  " I have consumed them and wounded them
that they could not arise ; yea, they are fallen under my
feet. . . . Then did I beat them as small as the dust of
the earth, I did stamp them as the mire of the street,
and did spread them abroad."   It is the military spirit
which we have so often observed, looking on his
enemies in one light only, as identified with everything evil and enemies of all that was good.   To
show mercy to them would be like showing mercy to
destructive wild beasts, raging bears, venomous serpents, and rapacious vultures.   Mercy to them would
be cruelty to all God's servants ; it would be ruin to
God's cause.   No ! for them the only fit doom was
destruction, and that destruction he had dealt to them
with no unsparing hand.

But while we perceive his spirit, and harmonise it
with his general character, we cannot but regard it as
the spirit of one who was imperfectly enlightened.   We
tremble when we think what fearful wickedness persecutors and inquisitors have committed, under the idea
that the same course was to be followed against those
whom they deemed enemies of the cause of God.   We
rejoice in the Christian spirit that teaches us to regard
even public enemies as our brothers, for whom individually kindly and brotherly feelings are to be cherished.
And we remember the new aspect in which our relations
to such have been placed by our Lord : "Love your
enemies, bless them that curse you, do good to them

that hate you, and pray for them that despitefully use you and persecute you."

In the closing verses of the Psalm, the views of the Psalmist seem to sweep beyond the limits of an earthly kingdom.  His eye seems to embrace the wide-spreading dominion of Messiah; at all events, he dwells on those features of his own kingdom that were typical of the all-embracing kingdom of the Gospel: "Thou hast made me the head of the nations; a people whom I have not known shall serve me.  As soon as they hear of me they shall obey me; the strangers shall submit themselves unto me."  The forty-ninth verse is quoted by St. Paul (Rom. xv. 9) as a proof that in the purpose of God the salvation of Christ was designed for Gentiles as well as Jews.  "It is beyond doubt," says Luther, "that the wars and victories of David prefigured the passion and resurrection of Christ."  At the same time, he admits that it is very doubtful how far the Psalm applies to Christ, and how far to David, and he declines to press the type to particulars.  But we may surely apply the concluding words to David's Son: "He showeth loving-kindness to his anointed, to David and to his seed for evermore."

It is interesting to mark the military aspect of the kingdom gliding into the missionary.  Other psalms bring out more clearly this missionary element, exhibit David rejoicing in the widening limits of his kingdom, in the wider diffusion of the knowledge of the true God, and in the greater happiness and prosperity accruing to men.  And yet, perhaps, his views on the subject were comparatively dim; he may have been disposed to identify the conquests of the sword and the conquests of the truth instead of regarding the one as but typical of the other.  The visions and revelations of his later years seem to have thrown new light on this glorious subject, and though not immediately, yet ultimately, to have convinced nim that truth, righteousness, and meekness were to be the conquering weapons of Messiah's reign.

# CHAPTER XXXI.

## THE LAST WORDS OF DAVID.

2 SAMUEL xxiii. 1—7. (*See Revised Version and margin.*)

OF these "the last words of David," we need not understand that they were the last words he ever spoke, but his last song or psalm, his latest vision, and therefore the subject that was most in his mind in the last period of his life. The Psalm recorded in the preceding chapter was an earlier song, and its main drift was of the past. Of this latest Psalm the main drift is of the future. The colours of this vision are brighter than those of any other. Aged though the seer was, there is a glory in this his latest vision unsurpassed in any that went before. The setting sun spreads a lustre around as he sinks under the horizon unequalled by any he diffused even when he rode in the height of the heavens.

The song falls into four parts. First, there is an elaborate introduction, descriptive of the singer and the inspiration which gave birth to his song; secondly, the main subject of the prophecy, a Ruler among men, of wonderful brightness and glory; thirdly, a reference to the Psalmist's own house and the covenant God had made with him; and finally, in the way of contrast to the preceding, a prediction of the doom of the ungodly.

I. In the introduction, we cannot but be struck with

the formality and solemnity of the affirmation respecting the singer and the inspiration under which he sang.

> " David, the son of Jesse, saith,
> And the man who was raised on high saith,
> The anointed of the God of Jacob,
> And the sweet psalmist of Israel :
> The Spirit of the Lord spake by me,
> And His word was upon my tongue ;
> The God of Israel said,
> The Rock of Israel spake to me "    (R.V.).

The first four clauses represent David as the speaker; the second four represent God's Spirit as inspiring his words. The introduction to Balaam's prophecies is the only passage where we find a similar structure, nor is this the only point of resemblance between the two songs.

> " Balaam, the son of Beor, saith,
> And the man whose eye was closed saith ;
> He saith which heareth the words of God,
> And knoweth the knowledge of the Most High ;
> Which seeth the vision of the Almighty,
> Falling down, and having his eyes open "
> (Num. xxiv. 15, 16, R.V.).

In both prophecies, the word translated "saith" is peculiar. While occurring between two and three hundred times in the formula "Thus saith the Lord," it is used by a human speaker only in these two places and in Prov. xxx. 1. Both Balaam and David begin by giving their own name and that of their father, thereby indicating their native insignificance, and disclaiming any right to speak on subjects so lofty through any wisdom or insight of their own. Immediately after, they claim to speak the words of God. All the grounds on which David should be listened to fall under this head. Was he not "raised up on high"? Was he not the

anointed of the God of Jacob? Was he not the sweet
Psalmist of Israel? Having been raised up on high,
David had established the kingdom of Israel on a firm
and lasting basis, he had destroyed all its enemies,
and he had established a comely order and prosperity
throughout all its borders; as the sweet singer of Israel,
or, as it has been otherwise rendered, "the lovely one
in Israel's songs of praise"—that is, the man who had
been specially gifted to compose songs of praise in
honour of Israel's God—it was fitting that he should be
made the organ of this very remarkable and glorious communication. It is interesting to to observe how David
must have been attracted by Balaam's vision. The dark
wall of the Moabite mountains was a familiar object to
him, and must often have recalled the strange but unworthy prophet who spoke of the Star that was to shine
so gloriously, and the Sceptre that was to have such a
wonderful rule. Often during his life we may believe
that David devoutly desired to know something more
of that mysterious Star and Sceptre; and now that
desire is fulfilled; the Star is as the light of the morning star; the Sceptre is that of a blessed ruler, "one
that ruleth over men righteously, that ruleth in the fear
of God."

The second part of the introduction stamps the
prophecy with a fourfold mark of inspiration. 1. "The
Spirit of the Lord spake by me." For "the prophecy
came not of old time by the will of man; but holy men
of God spake as they were moved by the Holy Ghost."
2. "His word was in my tongue." For in high
visions like this, of which no wisdom of man can create
even a shadow, it is not enough that the Spirit should
merely guide the writer; this is one of the utterances
where verbal inspiration must have been enjoyed.

3. "The God of Israel said," He who entered into covenant with Israel, and promised him great and peculiar mercies. 4. "The Rock of Israel spake to me," the faithful One, whose words are stable as a rock, and who provides for Israel a foundation-stone, elect and precious, immovable as the ever-lasting hills.

So remarkable an introduction must be followed by no ordinary prophecy. If the prophecy should bear on nothing more remarkable than some earthly successor of David, all this preliminary glorification would be singularly out of place. It would be like a great procession of heralds and flourishing of trumpets in an earthly kingdom to announce some event of the most ordinary kind, the repeal of a tax or the appointment of an officer.

II. We come then to the great subject of the prophecy —a Ruler over men. The rendering of the Authorized Version is somewhat lame and obscure, "He that ruleth over men must be just," there being nothing whatever in the original corresponding to "must be." The Revised Version is at once more literal and more expressive :—

> "One that ruleth over men righteously,
>   Ruling in the fear of God,
>   He shall be as the light of the morning."

It is a vision of a remarkable Ruler, not a Ruler over the kingdom of Israel merely, but a Ruler "over men." The Ruler seen is One whose government knows no earthly limits, but prevails wherever there are men. Solomon could not be the ruler seen, for, wide though his empire was, he was king of Israel only, not king of men. It was but a speck of the habitable globe, but a morsel of that part of it that was inhabited even then, over which Solomon reigned. If the term "One that ruleth over men" could have been appropriated by any monarch, it would have been Ahasuerus, with his hundred and twenty-seven provinces, or Alexander the Great, or some other universal monarch, that would have had the right to claim it. But every such application is out of the question. The "Ruler over men" of this vision must have been identified by David with Him "in whom all the nations of the earth were to be blessed."

It is worthy of very special remark that the first characteristic of this Ruler is "righteousness." There is no grander or more majestic word in the language of men. Not even love or mercy can be preferred to righteousness. And this is no casual expression, happening in David's vision, for it is common to the whole class of prophecies that predict the Messiah. "Behold, a King shall reign in righteousness, and princes shall rule in judgment." "There shall come forth a rod out of the stem of Jesse, and the spirit of the fear of the Lord . . . shall rest on Him, . . . and righteousness shall be the girdle of His loins." There is no lack in the New Testament of passages to magnify the love and mercy of the Lord Jesus, yet it is made very plain that righteousness was the foundation of all His work. "Thus it becometh us to fulfil all righteousness," were the words with which He removed the objections of John to His baptism, and they were words that described the business of His whole life: to fulfil all righteousness *for* His people and *in* His people— for them, to satisfy the demands of the righteous law and bear the righteous penalty of transgression; in them to infuse His own righteous spirit and mould them into the likeness of His righteous example, to sum up the whole law of righteousness in the law of love, and by His grace instil that law into their hearts. Such essentially was the work of Christ. No man can say of the religious life that Christ expounded that it was a life of loose, feverish emotion or sentimental spirituality that left the Decalogue far out of view. Nothing could have been further from the mind of Him that said, "Except your righteousness shall exceed the righteousness of the scribes and Pharisees, ye shall in no wise enter into the kingdom of heaven." Nothing could have been more unlike the spirit of Him who was not content with maintaining the letter of the Decalogue, but with His "again, I say unto you," drove its precepts so much further as into the very joints and marrow of men's souls.

It is the grand characteristic of Christ's salvation in theory that it is through righteousness ; it is not less its effect in practice to promote righteousness. To any who would dream, under colour of free grace, of breaking down the law of righteousness, the words of "the Holy One and the Just" stand out as an eternal rebuke, "Think not that I am come to destroy the law and the prophets ; I am not come to destroy, but to fulfil."

And as Christ's work was founded on righteousness, so it was constantly done "in the fear of God,"—with the highest possible regard for His will, and reverence for His law. "Wist ye not that I must be about My Father's business ?" is the first word we hear from Christ's lips; and among the last is, "Not My will, but Thine, be done." No motto could have been more appropriate for His whole life than this : "I delight to do Thy will, O My God."

Having shown the character of the Ruler, the vision next pictures the effects of His rule :—

" He shall be as the light of the morning when the sun riseth,
   A morning without clouds,
   When the tender grass springeth out of the earth
   Through clear shining after rain. "

But why introduce the future " shall be " in the translation when it is not in the original ? May we not conceive the Psalmist reading off a vision—a scene unfolding itself in all its beauty before his mind's eye ? A beautiful influence seems to come over the earth as the Divine Ruler makes His appearance, like the rising of the sun on a cloudless morning, like the appearance of the grass when the sun shines out clearly after rain. No imagery could be more delightful, or more fitly applied to Christ. The image of the morning sun presents Christ in His gladdening influences, bringing pardon to the guilty, health to the diseased, hope to the despairing ; He is indeed like the morning sun, lighting up the sky with splendour and the earth with beauty, giving brightness to the languid eye, and colour to the faded cheek, and health and hope to the sorrowing heart. The chief idea under the other emblem, the grass shining clearly after rain, is that of renewed beauty and growth. The heavy rain batters the grass, as heavy trials batter the soul, but when the morning sun shines out clearly, the grass recovers, it sparkles with a fresher lustre, and grows with intenser activity. So when Christ shines on the heart after trial, a new beauty and a new growth and prosperity come to it. When this Sun of righteousness shines forth thus, in the case of individuals the understanding becomes more clear, the conscience more vigorous, the will more firm, the habits more holy, the temper more serene, the affections more pure, the desires more heavenly. In communities, conversions are multiplied, and souls advanced steadily in holy beauties; intelligence spreads, love triumphs over selfishness, and the spirit of Christ modifies the spirit of strife and the spirit of mammon. It is with the happiest skill that Solomon, appropriating part of his father's imagery, draws the picture of the bride, with the radiance of the bridegroom falling on her: " Who is she that looketh forth as the morning, fair as the moon, clear as the sun, and terrible as an army with banners ? "

III. Next comes David's allusion to his own house. In our translation, and in the text of the Revised Version, this comes in to indicate a sad contrast between the bright vision just described and the Psalmist's own family. It indicates that his house or family did not correspond to the picture of the prophecy, and would not realize the emblems of the rising sun and the growing grass ; but as God had made with himself an everlasting covenant, ordered in all things and sure, that satisfied him ; it was all his salvation and all his desire, although his house was not to grow.

But in the margin of the Revised Version we have another translation, which reverses all this :—

> " For is not my house so with God ?
> For He hath made with me an everlasting covenant,
> Ordered in all things and sure :
> For all my salvation and all my desire,
> Will He not make it to grow ? "

Corresponding as this does with the translation of many scholars (*e.g.*, Boothroyd, Hengstenberg, Fairbairn), it must be regarded as admissible on the strength of outward evidence. And if so, certainly it

is very strongly recommended by internal evidence.
For what reason could David have for introducing his
family at all after the glorious vision if only to say
that they were excluded from it ?  And can it be
thought that David, whose nature was so intensely
sympathetic, would be so pleased because he was
personally provided for, though not his family ?  And
still further, why should he go on in the next verses
(6, 7) to describe the doom of the ungodly by way of
contrast to what precedes if the doom of ungodly
persons is the matter already introduced in the fifth
verse ?  The passage becomes highly involved and
unnatural in the light of the older translation.

The key to the passage will be found, if we mistake
not, in the expression "my house."  We are liable to
think of this as the domestic circle, whereas it ought to
be thought of as the reigning dynasty.  What is denoted
by the house of Hapsburg, the house of Hanover, the
house of Savoy, is quite different from the personal
family of any of the kings.  So when David speaks of
his house, he means his dynasty.  In this sense his
" house" had been made the subject of the most gracious promise.  "Moreover, the Lord telleth thee that
He will make thee an house. . . . And thine house and
thy kingdom shall be made sure for ever before
thee. . . . Then David said, . . . What is my house, that
Thou hast brought me thus far ? . . . Thou hast spoken
also of Thy servant's house for a great while to come."
The king felt profoundly on that occasion that his house
was even more prominently the subject of Divine
promise than himself.  What roused his gratitude to
its utmost height was the gracious provision for his
house.  Surely the covenant referred to in the passage
now before us, "ordered in all things and sure," was

this very covenant announced to him by the prophet Nathan, the covenant that made this provision for his house. It is impossible to think of him recalling this covenant and yet saying, " Verily my house is not so with God " (R.V.).

But take the marginal reading—" Is not my house so with God ? "  Is not my dynasty embraced in the scope of this promise ?  Hath He not made with me an ever-lasting covenant, ordered in all things and sure ?  And will He not make this promise, which is all my salvation and all my desire, to grow, to fructify ?  It is infinitely more natural to represent David on this joyous occasion congratulating himself on the promise of long continu-ance and prosperity made to his dynasty, than dwell-ing on the unhappy condition of the members of his family circle.

And the facts of the future correspond to this explanation.  Was not the government of David's house or dynasty in the main righteous, at least for many a reign, conducted in the fear of God, and followed by great prosperity and blessing ?  David himself, Solomon, Asa, Jehoshaphat, Hezekiah, Josiah—what other nation had ever so many Christlike kings ? What a contrast was presented to this in the main by the apostate kingdom of the ten tribes, idolatrous, God-dishonouring, throughout !  And as to the growth or continued vitality of his house, its "clear shining after rain," had not God promised that He would bless it, and that it would continue for ever before Him ?  He knew that, spiritually dormant at times, his house would survive, till a living root came from the stem of Jesse, till the Prince of life should be born from it, and once that plant of renown was raised up, there was no fear but the house would be preserved for ever.  From this point it would start on a new career of glory ; nay, this was the very Ruler of whom he had been prophesying, at once David's Son and David's Lord ; this was the root and the offspring of David, the bright and the morning star.   Conducted to this stage in the future experience of his house, he needed no further assurance, he cherished no further desire.   The covenant that rested on Him and that promised Him was ordered in all things and sure.   The glorious prospect exhausted his every wish.   "This is all my salvation and all my desire."

IV. The last part of the prophecy, in the way of contrast to the leading vision, is a prediction of the doom of the ungodly.   The revised translation is much the clearer :—

" But the ungodly shall be all of them as thorns to be thrust away,
For they cannot be taken with the hand,
But the man that toucheth them
Must be armed with iron and the staff and spear,
And they shall be utterly burned with fire in their place."

While some would fain think of Christ's sceptre as one of mercy only, the uniform representation of the Bible is different.   In this, as in most predictions of Christ's kingly office, there is an instructive combination of mercy and judgment.   In the bosom of one of Isaiah's sweetest predictions, he introduces the Messiah as anointed by the Spirit of God to proclaim "the day of vengeance of our God."   In a subsequent vision, Messiah appears marching triumphantly "with dyed garments from Bozrah, after treading the people in His anger and trampling them in His fury."   Malachi proclaimed Him " the Sun of righteousness, with healing under His wings," while His day was to burn as an oven and consume the proud and the

wicked like stubble.   John the Baptist saw Him " with
His fan in His hand, throughly purging His floor,
gathering the wheat into His garner, while the chaff
should be burnt with unquenchable fire."   In His own
words, " the Son of man shall gather out of His kingdom all things that offend, and them that do iniquity,
and cast them into a furnace of fire ; there shall be
weeping and gnashing of teeth."   And in the Apocalypse, when the King of kings and the Lord of lords
is to be married to His bride, He appears " clothed
with a garment dipped in blood, and out of His mouth
goeth a sharp sword, that He should smite the nations,
and He treadeth the winepress of the fierceness and
wrath of Almighty God."

Nor could it be otherwise.   The union of mercy
and judgment is the inevitable result of the righteousness which is the foundation of His government.   Sin
is the abominable thing which He hates.   To separate
men from sin is the grand purpose of His government.
For this end, He draws His people into union with
Himself, thereby for ever removing their guilt, and
providing for the ultimate removal of all sin from their
hearts and the complete assimilation of their natures
to His holy nature.   Blessed are they who enter into
this relation ; but alas for those who, for all that He
has done, prefer their sins to Him !   " The ungodly
shall be all of them as thorns to be thrust away."

Oh, let us not be satisfied with admiring beautiful
images of Christ !   Let us not deem it enough to think
with pleasure of Him as the light of the morning, a
morning without clouds, brightening the earth, and
making it sparkle with the lustre of the sunshine on
the grass after rain !   Let us not satisfy ourselves
with knowing that Jesus Christ came to earth on a

beneficent mission, and with thinking that surely we shall one day share in the blessed effects of His work ! Nothing of that kind can avail us if we are not personally united to Christ. We must come as sinners individually to Him, cast ourselves on His free, unmerited grace, and deliberately accept His righteousness as our clothing. Then, but only then, shall we be able to sing : " I will greatly rejoice in the Lord ; my soul shall be joyful in my God; for He hath clothed me with the garments of salvation, He hath covered me with the robe of righteousness, as a bridegroom decketh himself with ornaments, and as a bride adorneth herself with her jewels."

## CHAPTER XXXII.

### *THE NUMBERING OF ISRAEL.*

2 SAMUEL xxiv.

THOUGH David's life was now drawing to its close, neither his sins nor his chastisements were yet exhausted. One of his chief offences was committed when he was old and grey-headed. There can be little doubt that what is recorded in this chapter took place toward the close of his life; the word "again" at the beginning indicates that it was later in time than the event which gave rise to the last expression of God's displeasure to the nation. Surely there can be little ground for the doctrine of perfectionism, otherwise David, whose religion was so earnest and so deep, would have been nearer it now than this chapter shows that he was.

The offence consisted in taking a census of the people. At first it is difficult to see what there was in this that was so sinful; yet highly sinful it was in the judgment of God, in the judgment of Joab, and at last in the judgment of David too; it will be necessary, therefore, to examine the subject very carefully if we would understand clearly what constituted the great sin of David.

The origin of the proceeding was remarkable. It may be said to have had a double, or rather a triple, origin: God, David, and Satan, or, as some propose to render in place of Satan, "*an* enemy."

In Samuel we read that "the Lord's anger was again kindled against Israel." The nation required a chastisement. It needed a smart stroke of the rod to make it pause and think how it was offending God. We do not require to know very specially what it was that displeased God in a nation that had been so ready to side with Absalom and drive God's anointed from the throne. They were far from steadfast in their allegiance to God, easily drawn from the path of duty ; and all that it is important for us to know is simply that at this particular time they were farther astray than usual, and more in need of chastisement. The cup of sin had filled up so far that God behoved to interpose.

For this end "the Lord moved David against them to say, Go, number Israel and Judah." The action of God in the matter, like His action in sinful matters generally, was, that He permitted it to take place. He allowed David's sinful feeling to come as a factor into His scheme with a view to the chastising of the people. We have seen many times in this history how God is represented as doing things and saying things which He does not do nor say directly, but which He takes up into His plan, with a view to the working out of some great end in the future. But in Chronicles it is said that Satan stood up against Israel and provoked David to number Israel. According to some commentators, the Hebrew word is not to be translated " Satan," because it has no article, but "an adversary," as in parallel passages : " The Lord stirred up an adversary unto Solomon, Hadad the Edomite " (1 Kings xi. 14); " God stirred up another adversary to Israel, Razon, the son of Eliadib " (1 Kings xi. 23). Perhaps it was some one in the garb of a friend, but with the spirit of an enemy, that moved David in this matter. If we suppose Satan to have been the active mover, then Bishop Hall's words will indicate the relation between the three parties : " Both God and Satan had then a hand in the work—God by permission, Satan by suggestion ; God as a Judge, Satan as an enemy ; God as in a just punishment for sin, Satan as in an act of sin ; God in a wise ordination of it for good, Satan in a malicious intent of confusion. Thus at once God moved and Satan moved, neither is it any excuse to Satan or to David that God moved, neither is it any blemish to God that Satan moved. The ruler's sin is a punishment to a wicked people ; if God were not angry with a people, He would not give up their governors to evils that provoke His vengeance ; justly are we charged to make prayers and supplications as for all men, so especially for rulers."

But what constituted David's great offence in numbering the people ? Every civilised State is now accustomed to number its people periodically, and for many good purposes it is a most useful step. Josephus represents that David omitted to levy the atonement money which was to be raised, according to Exod. xxx. 12, etc., from all who were numbered, but surely, if this had been his offence, it would have been easy for Joab, when he remonstrated, to remind him of it, instead of trying to dissuade him from the scheme altogether. The more common view of the transaction has been that it was objectionable, not in itself, but in the spirit by which it was dictated. That spirit seems to have been a self-glorifying spirit. It seems to have been like the spirit which led Hezekiah to show his treasures to the ambassadors of the king of Babylon. Perhaps it was designed to show, that in the number of his forces David was quite a match for the great

empires on the banks of the Nile and the Euphrates.
If their fighting men could be counted by the hundred
thousand or the thousand thousand, so could his.    In
the fighting resources of his kingdom, he was able to
hold his head as high as any of them.    Surely such
a spirit was the very opposite of what was becoming
in such a king as David.    Was this not measuring the
strength of a spiritual power with the measure of a
carnal ?    Did it not leave God most sinfully out of
reckoning ?    Nay, did it not substitute a carnal for
a spiritual defence ?    Was it not in the very teeth of
the Psalm, " There is no king saved by the multitude
of an host ; a mighty man is not delivered by much
strength.    An horse is a vain thing for safety ; neither
shall he deliver any by his great strength.    Behold, the
eye of the Lord is upon them that fear Him, upon them
that hope in His mercy, to deliver their soul from
death, and to keep them alive in famine " ?

That David's project was very deeply seated in his
heart is evident from the fact that he was unmoved by
the remonstrance of Joab.    In ordinary circumstances
it must have startled him to find that even he was
strongly opposed to his project.    It is indeed strange
that Joab should have had scruples where David had
none.    We have been accustomed to find Joab so
seldom in the right that it is hard to believe that he
was in the right now.    But perhaps we do Joab
injustice.    He was a man that could be profoundly
stirred when his own interests were at stake, or his
passions roused, and that seemed equally regardless
of God and man in what he did on such occasions.
But otherwise Joab commonly acted with prudence
and moderation.    He consulted for the good of the
nation.    He was not habitually reckless or habitually

cruel, and he seems to have had a certain amount of regard to the will of God and the theocratic constitution of the kingdom, for he was loyal to David from the very beginning, up to the contest between Solomon and Adonijah. It is evident that Joab felt strongly that in the step which he proposed to take David would be acting a part unworthy of himself and of the constitution of the kingdom, and by displeasing God would expose himself to evils far beyond any advantage he might hope to gain by ascertaining the number of the people.

For once—and this time, unhappily—David was too strong for the son of Zeruiah. The enumerators of the people were despatched, no doubt with great regularity, to take the census. The boundaries named were not beyond the territory as divided by Joshua among the Israelites, save that Tyre and Zidon were included; not that they had been annexed by David, but probably because there was an understanding that in all his military arrangements they were to be associated with him. Nine months and twenty days were occupied in the business. At the end of it, it was ascertained that the fighting men of Israel were eight hundred thousand, and those of Judah five hundred thousand; or, if we take the figures in Chronicles, eleven hundred thousand of Israel and four hundred and seventy thousand of Judah. The discrepancy is not easily accounted for; but probably in Chronicles in the number for Israel certain bodies of troops were included which were not included in Samuel, and *vice versâ* in the case of Judah.

Just as in the case of his sin in the matter of Uriah, David was long of coming to a sense of it. How his view came to change we are not told, but when the change did occur, it seems, as in the other case, to have

come with extraordinary force. " David's heart smote
him after that he had numbered the people. And
David said unto the Lord, I have sinned greatly in that
which I have done ; and now, I beseech Thee, O Lord,
take away the iniquity of Thy servant, for I have done
very foolishly." Once alive to his sin, his humiliation
is very profound. His confession is frank, hearty,
complete. He shows no proud desire to remain on
good terms with himself, seeks nothing to break his
fall or to make his humiliation less before Joab and
before the people. He says, " I will confess my transgression to the Lord ;" and his plea is one with which
he is familiar from of old—" For Thy name's sake,
O Lord, pardon mine iniquity, for it is great." He is
never greater than when acknowledging his sin.

Next comes the chastisement. The moment for
sending it is very seasonable. It did not come while
his conscience was yet slumbering, but after he had
come to feel his sin. His confessions and relentings
were proofs that he was now fit for chastisement; the
chastisement, as in the other case, was solemnly
announced by a prophet ; and, as in the other case too,
it fell on one of the tenderest spots of his heart. Then
the first blow fell on his infant child ; now it falls upon
his sheep. His affections were divided between his
children and his people, and in both cases the blow
must have been very severe. It was, as far as we can
judge, after a night of very profound humiliation that
the prophet Gad was sent to him. Gad had first
come to him when he was hiding from Saul, and had
therefore been his friend all his kingly life. Sad that
so old and so good a friend should be the bearer to
the aged king of a bitter message ! Seven years of
famine (in 1 Chron. xxi. 12, three years), three months

of unsuccessful war, or three days of pestilence,—the choice lies between these three. All of them were well fitted to rebuke that pride in human resources which had been the occasion of his sin. Well might he say, " I am in a great strait." Oh the bitterness of the harvest when you sow to the flesh ! Between these three horrors even God's anointed king has to choose. What a delusion it is that God will not be very careful in the case of the wicked to inflict the due retribution of sin ! " If these things were done in the green tree, what shall be done in the dry ? "

David chose the three days of pestilence. It was the shortest, no doubt, but what recommended it, especially above the three months of unsuccessful war, was that it would come more directly from the hand of God. " Let me fall now into the hand of the Lord, for His mercies are great, and let me not fall into the hand of man." What a frightful time it must have been ! Seventy thousand died of the plague. From Dan to Beersheba nothing would be heard but a bitter cry, like that of the Egyptians when the angel slew the first-born. What days and nights of agony these must have been to David ! How slowly would they drag on ! What cries in the morning, " Would God it were evening !" and in the evening, " Would God it were morning !"

The pestilence, wherever it originated, seems to have advanced from every side like a besieging army, till it was ready to close upon Jerusalem. The destroying angel hovered over Mount Moriah, and, like Abraham on the same spot a thousand years before, was brandishing his sword for the work of destruction. It was a spot that had already been memorable for one display of Divine forbearance, and now it became the scene

of another. Like the hand of Abraham when ready
to plunge the knife into the bosom of his son, the
hand of the angel was stayed when about to fall on
Jerusalem. For Abraham a ram had been provided
to offer in the room of Isaac ; and now David is commanded to offer a burnt-offering in acknowledgment
of his guilt and of his need of expiation. Thus the
Lord stayed His rough wind in the day of His east
wind. In sparing Jerusalem, on the very eve of
destruction, He caused His mercy to rejoice over
judgment.

No one but must admire the spirit of David when
the angel appeared on Mount Moriah. Owning frankly
his own great sin, and especially his sin as a shepherd,
he bared his own bosom to the sword, and entreated
God to let the punishment fall on him and on his
father's house. Why should the sheep suffer for the
sin of the shepherd ? The plea was more beautiful
than correct. The sheep had been certainly not less
guilty than the shepherd, though in a different way.
We have seen how the anger of the Lord had been
kindled against Israel when David was induced to go
and number the people. And as both had been guilty,
so both had been punished. The sheep had been
punished in their own bodies, the shepherd in the
tenderest feelings of his heart. It is a rare sight to
find a man prepared to take on himself more than his
own share of the blame. It was not so in paradise,
when the man threw the blame on the woman and the
woman on the serpent. We see that, with all his
faults, David had another spirit from that of the vulgar
world. After all, there is much of the Divine nature
in this poor, blundering, sinning child of clay.

On the day when the angel appeared over Jerusalem,

Gad was sent back to David with a more auspicious
message.   He is required to build an altar to the Lord
on the spot where the angel stood.   This was the
fitting counterpart to Abraham's act when, in place
of Isaac, he offered the ram which Jehovah-jireh had
provided for the sacrifice.   The circumstances connected with the rearing of the altar and the offering
of the burnt-offering were very peculiar, and seem to
have borne a deep typical meaning.   The place where
the angel's arm was arrested was by the threshing-floor
of Araunah the Jebusite.   It was there that David was
commanded to rear his altar and offer his burnt-offering.
When Araunah saw the king approaching, he bowed
before him and respectfully asked the purpose of his
visit.   It was to buy the threshing-floor and build an
altar, that the plague might be stayed.   But if the
threshing-floor was needed for that purpose, Araunah
would give it freely ; and offer it as a free gift he did,
with royal munificence, along with the oxen for a burnt-
offering and their implements also as wood for the
sacrifice.   David, acknowledging his goodness, would
not be outdone in generosity, and insisted on making
payment.   The floor was bought, the altar was built,
the sacrifice was offered, and the plague was stayed.
As we read in Chronicles, fire from heaven attested
God's acceptance of the offering.   "And David said,
This is the house of the Lord God, and this is the altar
of the burnt-offering for Israel."   That is to say, the
threshing-floor was appointed to be the site of the temple
which Solomon was to build ; and the spot where David
had hastily reared his altar was to be the place where,
for hundreds of years, day after day, morning and
evening, the blood of the burnt-offering was to flow,
and the fumes of incense to ascend before God.

No doubt it was to save time in so pressing an emergency that Araunah gave for sacrifice the oxen with which he was working, and the implements connected with his labour. But in the purpose of God, a great truth lay under these symbolical arrangements. The oxen that had been labouring for man were sacrificed for man ; both their life and their death were given for man, just as afterwards the Lord Jesus Christ, after living and labouring for the good of many, at last gave His life a ransom. The wood of the altar on which they suffered was, part of it at all events, borne on their own necks, " the threshing instruments and other instruments of the oxen," just as Isaac had borne the wood and as Jesus was to bear the cross on which, respectively, they were stretched. The sacrifice was a sacrifice of blood, for only blood could remove the guilt that had to be pardoned. The analogy is clear enough. Isaac had escaped ; the ram suffered in his room. Jerusalem escaped now ; the oxen were sacrificed in its room. Sinners of mankind were to escape ; the Lamb of God was to die, the just for the unjust, to bring them to God.

There were other circumstances, however, not without significance, connected with the purchase of the temple site. The man to whom the ground had belonged, and whose oxen had been slain as the burnt-offering, was a Jebusite ; and from the way in which he designated David's Lord, " the Lord *thy* God," it is not certain whether he was even a proselyte. Some think that he had formerly been king of Jerusalem, or rather of the stronghold of Zion, but that when Zion was taken he had been permitted to retire to Mount Moriah, which was separated from Zion only by a deep ravine. Josephus calls him a great friend of David's.

He could not have shown a more friendly spirit or a more princely liberality. The striking way in which the heart of this Jebusite was moved to co-operate with King David in preparing for the temple was fitted to remind David of the missionary character which the temple was to sustain. " My house shall be called an house of prayer for all nations." In the words of the sixty-eighth Psalm, " Because of thy temple at Jerusalem shall kings bring presents unto thee." As Araunah's oxen had been accepted, so the time would come when " the sons of the stranger that join themselves to the Lord, to serve Him and to love the name of the Lord, even them will I bring to My holy mountain, and make them joyful in My house of prayer; their burnt-offerings and their sacrifices shall be accepted upon Mine altar." What a wonderful thing is sanctified affliction! While its root lies in the very corruption of our nature, its fruit consists of the best blessings of Heaven. The root of David's affliction was carnal pride; but under God's sanctifying grace, it was followed by the erection of a temple associated with heavenly blessing, not to one nation only, but to all. When affliction, duly sanctified, is thus capable of bringing such blessings, it makes the fact all the more lamentable that affliction is so often unsanctified. It is vain to imagine that everything of the nature of affliction is sure to turn to good. It can turn to good on one condition only—when your heart is humbled under the rod, and in the same humble, chastened spirit as David you say, and feel as well as say, " I have sinned."

One other lesson we gather from this chapter of David's history. When he declined to accept the generous offer of Araunah, it was on the ground that he would not serve the Lord with that which cost him nothing. The thought needs only to be put in words to commend itself to every conscience. God's service is neither a form nor a sham ; it is a great reality. If we desire to show our honour for Him, it must be in a way suited to the occasion. The poorest mechanic that would offer a gift to his sovereign tries to make it the product of his best labour, the fruit of his highest skill. To pluck a weed from the roadside and present it to one's sovereign would be no better than an insult. Yet how often is God served with that which costs men nothing ! Men that will lavish hundreds and thousands to gratify their own fancy,—what miserable driblets they often give to the cause of God ! The smallest of coins is good enough for His treasury. And as for other forms of serving God, what a tendency there is in our time to make everything easy and pleasant,—to forget the very meaning of self-denial ! It is high time that that word of David were brought forth and put before every conscience, and made to rebuke ever so many professed worshippers of God, whose rule of worship is to serve God with what does cost them nothing. The very heathen reprove you. Little though there has been to stimulate their love, their sacrifices are often most costly—far from sacrifices that have cost them nothing. Oh, let us who call ourselves Christians beware lest we be found the meanest, paltriest, shabbiest of worshippers ! Let souls that have been blessed as Christians have devise liberal things. Let your question and the answer be : " What shall I render to the Lord for all His benefits toward me ? I will take the cup of salvation and call on the name of the Lord. I will pay my vows unto the Lord, now in the presence of His people."

# CHAPTER XXXIII.

## *THE TWO BOOKS OF SAMUEL.*

HAVING now surveyed the events of the history of Israel, one by one, during the whole of that memorable period which is embraced in the books of Samuel, it will be profitable, before we close, to cast a glance over the way by which we have travelled, and endeavour to gather up the leading lessons and impressions of the whole.

Let us bear in mind all along that the great object of these books, as of the other historical books of Scripture, is peculiar : it is not to trace the history of a nation, in the ordinary sense, but to trace the course of Divine revelation, to illustrate God's manner of dealing with the nation whom He chose that He might instruct and train them in His ways, that He might train them to that righteousness which alone exalteth a people, and that He might lay a foundation for the work of Christ in future times, in whom all the families of the earth were to be blessed. The history delineated is not that of the kingdom of Israel, but that of the kingdom of God.

The history falls into four divisions, like the acts of a drama. I. It opens with Eli as high-priest, when the state of the nation is far from satisfactory, and God's holy purpose regarding it appears a failure. II. With Samuel as the Lord's prophet, we see a remarkable

revival of the spirit of God's nation. III. With Saul a
king, the fair promise under Samuel is darkened, and an
evil spirit is again ascendant. IV. But with David, the
conditions are again reversed ; God's purpose regarding
the people is greatly advanced, but in the later part of
his reign the sky again becomes overcast, through his
infirmities and the people's perversity, and the great
forces of good and evil are left still contending, though
not in the same proportion as before.

I. The opening scene, under the high-priesthood of
Eli, is sad and painful. It is the sanctuary itself, the
priestly establishment at Shiloh, that which ought to be
the very centre and heart of the spiritual life of the
nation, that is photographed for us ; and it is a deplorable picture. The soul of religion has died out; little
but the carcase is left. Formality and superstition are
the chief forces at work, and a wretched business they
make of it. Men still attend to religious service, for
conscience and the force of habit have a wonderful
tenacity ; but what is the use ? Religion does not
even help morality. The acting priests are unblushing
profligates, defiling the very precincts of God's house
with abominable wickedness. And what better could
you expect of the people when their very spiritual
guides set them such an example ? " Men abhor the
offering of the Lord." No wonder ! It irritates them
in the last degree to have to give their wealth ostensibly
for religion, but really to feed the lusts of scoundrels.
People feel that instead of getting help from religious
services for anything good, it strains all that is best in
them to endure contact with such things. How can
belief in a living God prevail when the very priests
show themselves practical atheists ? The very idea
of a personal God is blotted out of the people's mind,

and superstition takes its place. Men come to think that certain words, or things, or places have in some way a power to do them good. The object of religion is not to please God, but to get the mysterious good out of the words, or things, or places that have it in them. When they are going to war, they do not think how they may get the living God to be on their side, but they take hold of the dead ark, believing that there is some spell in it to frighten their enemies. Israelites who believe such things are no better than their pagan neighbours. The whole purpose of God to make them an enlightened, orderly, sanctified people seems grievously frustrated.

Even good men become comparatively useless under such a system. The very high-priest is a kind of nonentity. If Eli had asserted God's claims with any vigour, Hophni and Phinehas would not have dared to live as they did. It is a mournful state of things when good men get reconciled to the evil that prevails, or content themselves with very feebly protesting against it. No doubt Eli most sincerely bewailed it. But the very atmosphere was drowsy, inviting to rest and quiet. There was no stir, no movement anywhere. Where all death lived, life died.

And yet, as in the days of Elijah, God had His faithful ones in the land. There were still men and women that believed in a living God, and in their closets prayed to their Father that seeth in secret. And God has wonderful ways of reviving His cause when it seems extinct. When all flesh had corrupted their way, there was yet one man left who was righteous and godly; and through Noah God peopled the world. When the new generation had become idolatrous, He chose one man, Abraham, and by him alone He built up a holy Church, and a consecrated nation. And now, when all Israel seems to be hopelessly corrupt, God finds in an obscure cottage a humble woman, through whose seed it is His purpose that His Church be revived, and the nation saved. Take heed that ye despise not one of these little ones. Be thankful for every man and woman, however insignificant, in whose heart there is a living faith in a living God. No one can tell what use God may not make of the poorest saint. For God's power is unlimited. One man, one woman, one child, may be His instrument for arresting the decline of ages, and introducing a new era of spiritual revival and holy triumph.

II. For it was no less a change than this that was effected through Samuel, Hannah's child. From his infancy Samuel was a consecrated person. Brought up as a child to reverence the sanctuary and all its worship, he learned betimes the true meaning of it all ; and the reverence that he had been taught to give to His outward service, he learned to associate with the person of the living God. And Samuel had the courage of his convictions, and told the people of their sins, and of God's claims. It was his function to revive belief in the spiritual God, and in His relation to the people of Israel ; and to summon the nation to honour and serve Him. What Samuel did in this way, he did mainly through his high personal character and intense convictions. In office he was neither priest nor king, though he had much of the influence of both. No doubt he judged Israel ; but that function came to him not by formal appointment, but rather as the fruit of his high character and commanding influence. The whole position of Samuel and the influence which he wielded were due not to temporal but spiritual considerations.  He manifestly walked with God ; he was conspicuous for his fellowship with Jehovah, Israel's Lord ; and his life, and his character, and his words, all combined to exalt Him whose servant he evidently was.

And that was the work to which Samuel was appointed.  It was to revive the faith of an unbelieving people in the reality of God's existence in the first place, and in the second in the reality of His covenant relation to Israel.  It was to rivet on their minds the truth that the supreme and only God was the God of their nation, and to get them to have regard to Him and to honour Him as such.  He was to impress on them the great principle of national prosperity, to teach them that the one unfailing source of blessing was the active favour of God.  It was their sin and their misery alike that they not only did not take the right means to secure God's favour, but, on the contrary, provoked Him to anger by their sins.

Now there were two things about God that Samuel was most earnest in pressing.  The one was His holiness, the other His spirituality.  The righteous Lord loved righteousness.  No amount of ritual service could compensate the want of moral obedience.  " Behold, to obey is better than sacrifice, and to hearken than the fat of rams."  If they would enjoy His favour, they must search out their sins, and humble themselves for them before this holy God.  The other earnest lesson was God's spirituality.  Not only was all idolatry and image-worship most obnoxious to Him, but no service was acceptable which did not come from the heart.  Hence the great value of prayer.  It was Samuel's privilege to show the people what prayer could do.  He showed them prayer, when it arose from a humble, penitent spirit, moving the Hand that moved the universe. He endeavoured to inspire them with heartfelt regard to God as their King, and with supreme honour for Him in all the transactions both of public and private life. That was the groove in which he tried to move the nation, for in that course alone he was persuaded that their true interest lay. To a large extent, Samuel was successful in this endeavour. His spirit was very different from the languid timidity of Eli. He spoke with a voice that evoked an echo. He raised the nation to a higher moral and spiritual platform, and brought them nearer to their heavenly King. Seldom has such proof been given of the almost unbounded moral power attainable by one man, if he but be of single eye and immovable will.

But, as we have said, Samuel was neither priest nor king; his conquests were the conquests of character alone. The people clamoured for a king, certainly from inferior motives, and Samuel yielded to their clamour. It would have been a splendid thing for the nation to have got an ideal king, a king adapted for such a kingdom, as deeply impressed as Samuel was with his obligation to honour God, and ruling over them with the same regard for the law and covenant of Israel. But such was not to be their first king. Some correction was due to them for having been impatient of God's arrangements, and so eager to have their own wishes complied with. Saul was to be as much an instrument of humiliation as a source of blessing.

III. And this brings us to the third act of the drama. Saul the son of Kish begins well, but he turns aside soon. He has ability, he has activity, he has abundant opportunity to make the necessary external arrangements for the welfare of the nation; but he has no

heart for the primary condition of blessing. At first
he feels constrained to honour God; he accepts from
Samuel the law of the kingdom and tries to govern
accordingly. He could not well have done otherwise.
He could not decently have accepted the office of king
at the hands of Samuel without promising and without
trying to have regard to the mode of ruling which the
king-maker so earnestly pressed on him. But Saul's
efforts to honour God shared the fate of all similar
efforts when the force that impels to them is pressure
from without, not heartiness within. Like a rower
pulling against wind and tide, he soon tired. And
when he tired of trying to rule as God would have him,
and fell back on his own way of it, he seemed all the
more wilful for the very fact that he had tried at first
to repress his own will. Externally he was active and
for a time successful, but internally he went from bad
to worse. Under Saul, the process of training Israel
to fear and honour God made no progress whatever.
The whole force of the governing power was in the
opposite direction. One thing is to be said in favour
of Saul—he was no idolater. He did not encourage
any outward departure from the worship of God.
Neither Baal nor Ashtaroth, Moloch nor Chemosh,
received any countenance at his hands. The Second
Commandment was at least outwardly observed.

But for all that, Saul was the active, inveterate, and
bitter persecutor of what we may call God's interest
in the kingdom. There was no real sympathy between
him and Samuel; but as Samuel did not cross his path,
he left him comparatively alone. It was very different
in the case of David. In Saul's relation to David we
see the old antagonism—the antagonism of nature and
grace, of the seed of the serpent and the seed of the

woman, of those born after the flesh and those born after the Spirit. Here is the most painful feature of Saul's administration. Knowing, as he did, that David enjoyed God's favour in a very special degree, he ought to have respected him the more. In reality he hated him the more. Jealousy is a blind and stupid passion. It mattered nothing to Saul that David was a man after God's own heart, except that it made him more fierce against him. How could a theocratic kingdom prosper when the head of it raged against God's anointed one, and strained every nerve to destroy him ? The whole policy of Saul was a fatal blunder. Under him, the nation, instead of being trained to serve God better, and realise the end of their selection more faithfully, were carried in the opposite direction. And Saul lived to see into what confusion and misery he had dragged them by his wilful and godless rule. No man ever led himself into a more humiliating maze, and no man ever died in circumstances that proclaimed more clearly that his life had been both a failure and a crime.

IV. The fourth act of the drama is a great contrast to the third. It opens at Hebron, that place of venerable memories, where a young king, inheriting Abraham's faith, sets himself, heart and soul, to make the nation of Israel what God would have it to be. Trained in the school of adversity, his feet had sometimes slipped ; but on the whole he had profited by his teacher ; he had learned a great lesson of trust, and knowing something of the treachery of his own heart, he had committed himself to God, and his whole desire and ambition was to be God's servant. For a long time he is occupied in getting rid of enemies, and securing the tranquillity of the kingdom. When that object is gained, he sets himself to the great business of his life. He places the symbol of God's presence and covenant in the securest spot in the kingdom, and where it is at once most central and most conspicuous. He proposes, after his wars are over, and when he has not only become a great king, but amassed great treasure, to employ this treasure in building a stately temple for God's worship, although he is not allowed to carry out that purpose. He re-models the economy of priests and Levites, making arrangements for the more orderly and effective cele-bration of all the service in the capital and throughout the kingdom for which they were designed. He places the whole administration of the kingdom under distinct departments, putting at the head of each the officer that is best fitted for the effective discharge of its duties. In all these arrangements, and in other arrangements more directly adapted to the end, he sought to promote throughout his kingdom the spirit that fears and honours God. And more especially did he labour for this in that most interesting field for which he was so well adapted—the writing of songs fitted for God's public service, and accom-panied by the instruments of music in which he so greatly delighted. Need we say how his whole soul was thrown into this service? Need we say how wonderfully he succeeded in it, not only in the songs which he wrote personally, but in the school of like-minded men which he originated, whose songs were worthy to rank with his own? The whole col-lection, for well-nigh three thousand years, has been by far the best aid to devotion the Church of God has ever known, and the best means of promoting that fellowship with God of which his own life and experience furnished the finest sample. No words can tell the effect of this step in guiding the nation to a due reverence for God, and stimulating them to the faithful discharge of the high ends for which they had been chosen.

Beautiful and most promising was the state of the nation at one period of his life. Unbounded prosperity had flowed into the country. Every enemy had been subdued. There was no division in the kingdom, and no one likely to cause any. The king was greatly honoured by his people, and highly popular. The arrangements which he had made, both for the civil and spiritual administration of the kingdom, were working beautifully, and producing their natural fruits. All things seemed to be advancing the great purpose of God in connection with Israel. Let this state of things but last, and surely the consummation will be reached. The promise to Abraham and Isaac and Jacob will be fulfilled, and the promised Seed will come very speedily to diffuse His blessing over all the families of the earth.

But into this fair paradise the serpent contrived to creep, and the consequence was another fall. Never did the cause of God seem so strong as it was in Israel under David, and never did it seem more secure from harm. David was an absolute king, without an opponent, without a rival; his whole soul was on the side of the good cause; his influence was paramount; whence could danger come? Alas, it could come and it did come from David himself. His sin in the matter of Uriah was fraught with the most fatal consequences. It brought down the displeasure of God; it lowered the king in the eyes of his subjects; it caused the enemy to blaspheme; it made rebellion less difficult; it made the success of rebellion possible. It threw back the cause of God, we cannot tell for how long.  Disaster followed disaster in the latter part of David's reign ; and though he bequeathed to his son a splendid and a peaceful empire, the seeds of division had been sown in it; the germ of disruption was at work ; and when the disruption came, in the days of David's grandson, no fewer than ten tribes broke away from their allegiance, and of the new kingdom which they founded idolatry was the established religion, and the worship of calves was set up by royal warrant from Bethel even to Dan.

It is sad indeed to dwell on the reverse which befel the cause of God in the latter part of the reign of David.  But this event has been matched, over and over again, in the chequered history of religious movements.  The story of Sisyphus has often been realized, rolling his stone up the hill, but finding it, near the top, slip from his hands and go thundering to the bottom.  Or rather, to take a more Biblical similitude, the burden of the watchman of Dumah has time after time come true : "The morning cometh, and also the night."  Strange and trying is often the order of Providence.  The conflict between good and evil seems to go on for ever, and just when the good appears to be on the eve of triumph something occurs to throw it back, and restore the balance.  Was it not so after the Reformation ?  Did not the Catholic cause, by diplomacy and cruelty in too many cases, regain much of what Luther had taken from it ?  And have we not from time to time had revivals of the Church at home that have speedily been followed by counter-acting forces that have thrown us back to where we were ?  What encouragement is there to labour for truth and righteousness when, even if we are apparently successful, we are sure to be overtaken by some counter-current that will sweep us back to our former position ?

But let us not be too hasty or too summary in our inferences.   When we examine carefully the history of David, we find that the evil that came in the end of his reign did not counteract all the good at the beginning.   Who does not see that, after all, there was a clear balance of gain ?   The cause of God was stronger in Israel, its foundation firmer, its defences surer, than it had ever been before.   Why, even if nothing had remained but those immortal psalms that ever led the struggling Church to her refuge and her strength, the gain would have been remarkable. And so it will be found that the Romish reaction did not swallow up all the good of the Reformation, and that the free-thinking reaction of our day has not neutralized the evangelical revival of the nineteenth century.   A decided gain remains, and for that gain let us ever be thankful.

And if the gain be less decided and less full than once it promised, and if Amalek gains upon Israel, and recovers part of the ground he had lost, let us mark well the lesson which God designs to teach us.   In the first place, let us learn the lesson of vigilance.   Let us watch against the decline of spiritual strength, and against the decline of that fellowship with God from which all spiritual strength is derived.   Let those who are prominent in the Church watch their personal con-duct let them be intensely careful against those in-consistencies and indulgences by which, when they take place, such irreparable injury is done to the cause. And in the second place, let us learn the lesson ot patient waiting and patient working.   As the early Church had to wait for the promise of the Father, so let the Church wait in every age. As the early Church continued with one accord in prayer and supplication, so let each successive age ply with renewed earnestness its applications to the throne of grace. And let us be encouraged by the assurance that long though the tide has ebbed and flowed, and flowed and ebbed, it will not be so for ever. To them that look for Him, the great Captain shall appear the second time without sin unto salvation. "The Redeemer shall come to Zion, and unto them that turn from transgression in Jacob, saith the Lord. As for Me, this is My covenant with them, saith the Lord; My spirit that is upon thee, and My words which I have put in thy mouth, shall not depart out of thy mouth, nor out of the mouth of thy seed, nor out of the mouth of thy seed's seed, saith the Lord, from henceforth and for ever" (Isa. lix. 20, 21).

**THE END.**

# John Eadie Titles

Solid Ground is delighted to announce that we have republished several volumes by John Eadie, gifted Scottish minister. The following are in print:

*Commentary on the Greek Text of Paul's Letter to the Galatians*
Part of the classic five-volume set that brought world-wide renown to this humble man, Eadie expounds this letter with passion and precision. In the words of Spurgeon, "This is a most careful attempt to ascertain the meaning of the Apostle by painstaking analysis of his words."

*Commentary on the Greek Text of Paul's Letter to the Ephesians*
Spurgeon said, "This book is one of prodigious learning and research. The author seems to have read all, in every language, that has been written on the Epistle. It is also a work of independent criticism, and casts much new light upon many passages."

*Commentary on the Greek Text of Paul's Letter to the Philippians*
Robert Paul Martin wrote, "Everything that John Eadie wrote is pure gold. He was simply the best exegete of his generation. His commentaries on Paul's epistles are valued highly by careful expositors. Solid Ground Christian Books has done a great service by bringing Eadie's works back into print."

*Commentary on the Greek Text of Paul's Letter to the Colossians*
According to the New Schaff-Herzog Encyclopedia of Religious Knowledge, "These commentaries of John Eadie are marked by candor and clearness as well as by an evangelical unction not common in works of the kind." Spurgeon said, "Very full and reliable. A work of utmost value."

*Commentary on the Greek Text of Paul's Letters to the Thessalonians*
Published posthumously, this volume completes the series that has been highly acclaimed for more than a century. Invaluable.

*Paul the Preacher: A Popular and Practical Exposition of His Discourses and Speeches as Recorded in the Acts of the Apostles*
Very rare volume intended for a more popular audience, this volume begins with Saul's conversion and ends with Paul preaching the Gospel of the Kingdom in Rome. It perfectly fills in the gaps in the commentaries. Outstanding work!

*DIVINE LOVE: A Series of Doctrinal, Practical and Experimental Discourses*
Buried over a hundred years, this volume consists of a dozen complete sermons from Eadie's the pastoral ministry. "John Eadie, the respected nineteenth-century Scottish Secession minister-theologian, takes the reader on an edifying journey through this vital biblical theme." - Ligon Duncan

*Lectures on the Bible to the Young for Their Instruction and Excitement*
"Though written for the rising generation, these plain addresses are not meant for mere children. Simplicity has, indeed, been aimed at in their style and arrangement, in order to adapt them to a class of young readers whose minds have already enjoyed some previous training and discipline." – Author's Preface

# Other Solid Ground Titles

In addition to the Blaikie volume which you hold in your hand, Solid Ground is honored to offer many other uncovered treasure, many for the first time in more than a century:

THE CHILD AT HOME by John S.C. Abbott

THE KING'S HIGHWAY: *The 10 Commandments for the Young* by Richard Newton

HEROES OF THE REFORMATION by Richard Newton

FEED MY LAMBS: *Lectures to Children on Vital Subjects* by John Todd

LET THE CANNON BLAZE AWAY by Joseph P. Thompson

THE STILL HOUR: *Communion with God in Prayer* by Austin Phelps

COLLECTED WORKS of James Henley Thornwell (4 vols.)

CALVINISM IN HISTORY *by Nathaniel S. McFetridge*

OPENING SCRIPTURE: *Hermeneutical Manual by Patrick Fairbairn*

THE ASSURANCE OF FAITH *by Louis Berkhof*

THE PASTOR IN THE SICK ROOM *by John D. Wells*

THE BUNYAN OF BROOKLYN: *Life & Sermons of I.S. Spencer*

THE NATIONAL PREACHER: *Sermons from 2nd Great Awakening*

FIRST THINGS: *First Lessons God Taught Mankind Gardiner Spring*

BIBLICAL & THEOLOGICAL STUDIES *by 1912 Faculty of Princeton*

THE POWER OF GOD UNTO SALVATION *by B.B. Warfield*

THE LORD OF GLORY *by B.B. Warfield*

A GENTLEMAN & A SCHOLAR: *Memoir of J.P. Boyce* by J. Broadus

SERMONS TO THE NATURAL MAN *by W.G.T. Shedd*

SERMONS TO THE SPIRITUAL MAN *by W.G.T. Shedd*

HOMILETICS AND PASTORAL THEOLOGY *by W.G.T. Shedd*

A PASTOR'S SKETCHES 1 & 2 *by Ichabod S. Spencer*

THE PREACHER AND HIS MODELS *by James Stalker*

IMAGO CHRISTI: *The Example of Jesus Christ by James Stalker*

A HISTORY OF PREACHING *by Edwin C. Dargan*

LECTURES ON THE HISTORY OF PREACHING *by J. A. Broadus*

THE SCOTTISH PULPIT *by William Taylor*

THE SHORTER CATECHISM ILLUSTRATED *by John Whitecross*

THE CHURCH MEMBER'S GUIDE *by John Angell James*

THE SUNDAY SCHOOL TEACHER'S GUIDE *by John A. James*

CHRIST IN SONG: *Hymns of Immanuel from All Ages* by Philip Schaff

COME YE APART: *Daily Words from the Four Gospels* by J.R. Miller

DEVOTIONAL LIFE OF THE S.S. TEACHER *by J.R. Miller*

Call us Toll Free at 1-877-666-9469

Send us an e-mail at sgcb@charter.net

Visit us on line at solid-ground-books.com

*Uncovering Buried Treasure to the Glory of God*

CPSIA information can be obtained
at www.ICGtesting.com
Printed in the USA
FFOW03n1248010618
47039284-49329FF